P O W E R,
EMPLOYMENT,
AND
ACCUMULATION

P O W E R,
EMPLOYMENT,
AND
ACCUMULATION

Social Structures in
Economic Theory and Practice

Jim Stanford, Lance Taylor,
and Ellen Houston
Editors

M.E. Sharpe
Armonk, New York
London, England

Library of Congress Cataloging-in-Publication Data

Power, employment, and accumulation : social structures in economic theory and
practice / edited by Jim Stanford, Lance Taylor, and Ellen Houston.
　　p. cm.
Includes bibliographical references and index.
ISBN 0-7656-0630-5 (alk. paper)
　　1. Economics—Sociological aspects. 2. Institutional economics. 3. Power (Social
sciences)—Economic aspects. 4. Macroeconomics. 5. Labor market. 6. International
economic relations. I. Stanford, Jim. II. Taylor, Lance. III. Houston, Ellen, 1965–

HM548.P69 2001
306.3—dc21   00-032978

Printed in the United States of America

The paper used in this publication meets the minimum requirements of
American National Standard for Information Sciences
Permanence of Paper for Printed Library Materials,
ANSI Z 39.48-1984.

BM (c)   10   9   8   7   6   5   4   3   2   1

This volume is dedicated
to the memory of David M. Gordon,
whose careful, creative scholarship and egalitarian social vision
continue to inspire a legion of progressive economists
around the world.

TABLE OF CONTENTS

Part III: Power and the Global Economy

LIST OF TABLES AND FIGURES

Tables

Figures

ACKNOWLEDGMENTS

The editors would like to thank all of the authors for their valuable contributions to the volume. The book is based on an initial 1997 conference at the New School for Social Research hosted by the Center for Economic Policy Analysis, which David Gordon helped to found and which he served as its first director. The major organizational responsibilities for that conference were undertaken by Ellen Houston, William Milberg, David Kucera, and Lance Taylor (who succeeded Gordon as director of the CEPA). Additional thanks go to John Eatwell and Diana Gordon for their support for that conference and subsequent activities at CEPA. The enthusiasm of Sean Culhane at M.E. Sharpe for this volume is gratefully recognized, as is the technical oversight of Esther Clark. Valuable word processing and organizational support was provided by Nancy Kearnan, Maureen Gale, Kim O'Neil, and Bess King of the Canadian Auto Workers in Toronto.

We conclude with our collective thanks to David M. Gordon for his lasting contribution to the development of a vibrant, creative community of progressive economists.

P O W E R,
EMPLOYMENT,
AND
ACCUMULATION

1

Jim Stanford

INTRODUCTION

Power, Employment, and Accumulation

I. Social Structures and Economic Processes

Free markets. Free competition. Free trade. Free exchange.

These are the ideologically loaded buzzwords of conventional, market-oriented economics. The underlying assumption is that the private economy will function in an efficient and mutually beneficial manner, so long as it is allowed to operate free from government regulation, taxation, and other forms of interference. The choice of terms is not accidental: who could be opposed to "free" competition and "free" trade? Indeed, free-market economics has always been closely associated with philosophical liberalism, and in this tradition it is hard to imagine being "free" at all, without being able to truck and trade in a free private market.[1]

The profession of mainstream "neoclassical" economics is premised on the propagation and elaboration of a huge and elegant complex of partial and general equilibrium models, all rooted within this core notion of free, utility-enhancing exchange. We start with an initial endowment of factor resources (capital, labor, and natural resources), the distribution of which is taken as some irreversible accident of chance. The model then proves how the well-being of individuals can be improved (all relative to that accidental, exogenous starting point) through mutual and voluntary trade. The resources can be traded directly in their original form, or indirectly through the process of production, which converts those initial resources into other, more useful commodities. Strangely (for a profession purportedly concerned with the output of actual goods and services), the concrete mechanics of those processes of *production* and *work* are seldom directly considered. Neoclassical production functions and other abstract conveniences allow the theorists to abstract from details like the organization and supervision of real work activity (mundane topics best left for the business school to deal with), focusing instead on the more interesting and pure processes of trade and exchange. Meanwhile, the allocative magic of flexible, competitive price determination ensures that supply and demand will always (absent misguided government interference or rare instances of "market failure") match one another, ensuring the productive utilization of all offered resources. In return for their supplies of factor services, individuals receive compensation that reflects—thanks again to that competitive process of price determination—their true "value" from the perspective of those who are doing the buying. Everyone is employed, everyone is paid what they are worth, and everyone is better off than they were given their initial position (or "endowment"). Isn't freedom great?

This approach to economics is fundamentally *ahistorical* and *asocial*. A "market" is seen as some natural, anonymous forum in which human beings productively interact. Economic history is reduced largely to a unidimensional process in which countries move at varying speeds along a continuum toward a state in which their citizens are able to fully participate in market exchanges to their mutual benefit. (It is not surprising, in this light, that economic history is rarely taught anymore within the economics departments of universities: it does not take too much research before this unidimensional approach to economic history is "all done," having exhausted its potential lines of inquiry.) And since endowments are specified across individuals, and each individual possesses his own objective function which he will creatively and perpetually strive to maximize, the whole process is fundamentally atomistic in nature. Indeed, in the most perfect neoclassical vision of the world, there is no such thing as the study of macroeconomics (that is, the study of broader issues such as aggregate demand, expenditure, and unemployment). The microeconomic behavior of individual actors, in the context of free competitive markets, ensures that no macroeconomic problems (such as unemployment) can exist. Hence the "macro" is simply the sum of the "micros"—no more and no less.

In reality, of course, markets are not "natural," "neutral," or even rooted purely in the actions of "individuals." Markets, rather, are fundamentally *social* institutions that took centuries to evolve, and that are fundamentally influenced by a complex set of economic and noneconomic factors (such as laws, attitudes, political processes, and culture) that determine who owns what, how much they get paid for it, and what they are and are not willing to put up with at the end of the economic day. The so-called free market is not the only means by which human beings have chosen to conduct their economic relationships with one another, and—the "end of history" notwithstanding—it is not likely to be the last. This sense of historical and systemic relativity, however, is almost entirely absent from the tradition of mainstream, free-market economics.

What we think of as free-market interactions are actually shaped by powerful social, institutional, and cultural influences. The "goal" of free markets may not necessarily be to "clear" (that is, to match every supply with a demand). Market exchanges do not usually occur between equal consenting parties. The exercise of *power*—in its economic and noneconomic forms—is an important part of explaining how economies work. Economists who focus too much on a reified model of pure exchange among equals are thus missing many features of the phenomena they are studying.

As an example of the potential errors produced by this myopic view on the economic world, consider the analysis of key labor market issues such as employment, employee turnover, and wage inflation. The words of Alan Greenspan, chairman of the U.S. Federal Reserve Board, are illuminating in this regard—perhaps accidentally so. Greenspan described the labor-market features that contributed to the success of the U.S. economy in the late 1990s as follows:

> Increases in hourly compensation . . . have continued to fall far short of what they would have been had historical relationships between compensation gains and the degree of labor market tightness held. . . . As I see it, heightened job insecurity explains a significant part of the restraint on compensation and the consequent muted price inflation. . . . The continued reluctance of workers to leave their jobs to seek other employment as the labor market has tightened provides further evidence of such concern, as does the tendency toward longer labor union contracts. . . . The low level of work stoppages of recent years also attests to concern about job security. . . . The continued decline in the share of the private workforce in labor unions has likely made wages more responsive to market forces. . . . Owing in part to the subdued behavior of wages, profits and rates of return on capital have risen to high levels. (Greenspan 1997)

The mechanisms described by Greenspan as being so crucial to the success of the U.S. economy are not, it seems, rooted solely in the competitive interaction of individual economic agents meeting in a faceless, neutral "marketplace." Greenspan is speaking of matters of power, security, and fear—things that are not supposed to matter in a free-market exchange between free individuals. And hence any analysis of macroeconomic issues that ignored these structural and institutional features would be missing, even according to Greenspan's eclectically pragmatic view, important pieces of the story.

The late-1990s success of the U.S. economy is typically ascribed by mainstream economists to that country's more deregulated, business-oriented economy. In the context of labor market policies, this deregulation is often described (with a typically misleading and non-neutral choice of words) as "flexibility," and the U.S. labor market is now held up internationally as a paradigmatic example of this policy approach.[2] Yet many of the features highlighted by Greenspan reflect precisely a *lack* of flexibility in the labor market: a lack of response by compensation levels to tight labor markets, a reluctance of workers to leave their jobs, and the prevalence of long-term contracts that lock in employment arrangements for six or more years at a time. This suggests that something other than flexibility—something other than the anonymous interaction of consenting and equal adults through a free labor market—is a key ingredient at work. The unique features and functioning of the U.S. labor market may have more to do with forces of power and fear than with the freely flexible forces of supply and demand. American workers remain fundamentally insecure despite a relatively low unemployment rate, and hence compensation gains are muted. A consequent redistribution of income from labor to capital is part of the equation, reflected in strong business profitability and soaring stock markets. In this environment, the monetary authority is willing to allow the unemployment rate to fall below previously acceptable levels, with less fear of shrinking profit margins and accelerating inflation. Greenspan's story is more about *fear* than it is about flexibility—and hence this famous quotation has come to be known as Greenspan's "fear factor" testimony, in which he concisely described the importance of evolving labor market structures for his conduct of monetary policy. Any theory of monetary policy and interest rates that ignores these structural issues of economic power and its uneven distribution will be incomplete at best, misleading at worst.[3]

In this light, free-market economics can produce errors of at least two kinds: errors of description, and errors of prescription. In the preceding example, a lack of *descriptive* understanding of the institutional factors behind the relative acquiescence of U.S. workers during the latter 1990s would promote an incorrect *prescriptive* bias in favor of a tighter monetary policy to ward off wage-led inflation that was simply not on the horizon. Indeed, conventional economists, who did not comprehend the broad-based institutional disempowerment of American workers that was successfully engineered in the 1980s and 1990s, called repeatedly for monetary tightening as the 1990s recovery wore on and the unemployment rate dropped ever lower. Those calls, in retrospect, were premature. A richer institutional analysis of the U.S. labor market would help to explain not only why the feared wage-led inflation did not arise, but also why the distribution of the economic fruits of that recovery was so unbalanced. It was not until the U.S. unemployment rate fell to near 4 percent later in the decade that average American real wages began to grow *at all*—let alone by a pace that could possibly be considered inflationary, in relation to productivity growth.

On the other hand, this institutional or structural perspective on U.S. labor markets and monetary policy might also suggest that the happy confluence of low unemployment and low inflation attained in the U.S. in the late 1990s will not necessarily be a permanent state of affairs. Many pundits optimistically declared the advent of a "new paradigm" at the turn of the century, in which the economic magic of the Internet and other technological breakthroughs allows the economy to break free of former trade-offs between unemployment and inflation. In contrast to this happy view, the preceding structural analysis suggests perhaps that the combination of low unemployment and sluggish wage growth will persist only for as long as U.S. workers remain as precariously insecure as in Greenspan's 1997 description. It is unlikely, however, that the workforce would remain permanently acquiescent in the face of growing inequality and continuing decline in real wages for many workers, and low unemployment should eventually have a positive impact on the economic and political confidence of U.S. labor. American unions, for example, increased their membership by more in 1999 than in any other single year in the past three decades. Once workers regain more confidence to demand and win a restored share of the economic pie, then the "old paradigm"—in which monetary policy proactively aims to maintain unemployment at levels sufficiently high to discipline the overall labor market—may suddenly find renewed currency.

Similar problems arise in the analysis of the complex of processes that is known as globalization. Ironically, in this case, the resulting errors of description are often shared by both the proponents and the opponents of the phenomenon. Globalization is typically interpreted as the breaking down of international barriers to economic activity, and the completion of more unified and harmonized international markets for both produced goods and productive factors (especially capital). In this context, globalization is viewed as involving both the strengthening and perfecting of market forces, and the weakening or dismantling of the ability of governments to interfere with those forces. Proponents and opponents of further international economic liberalization will naturally argue about *prescriptive* policy issues related to that process (with free-market adherents viewing it as desired and efficient, and critics viewing it as unwelcome and socially costly). But they seem largely to agree on what it is that is actually occurring.

But a closer reading of the institutional factors involved in the creation of this global economy suggests that this shared understanding of what globalization *is* might be less than complete. After all, it requires pro-active measures by national governments to undertake and enforce the trade and investment initiatives that have been heralded as the harbingers of this brave new global world. In many cases, it is not at all clear that governments have been disempowered by the process, or that the forces unleashed by globalization are rooted solely in the autonomous free-market interactions of private corporations and other agents (Panitch 1998). Think of the extensive new intellectual property provisions contained in many of the new trade agreements (including the NAFTA and the WTO agreements). These mandate far-reaching and aggressive forms of state intervention to protect and enforce private property claims over increasingly abstract and questionable terrain—ranging from music videos to pharmaceutical formulae to life forms. This hardly seems like the "powerless" state decried by many opponents of globalization; the problem is not a lack of state power, but rather a question of on whose side it is being exercised. Similar issues are at stake in understanding the tortuous, chaotic development of the post-Bretton Woods international financial system. One can take issue (as Lance Taylor does in chapter 10 of this volume) with the nature and terms of recent multilateral financial rescue efforts, such as those overseen by the IMF in response to the Asian financial crisis of 1997 and 1998. But one cannot deny that these quasi-state institutions are powerful, mobilizing incredible sums of wealth in the interests of preserving a particular, peculiar form of global financial "stability." One would also be hard-pressed to deny that the current financial regime would have collapsed in the absence of those powerful interventions. So portraying the whole process of globalization as one that disempowers governments and further empowers private markets is, in many cases, quite wrong. For critics of the whole process, a richer analysis of the structural and institutional forces at play in the course of globalization should produce both a stronger understanding of the process itself, and a more convincing view of the ways in which progressive policy initiatives may be hindered (or helped) by that process.

It seems evident, then, that debates over labor markets, monetary policy, globalization, and many other pressing economic issues would be enriched by an economics that focuses on the influence and importance of nonmarket institutional structures, forces, and practices. In this spirit, this volume presents a selection of current research, both theoretical and empirical, motivated by an alternative understanding of the relationships between economic behavior and the broader social and institutional context within which that behavior occurs. The unifying theme of the essays presented here is the core notion that economies cannot be described solely as the interaction of autonomous market forces. Rather, social structures and nonmarket institutions, and the differing degrees of power that various constituencies are able to exert over those structures and institutions, play a fundamental and defining role in shaping how economies (even so-called free-market economies) actually function. The practice of economics badly needs to incorporate these issues into its field of vision.

One main feature of this broader, "structuralist" approach to economics was defined by Lance Taylor, and seems highly relevant as a description of the common thread that runs through the present collection:

> Economically powerful actors—"institutions" such as the state or corporations, "groups" such as landlords or rentiers, and "classes" such as organized labor—are not price takers. They can influence price and/or quantity changes in certain markets. The seats of power differ from economy to economy, and change with local institutional arrangements and history. (1990, 2–3)

Economics practiced in this spirit will be an inherently more subjective and contingent exercise. No meta-model will be constructed to explain the purported universalities of the human economic experience. But we are nevertheless likely to emerge with a richer and more practical understanding of how the world actually works.

The essays in this volume represent outstanding examples of the application of heterodox economic principles—and in particular the general notion that social structures influence economic behavior and outcomes—to a range of highly current policy issues, including monetary policy, welfare reform, labor market regulations, and global financial regulation. The volume is thus relevant to academics and policy analysts in a range of different economic and related disciplines. The essays presented here are relatively descriptive and nontechnical by the standards of current professional economic literature, making the collection more accessible to a broader and more interdisciplinary audience of potential readers than most standard collections of current economic research.

II. David M. Gordon and the Economics of Power

This volume had its genesis in a 1997 conference that was organized at the New School for Social Research to commemorate the passing of David M. Gordon, one of that institution's leading scholars. The core notion that social factors such as *institutions* and *power* are key to the functioning of economic processes, and hence should be central objects of the science of economics, was an ongoing feature of Gordon's research into a range of economic subjects (including labor markets, macroeconomics, and international economics).

Gordon taught in the New School's graduate economics program from 1973 until his sadly premature death in 1996. All of the contributors to this volume worked closely with Gordon in one capacity or another—as colleague, collaborator, or student. Indeed, the former students of Gordon's who are represented within this collection span three decades of graduate study at the New School: economists who studied under him in the 1970s, the 1980s, and the 1990s, and who have since developed their own careers as heterodox theorists and practitioners, employed in both academic and nonacademic settings.

Gordon addressed an impressive range of economic topics during his career.[4] Three of these themes seem especially relevant to this collection's focus on the importance of social structures and institutions to economic processes. Gordon's early graduate and post-graduate research addressed problems of inequality and segmentation in the U.S. labor market, work which developed into important models of the functioning and distributional consequences of segmented labor markets.[5] Gordon fundamentally challenged the dominant understanding of the labor market as a site of purely competitive employment and compensation decisions. Instead, large and permanent differentials exist between the job and income prospects of different groups of workers. These differentials are rooted not in concrete individual characteristics (such as differences in skill or productivity), but rather in inherently social and institutional features of the economy—including the relationship between large "core" corporations and their network of smaller suppliers, and cleavages within the labor force based on race, gender, and ethnicity. Clearly the labor market is a place where power and social structures matter. Private employers attempt to enhance their bargaining power over workers by offering a select "core" group a degree of compensation and security that is not widely shared across the labor market as a whole. An important— and not entirely accidental—side effect of this segmentation is the creation of difficult divisions of interest and allegiance between workers in different segments of the labor market. Gordon's pioneering analysis of the concrete economic factors behind the inequalities that have long worried progressives considerably enriched the thinking of heterodox and mainstream labor economists alike. Several of the essays in this volume revisit and expand on Gordon's work in this area.

Gordon also applied his social and institutional analysis in his important contributions to the historical analysis of economic development and long cycles. Mainstream models of economic development traditionally describe the process as one of the simple application of a growing accumulation of capital (in both its physical and its human forms) to a standard production function. To the extent that issues of institutional change are even addressed in the traditional approach, the analysis focuses narrowly on the importance of private property rights for the self-interested optimization that underlies the whole neoclassical framework. Economists in the heterodox tradition have long rejected this ahistorical view of the development of capitalism, and Gordon added significantly to this long-standing thesis with his model of "social structures of accumulation."[6] A vibrant and sustainable capitalism requires much more than simply a "free market"—that is, an absence of government intrusion and widespread respect for private property. Rather, a whole congruence of economic and social institutions must be assembled to motivate private investment, establish a stable monetary and geopolitical context for accumulation, manage production in an efficient and profitable manner, and simultaneously manage the distributional and political conflicts inherent in any economic system rooted in profound inequality. When such a social and institutional congruence is attained, capitalism can enter a period of sustained and dynamic growth; but that growth will also tend to undermine the initial conditions for successful accumulation. Periodic episodes of economic and political crisis ensue, sparking processes of structural change as the system casts about for a new complex of economic and social institutions consistent with renewed profit-led accumulation in a changed technological and political context. This rich and subjective reading of the social and institutional prerequisites for economic development is quite compatible with similar insights from other streams of heterodox economic and historical analysis—ranging from more traditional Marxian accounts of the rise of capitalism, to modern structuralist approaches to development economics.

Later in his career, Gordon undertook a daunting, multidimensional project to compare the assumptions and implications of contrasting schools of macroeconomic thought. To this end he constructed and simulated sets of quantitative economic models incorporating contrasting theoretical and behavioral assumptions.[7] Gordon was imbued with an empirical positivism that has become unfashionable in the post-modern academy; he believed that a good test of the accuracy and relevance of a theory was how well it fit with observed facts. Hence one of his goals with this comparative modeling project was to make a case that consideration of the importance of social structures and institutional factors could measurably improve both the historical and predictive accuracy of quantitative economic models. Many are now skeptical, of course, that theories can stand or fall on the basis of empirical examination—although Gordon's concern with the real-world empirical and policy relevance of theoretical research now seems refreshing in contrast to the abstract introspection of many current streams of thought. But quite separate from this empirical "contest" between competing theoretical traditions, Gordon's comparative modeling exercise helped to illuminate the precise ways in which the consideration of different social and institutional factors affected the internal logic and functioning of the systems of equations postulated by respective schools of macroeconomics. This is useful not only in highlighting the failure of conventional approaches to consider the obvious real-world importance of institutional factors such as labor relations systems or international monetary regimes in their models. It also helps heterodox critics to systematically think through the implications of their own alternative views. This later macroeconomic research of Gordon's exerted an important influence in encouraging subsequent comparative modeling exercises, which are now a standard technique in the heterodox economist's toolbox.[8]

III. Overview of the Book

Threads from all of these major themes of David Gordon's writings are readily visible within the chapters contained in this volume. Nevertheless, however, the collection is not intended solely to pay tribute to the intellectual legacy of this important scholar and progressive activist. Rather, the volume is structured more as a "showcase" of current thinking within the broad school of modern heterodox economics. A rich variety of topics is addressed by the volume, from an equally diverse range of theoretical and political perspectives, and utilizing a rich array of methodological techniques. The important thing that all chapters hold in common is a shared realization that the capitalist economy does not simply consist of the amalgamation of an infinite number of individual, "free-market" transactions.

The remainder of the book is divided into three parts, each providing examples of the application of structural power analysis to three broad themes within economics. Part I, *Power, Work, and Distribution*, presents three applications of structural and institutional analysis to issues of labor market inequality, participation, and solidarity. These three articles, however, embody sharply contrasting analytical and methodological approaches.

Chapter 2, by David Howell, William Milberg, and Ellen Houston, provides an exhaustive and empirically based review of the possible causes of the notable growth in wage inequality evident in the U.S. labor market through the 1980s and 1990s. The standard free-market model of labor market functioning is clear on both the likely causes of this inequality (a shift in labor demand away from unskilled labor toward more highly trained labor), and on the appropriate policy response (encourage low-skill workers to get more training). From the authors' detailed reading of the empirical evidence, however, it is not at all clear that this standard story is accurate—in either its descriptive or its prescriptive dimensions. Disaggregated data on employment and earnings by detailed occupation show that skill differentials on their own explain hardly any of the rise in U.S. income inequality over the past fifteen years. A more nuanced analysis is required, one that incorporates the impact of labor market institutions (such as those that allowed professional workers in regulated public sector industries to enjoy relatively strong income gains during this period). Heterodox economists have always reacted against the simplistic neoclassical claim that distributional outcomes accurately and competitively reflect individual attributes such as skill or productivity; the data in this chapter provide more grist for this long-standing mill.

In chapter 3, Juliet Schor takes a very different methodological approach in surveying one recent trend in U.S. labor markets: the growing number of workers (in all income brackets, surprisingly) who voluntarily withdraw some or all of their labor services from the commercial labor market in pursuit of goals such as more time with loved ones or lower stress levels. This phenomenon of "downshifting" at least partially reflects a profound dissatisfaction among workers with the conditions of their working lives. Schor utilizes telephone surveys and in-depth interviews to map the dimensions, motives, and economic consequences of downshifting. Until such a time as the formal labor market responds to the demands of workers for more time and balance in their lives, downshifting may become an increasingly common expression of resistance by workers to the constraints and dictates of paid employment.

Chapter 4, written by Samuel Bowles and Herbert Gintis, provides a fascinating survey of the application of yet another economic methodology—game theory and behavioral experimentation—to the analysis of evolving public attitudes toward welfare and other wage-replacing or wage-supplementing social programs. The current pessimism of many egalitarians that public opinion has shifted to a more "selfish" and less compassionate position is quite wrong, Bowles and Gintis argue. Popular concern about modern welfare programs is motivated less by selfishness and a lack of concern for fellow citizens, they argue, than by a conviction that established income security programs violate long-held norms regarding fairness and reciprocity. They support their view with evidence collected from a range of game-theoretic behavioral experiments. These experiments suggest that simple game strategies in which mutuality is rewarded but a lack of mutuality is punished can prove superior to purely "selfish" strategies in repeated game interactions. These results challenge the neoclassical assumption that individual agents are interested solely in maximizing their personal gain with no attention to the collective good. In fact, the authors argue, traditions of mutuality are embedded deeply within our social and even our genetic patterns, and they can "pay off" in terms of greater economic gains. The challenge is to devise social policies that build on, rather than affront, this underlying sense of mutuality and reciprocity.

Part II of the book, *Power and the Macroeconomy*, presents two modern attempts to address issues in the macroeconomic realm—such as aggregate demand or full employment policies—from a perspective that admits the importance of social conflict and the institutions that mediate that conflict. In chapter 5, Thomas Palley presents a dense and synthetic overview of the contrasting assumptions and behavioral specifications embedded in comparative theoretical models of macroeconomic processes. This exercise is richly illustrated with references to various heterodox literatures, both current and historical, and builds (in a nonempirical manner) on David Gordon's own comparative macroeconomic modeling project. Mainstream macroeconomic models do not typically consider issues of power, conflict, and institutional change, and hence miss many important chains of causation and interaction within the milieux of aggregate demand, investment, and finance. Palley constructs a composite heterodox model incorporating insights from numerous theoretical traditions, including Post-Keynesian, Marxist, and Kaleckian, to explain the links between aggregate demand, labor market conditions, and investment and finance.

Chapter 6 provides a more concrete, empirically grounded exploration of the impacts of social structures on macroeconomic functions. Heather Boushey explores the macroeconomic dimensions of racial segmentation in the U.S. labor market. Not only are the incomes of African American workers consistently lower, and their incidence of unemployment consistently higher, than is the case for white Americans. It also turns out that African American incomes are more sensitive to *changes* in unemployment conditions. African Americans in this sense are the first to feel the chilling effects of weakening macroeconomic conditions on their job and income possibilities, whereas the jobs and incomes of white workers tend to be more insulated by social institutions from the ups and downs of the business cycle. This finding has important implications regarding the conduct of macroeconomic policy. When the central bank decides that the unemployment rate needs to increase so as to undercut wage-driven inflation pressures, the first and most sensitive victims of that tightening are likely to be African Americans, who already experienced lower incomes and employment rates even during the upswing.

Part III, *Power and the Global Economy*, explores the relevance of social structures and institutional power to economic theorizing at the international level. Many economists in the heterodox camp have expressed great concern in recent years regarding the impact of globalization on the future evolution of social institutions and standards. With investment and production more mobile than ever on an international scale, the story goes, profit-seeking firms will migrate to jurisdictions that impose less egalitarian, more business-friendly social, labor, and environmental rules. This will tend to spark a global "race to the bottom," as jurisdictions compete to attract private investment and production—but at the expense of the well-being of their residents.

Chapter 7, written by Jim Stanford, explores this concern with the help of a quantitative economic simulation model that incorporates non-neoclassical assumptions regarding the functioning of factor markets. In contrast to the near-universal optimism of neoclassical trade theory that international liberalization cannot but enhance economic efficiency and mutual well-being, Stanford's simulations suggest that—when key free-market assumptions regarding full employment and the determination of income distribution are abandoned, in favor of an approach that admits the influence of institutional structures—globalization may indeed have negative impacts on certain jurisdictions. On the other hand, there are important features of even this structuralist model of international economic integration that serve to limit the negative impacts of globalization. In particular, freer trade in commodities alone is seen to be a generally benign policy change. Widespread fears regarding the impact of integration between high-wage and low-wage economies are also seen as largely misplaced. It is not the level of wages per se that is crucial for the determination of competitiveness and success in the international economy; indeed, the experimental results suggest that integration will be especially damaging for those countries that are characterized by both low wages and a lack of international competitiveness. While many aspects of recent liberalization initiatives (particularly those concerned with enhancing the rights and protections of cross-border investors) raise legitimate concerns regarding the sustainability of progressive social and labor market policies, the single-minded focus of many critics on the supposedly all-powerful and destructive potential of globalization is not seen as justified.

Orthodox neoclassical trade theory also receives a critical review in chapter 8, by William Milberg, who also challenges recent mainstream models of economic growth. Milberg considers recent evidence suggesting that income inequality in the world economy—both across countries and within individual economies—has increased. This is not consistent with the expectation of standard trade theory that closer economic integration between countries should lead to a convergence of both relative factor prices (that is, the ratio of wages to profits) and absolute compensation levels. Recent models of endogenous economic growth, currently a hot topic in the mainstream profession, also emphasize the conditions under which economic convergence (measured variously according to different criteria) will occur. The persistence and the growth of inequality in the world economy suggest that both of these approaches are ignoring crucial dimensions of the processes of global integration and growth. Milberg argues that the mainstream models fail because of their failure to consider the effects of social and institutional structures on distributional outcomes, and their corresponding and related failure to consider the importance of demand-side conditions in the determination of patterns of growth and development. The often extreme segmentation of labor markets in most developing economies, for example, helps to explain the growth of inequality there, in contrast to neoclassical predictions that wages should equalize between skilled and unskilled workers in less developed countries as they are integrated with higher-income countries in the north. The consideration of the influences of institutions and demand—two lasting and fundamental features of most heterodox analysis—can considerably enhance our understanding of the income and growth dynamics presently visible in the global economy.

The gender dimensions of the analysis of the global economy are considered in chapter 9 by Isabella Bakker. Economics as a whole pretends, for the most part, to posit a "gender-neutral" world view. In a stylized competitive market system, in which resources (including people) are employed and compensated according to their real productivity, there is no particular reason to expect the analysis of men's economic lives to differ from that of women's. Both interact with the same set of natural, all-powerful market forces, and while there may be differences in the sorts of activity undertaken by men and women (for various reasons),[9] the same gender-neutral concepts and models explain the contrasting outcomes. Again, however, this view is ahistorical and ignores the profound impact of social institutions (such as the social construction of gender identities and practices) on the differing economic outcomes faced by men and women. In Bakker's words, mainstream theory is more "gender-blind" than gender-neutral, and she illustrates the different levels of economic analysis to which a gender-aware mode of thinking adds richness and explanatory detail. The implications of gender analysis have been well explored in certain areas of economic theory (mainly at the microeconomic level), but here Bakker applies the model in new ways to current global economic developments. For example, she considers the gendered nature and impact of budgetary policies and structural adjustment programs, among other current global issues.

The last essay in the book, chapter 10 by Lance Taylor, explores the limitation of standard free-market thinking in explaining the episodes of financial crisis that have repeatedly wracked the global economy over the past two decades. Mainstream analysis of most of these crises holds that an alert, rational, and efficient private financial sector—personified in the red-suspendered currency traders who work the front lines—acts as a disciplining force limiting the actions and abuses of self-interested national governments. Attempts to stabilize international financial affairs through regulation and controls on private financial flows would disengage this disciplinary mechanism, leading to all sorts of alleged inefficiencies and moral hazards, and this is why orthodox policy prescriptions almost universally accept the sanctity of the current global free reign enjoyed by private finance, no matter how chaotic and destructive that reign reveals itself to be. Taylor provides a critique of this standard view that is theoretically elegant but rooted in the concrete experiences of recent international financial crises. Far from playing an efficient disciplining role, the self-interested behavior of private financial investors is clearly an inherently destabilizing force that should be reigned in through the actions of public regulators (acting at both the national and the international levels). But regulators are constrained by a combination of the powerful vested opposition of the financiers, and a lack of regulatory resources and competence. Taylor makes numerous policy recommendations aimed at overcoming the current laxity of international financial regulation, and hence erecting tighter controls over the often-destructive actions of private finance. Once again, an institutional analysis—exploring the weakness of the present institutional regime, and highlighting areas of needed improvement—adds fundamentally to both our understanding of a current problem and our prescriptive options for solving that problem.

These nine essays, then, cover a remarkably wide range of topics, and utilize a surprising variety of different theoretical and methodological approaches. They share in common, however, the view that we cannot understand the functioning of the present-day economy—let alone figure out how to restructure that economy in more efficient and humane ways—without studying and analyzing the power of social structures and institutions. This is true whether the structures being considered are formal and legal (embodied in the constitution of an international lending agency, for instance, or in the edicts of a collective bargaining regime), or informal and cultural (such as the attitudes to work surveyed by Schor, or the racial and gendered divisions explored by Boushey and Bakker). If nothing else, the breadth and topical relevance of the ground covered by these essays proves the continuing vitality of heterodox approaches to economic theory and policy.

Notes

1. An interesting current example of this intellectual linkage between free markets and human freedom is provided by the Economic Freedom Project, a joint initiative of right-wing policy institutes in several countries that has attempted to rank the countries of the world according to their demonstrated degree of "economic freedom" (Gwartney, Lawson, and Block 1996). Freedom, in this context, is defined as freedom from various forms of government or community interference in private economic activity—whether that be taxation, public programs, inflation (which undermines the sanctity of private ownership of wealth), unionization, or regulation. Stanford (1998) challenges this one-sided and narrow conception of freedom, and presents an alternative mode of measurement.

2. The Organization for Economic Cooperation and Development (OECD 1994) has undertaken a concerted effort in recent years to push its member governments to adopt U.S.-style policies of labor market "flexibility." See Palley (1998) on the weaknesses and limitations of this policy agenda.

3. For one example of an analysis of monetary policy that attempts to incorporate these structural and institutional features, see Epstein and Schor (1992).

4. It is not the purpose of the present collection to present a detailed chronicle of David Gordon's life work. For a collection of some of his most important writings and a commentary on his multifaceted contributions to economics, see Bowles and Weisskopf (1998). See also the evaluation of Gordon's work provided by Boushey and Pressman (1997). The *Review of Radical Political Economics* devoted two special issues to Gordon's legacy (31, no. 1 [Winter 1999], and no. 4 [Fall 1999]).

5. See especially Gordon, Edwards, and Reich (1982) for the most complete statement of the model and its historical and distributional implications.

6. Gordon (1980) provides a first and classic statement of this model.

7. Unfortunately Gordon died before the full output of this work was com-

pleted, although important early results were published in various fora; see especially Gordon (1994).

8. The chapter by Thomas Palley in the current volume falls neatly within this tradition; see also Taylor (1991) for a dense summary statement of the comparative modeling approach.

9. Orthodox human capital theorists explain gender differentials as the outcome of the same competitive and supposedly mutually beneficial interactions as shape international trade between countries. See, for example, Becker (1981).

References

Becker, Gary. 1981. *A Treatise on the Family*. Cambridge: Harvard University Press.
Boushey, Heather, and Steven Pressman. 1997. "The Economic Contributions of David M. Gordon." *Review of Political Economy* 9, no. 2 (April): 225–246.
Bowles, Samuel, and Thomas E. Weisskopf, eds. 1998. *Economics and Social Justice: Essays on Power, Labor and Institutional Change by David M. Gordon.* Cheltenham, UK: Edward Elgar.
Epstein, Gerald A., and Juliet B. Schor. 1992. "Corporate Profitability as a Determinant of Restrictive Monetary Policy: Estimates for the Postwar United States." In *The Political Economy of American Monetary Policy*, ed. Thomas Mayer. Cambridge, UK: Cambridge University Press.
Gordon, David M. 1980. "Stages of Accumulation and Long Economic Cycles." In *Processes of the World-System*, ed. Terence K. Hopkins and Immanuel Wallerstein. Beverly Hills: Sage.
———. 1994. "Putting Heterodox Macro to the Test: Comparing Post-Keynesian, Marxian and Social-Structuralist Macroeconometric Models of the Postwar U.S. Economy." In *Competition, Technology and Money: Classical and Post-Keynesian Perspectives*, ed. Mark Glick and E.K. Hunt. Aldershot, UK: Edward Elgar.
Gordon, David M., Richard Edwards, and Michael Reich. 1982. *Segmented Work, Divided Workers: The Historical Transformation of Labor in the United States.* Cambridge, UK: Cambridge University Press.
Greenspan, Alan. 1997. "Testimony Before the Committee on the Budget, United States Senate, January 21." Washington: Federal Reserve Board.
Gwartney, James, Robert Lawson, and Walter Block. 1996. *Economic Freedom of the World: 1975–1995*. Vancouver, BC: Fraser Institute.
Organization for Economic Cooperation and Development (OECD). 1994. *The OECD Jobs Study: Facts, Analysis, Strategies*. Paris: OECD.
Palley, Thomas I. 1998. "Restoring Prosperity: Why the U.S. Model Is Not the Answer for the United States or Europe." *Journal of Post Keynesian Economics* 20, no. 3 (Spring): 337–353.
Panitch, Leo. 1998. " 'The State in a Changing World': Social-Democratizing Global Capitalism?" *Monthly Review* 50, no. 5 (October): 11–32.
Stanford, Jim. 1998. *Economic Freedom for the Rest of Us*. Ottawa: Canadian Centre for Policy Alternatives.
Taylor, Lance. 1990. "Structuralist CGE Models." In *Socially Relevant Policy Analysis*, ed. Lance Taylor. Cambridge: MIT Press.
———. 1991. *Income Distribution, Inflation, and Growth: Lectures on Structuralist Macroeconomic Theory*. Cambridge: MIT Press.

Part I

Power, Work, and Distribution

2

David R. Howell, Ellen Houston, and William Milberg

SKILL MISMATCH, BUREAUCRATIC BURDEN, AND RISING EARNINGS INEQUALITY IN THE U.S.

WHAT DO HOURS AND EARNINGS TRENDS BY OCCUPATION SHOW?

I. Introduction

Since the late 1970s the U.S. labor market has been characterized by sharply declining real wages for low-skilled workers, declining shares of middle income jobs, and a dramatic increase in earnings inequality for both men and women.[1] At the same time, the quality of the workforce has risen. Test scores have been fairly stable for white workers but have risen substantially for black and Hispanic workers, and the share of the workforce with just a high school degree or less fell from 60.9 percent in 1979, to 54.6 percent in 1989, and 44.3 percent in 1997. The share of workers with college or greater rose from 16 to 26 percent over this 18–year period (Mishel, Bernstein, and Schmitt 1999).

Viewing labor market outcomes through a simple demand and supply lens, these wage and labor supply trends have led most economists to conclude that an overwhelming shift in labor demand toward workers with high cognitive skills has characterized the last two decades (for example, see Levy 1998).[2] Within the standard textbook model, a simultaneous rise in the share of skilled workers in the workplace ("skill intensity") and in the wage gap between skilled and unskilled workers (the "skill premium") makes "a prima facie case for the importance of demand shifts in explaining changes in the earnings distribution in the

U.S." (Gottschalk and Smeeding 1997, 647). In essence, the conventional account rests upon the view that there has been a protracted (2–3 decade) skill mismatch between employer demand and worker supply. This "skill-biased demand shift" explanation, briefly outlined in Section II, has dominated the academic literature and policy circles for over a decade, although direct empirical support is remarkably limited (see Howell et al. 1999; Moss 1998; Mishel, Bernstein, and Schmitt 1999).

In his book *Fat and Mean: The Corporate Squeeze of Working Americans and the Myth of Managerial Downsizing* (1996), David Gordon proposed a strikingly different explanation for rising wage inequality, one that put relative management strategy, institutional shifts, and bargaining power at center stage. In Gordon's view, declining real wages for those at the bottom of the income distribution are the result of what he called the "wage squeeze": rising inequality and declining real wages have been the consequence of a broad-based effort on the part of corporate America to lower unit labor costs in order to become more competitive.[3] Supported by government policies, U.S. corporations have taken what Gordon called "the low road," a competitive strategy exemplified by such institutional developments as the decline in the value of the legal minimum wage, the declining coverage and power of labor unions, declining job security, and the expansion of irregular (part-time and temporary) employment.

Underlying these proximate causes is the shift in bargaining power within the firm, which has manifested itself in two ways. First, in order to boost productivity in an increasingly insecure work environment, management resorted to the "stick"—adversarial labor relations strategies. These include getting tougher on wages, slashing benefits, and attacking labor unions. This stance, Gordon argues, requires an increase in the number of managers and supervisors to monitor and discipline the workforce, imposing a "bureaucratic burden" on the economy and especially on non-supervisory workers. Second, the loss of bargaining strength on the part of workers coupled with a corporate "squeeze" on wages facilitates a shift in the distribution of earnings toward the growing legions of managers and supervisors. As Gordon put it:

> The connection between the wage squeeze and the bureaucratic burden runs in both directions. In one direction, stagnant or falling wages create the need for intensive managerial supervision of frontline employees. If workers do not share in the fruits of the enterprise, if they are not pro-

vided a promise of job security and steady wage growth, what incentive do they have to work as hard as their bosses would like? So the corporations need to monitor the workers' effort and be able to threaten credibly to punish them if they do not perform. The corporation must wield the Stick. Eventually the Stick requires millions of Stick-wielders.

In the other direction, once top-heavy corporate bureaucracies emerge, they acquire their own, virtually ineluctable expansionary dynamic. They push for more numbers in their ranks and higher salaries for their members. Where does the money come from? It can't come from dividends, since the corporations need to be able to raise money on equity markets. It can't come from interest obligations, since the corporations need to be able to borrow from lenders as well. One of the most obvious targets is frontline workers' compensation. The more powerful the corporate bureaucracy becomes, and the weaker the pressure with which employees can counter, the greater the downward pressure on production workers' wages. The wage squeeze intensifies. (1996, 5–6)

Gordon's vision of the dynamics of wage inequality in the United States directly challenges the conventional skill mismatch explanation. In the mainstream account, employment and earnings trends reflect the increasing demand for skill, caused principally by the growing use of new computer-based technologies. Those favored in this new economy are highly educated workers fluent in the latest information technologies. In contrast, according to Gordon, it is the top of the "top-heavy corporate bureaucracy" that is favored.[4] Some supervisory workers have more power than others, and this power includes the authority to increase their own employment and earnings.

While the skill mismatch account predicts that employment and earnings trends have most favored those commanding the skills necessary to perform in an information technology–intensive environment, the bureaucratic burden prediction is that supervisory standing will be decisive. Both perspectives appear consistent with the observed wage and employment collapse among low-skill workers, particularly in trade-sensitive industries. But according to Gordon's vision, employment and wage trends among non-supervisory workers should reflect less the level of skill a worker has to offer than the institutional shifts that have followed in the wake of the employer offensive. In sum, Gordon's bureaucratic burden story produces two separable predictions: (1) at the top of the distribution, employment and wage growth will reflect supervisory level (the "supervisory burden" prediction); and (2) among non-supervisory workers, the extent of employment and wage declines will reflect exposure to wage competition from the institutional trends that have reflected management's offensive (the "low-road" hypothesis).

Despite the wide acceptance of the skill mismatch account, we are aware of little research that has attempted to confirm it by observing patterns of wage and employment growth across the job structure.[5] In this paper, our main goal is to assess the conventional skill-biased technological change hypothesis with U.S. occupation data for the 1970–97 period. At the same time, these data allow us to assess the empirical support for Gordon's "supervisory burden" and "low-road" hypotheses. While some of our results are suggestive of the possible roles played in recent employment and wage trends by the specific institutional shifts Gordon calls attention to, we will address this more systematically in a forthcoming paper.

Our approach to testing the strength of the statistical links between skill and supervisory levels and employment and wage growth is to group workers by job, measured as narrowly defined occupations or, better yet, as occupation-industry cells (Howell and Wolff 1991; Gittleman and Howell 1995; Howell and Wieler 1998). We begin with individual-level data grouped by job category, using four alternative levels of Census occupation and industry detail: 13 one-digit large occupation groups; 44 two-digit occupation groups; 390 three-digit occupations; and 450 three-digit occupations in which the 6 largest occupations are broken out by industry group. We use the outgoing rotation group (ORG) data from the Current Population Survey (CPS) for our analyses of the 1984–92 and 1989–97 periods, and March CPS data (corrected for occupation redefinitions) for three alternatively defined periods: 1970–79, 1979–86, and 1986–94.

While distinguishing workers by "skill" lies at the heart of the conventional demand shift story, it is both poorly defined and poorly measured in the literature. We try to improve upon this record by adopting four alternative measures of job-related skill: "Factor 1," a measure of "substantive complexity" derived from a factor analysis of skill measures from the 4th edition of the *Dictionary of Occupational Titles* (U.S. Department of Labor); the average occupation National Adult Literacy Survey score (National Center for Education Statistics); the share of job employment with greater than a high school degree; and the mean hourly wage.

The remainder of the paper consists of four sections. Section II lays out in more detail the implications of the conventional model. Section

III describes our data and outlines our method. Section IV presents our results. In the first part of Section IV we summarize our findings on hours and wage growth for the 1984–97 period (separately for 1984–92 and 1989–97). In the second part we do the same using a different data set for the 1970–94 period (separately for 1970–79, 1979–86, and 1986–94). In Section V we conclude with a brief discussion of the results.

II. Implications of the Conventional Supply and Demand Model

The conventional wisdom is a skill mismatch story: the distribution of skills in the American labor force has simply not kept up with the skill needs of employers. As Rebecca Blank has put it, "Fundamentally, the demand for less-skilled workers appears to be declining faster than the number of less-skilled workers, and their wages are therefore drawn downward" (Blank 1994, 173).

Within the textbook competitive model, which has framed most of the recent research in the inequality area, there *had* to be a demand shift toward skilled workers that dominated the observed shift in supply toward the skilled in order to accommodate the observed rise in the relative (skilled/unskilled) wage. One way to show this appears in Figure 2.1 (derived from Snower 1998, figures 1–3). There are two categories of worker, those with high skills (the left side) and those with low skills (the right side, read from right to left). The horizontal axis shows employment for these two groups. The vertical lines indicate a movement toward greater "skill intensity": the share of high-skill workers increases from "skill mix 1" to "skill mix 2," which is consistent with the above mentioned decline in the share of workers with a high school degree or less.

At the same time, we know that during the 1980s, high-skill workers (college or more) experienced a real wage increase of about 5 percent, while low-skill workers were faced with a much larger 20 percent wage decline (Gottschalk 1997). Within this framework, these wage outcomes require sizable demand shifts: upwards for high-skill workers and downwards for the least skilled. With the high-skill wage on the left axis and the low-skill wage on the right, wage change for each group is depicted as an upward movement between points HS1 to HS2 for high-skill workers, and a downward movement from LS1 to LS2 for low-skill workers. The growth in wage inequality is shown by the difference between the gap between LS1 and HS1 at "skill mix 1" compared to LS2 and HS2 at "skill mix 2."

Figure 2.1 **Skill Premia and Skill Intensity: The Demand-Shift Explanation**

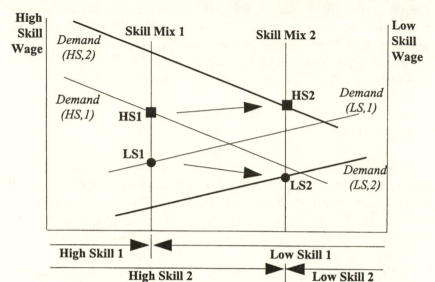

What could cause such a massive shift in the demand for skill? There is a broad consensus that the main culprit can be found in computer-based production technology.[6] As Bound and Johnson (1995, 12) put it, "At the risk of arguing tautologically, the source of this shift *had* to be technology" (emphasis in original).

In sum, the conventional view is that the massive restructuring of wages in recent years reflects a skill mismatch—too many low-skill workers chasing too few low-skill jobs (and vice-versa for high-skill workers)—caused mainly by skill-biased demand shifts that reflect some combination of technological change and globalization. This view implies the following three predictions that we assess in this paper. First, we should observe a strong and positive association between wage change and employment (hours) growth. Second, we should observe a strong association between the cognitive skill level of jobs and their rate of employment (or hours) and wage growth.[7] This suggests that across jobs, wage and employment (hours) growth should be strongly positively related to the skill levels. Thus, plotting wage change on the vertical axis and hours growth on the horizontal (both measured relative to the average for the economy as a whole), we should observe jobs arrayed by skill level from the upper right hand corner of the northeast quadrant (those with the greatest wage and hours growth) to the lower left hand

Figure 2.2 **The Skill-Biased Demand-Shift Prediction**

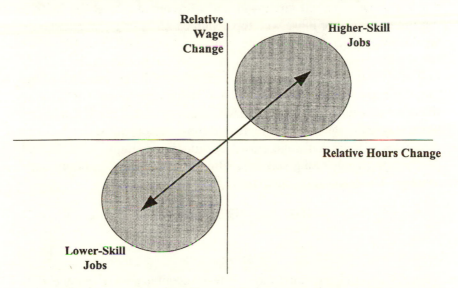

corner of the southwest quadrant (those with the lowest wage and hours growth). This is depicted in Figure 2.2.

The third prediction is that if the hypothesized demand shifts are primarily driven by the computerization of the workplace and globalization of the economy, then as these factors intensify over time, the positive relationship among skills, hours growth, and wage growth should also get stronger over time.

III. Data and Method

Our principal data are the outgoing rotation groups (ORG) of the Current Population Survey (CPS). Merged over 12 months, the ORG data offer a much larger sample than the other typical source of annual labor force data, the March CPS (140,000 observations, about 3 times the March figure). In addition, the ORG contains a direct measure of the hourly wage (in the previous week) for workers paid by the hour, whereas with the March CPS, the respondent is asked to recall last year's annual earnings, weeks worked, and usual hours per week, from which an approximate hourly wage can then be calculated (see Webster 1998).

We use data for all wage and salary workers with a strong labor market attachment. Self-employed are excluded. Included in our samples are those aged 16–64 who usually worked between 10 and 79 hours per week, who were not self-employed, and who earned at least one-half the minimum wage. For those with top coded earnings (e.g., the maximum weekly wage is coded at $999 per week in 1984, $1,923 in 1989), we use the Pareto-imputed mean from the upper tail of the earnings distribution (Webster 1998, Table B-2). This offers a better estimate of the top of the distribution, but in a period of rising relative earnings among those with the highest earnings, this procedure will still result in a downward bias (earnings will have increased more rapidly at the top than our data show). Hours and wage growth are measured simply as the annual percentage change of a given occupation relative to the economy-wide average. The formula for relative wage change is:

$$(1) \qquad \frac{100 \times [\,(W_i/W)^{t2}/(W_i/W)^{t1}\,] - 1}{t2 - t1}$$

where W_i is the occupation i wage, W is the economy-wide average, $t2$ is the last year of the period, and $t1$ is the initial year. The relative hours change measure is calculated similarly and indicates the change in total weekly hours worked in occupation i relative to the change in total weekly hours.

Three considerations determined our decision to focus most of our work on the 1984–97 period. First, there were extensive revisions in the Census occupation classifications that went into effect in the 1983 CPS. There are various (imperfect) ways to adjust the classifications to get consistency with earlier years, and we will present the results for such data in Section IV. But the bulk of our analysis is done with the "cleaner" 1980 classifications (with minor adjustments for changes made in the 1990 Census).

The nature of this limitation to the period since the 1980–82 recession can be seen in Figures 2.3 and 2.4. Figure 2.3 shows that male earnings inequality as measured by the 90/10 ratio took off in 1979, reflecting mainly the collapse at the bottom of the distribution during and just after the 1980–82 recession. This recession was particularly severe, and the wage and employment restructuring that took place during these years reflected the downturn as well as the adjustments firms made in reaction to the high inflation years of the 1970s (particularly for unionized firms whose workers were protected by cost-of-living contracts) and the sharp decline in trade competitiveness (following the

Figure 2.3 **Hourly Real Wage Decile Cutoffs, Male Workers** (1973=100)

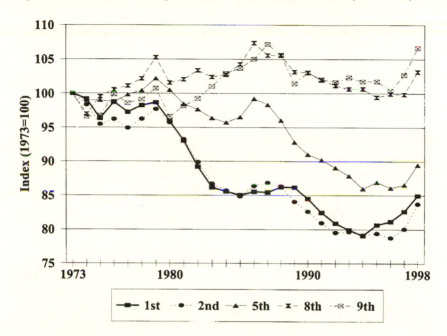

rise in the value of the dollar). Since computers did not play a substantial role in determining skill requirements in most workplaces until at least the mid-1980s, it seems clear that if technological change in the workplace played the key role in causing the demand shift, it would be observed after the 1980–82 recession.

As Figure 2.3 indicates, the decline in male real hourly wages at the tenth and twentieth percentiles continued in the late 1980s and early 1990s. It also shows a pronounced decline in the middle of the distribution. In 1996 dollars, the typical 1st decile worker experienced a decline from $5.37 in 1984 to $5.12 in 1996; the 2nd decile worker from $7.47 to $6.94; and the median (fiftieth percentile) worker from $13.73 to $12.62. In contrast, the ninetieth percentile worker saw an increase from $28.26 to $29 (Bernstein and Mishel 1997, Table 6). Figure 2.4 shows that for women, the growth in inequality since 1979 took place mainly after the recession, as real wages fell at the tenth percentile between 1982 and 1987, and rose steadily at the eightieth and ninetieth percentiles from 1982 through 1994. Our concern in this report is primarily with the post-recession (after 1983) rise in inequality. As Philip Moss

Figure 2.4 **Hourly Real Wage Decile Cutoffs, Female Workers** (1973=100)

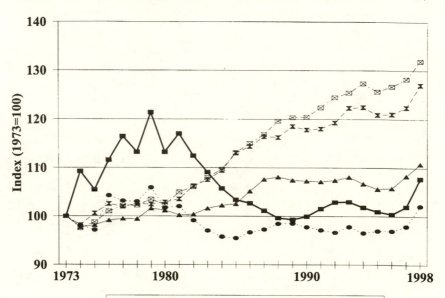

(1998, 24) has put it, "A reading of the statistical literature leaves the reader with a host of concerns with the explanations of why inequality continued to rise after the economy recovered from the severe 1981–82 recession."

For our analysis of the period since the 1980–82 recession, we chose to examine two overlapping intervals, 1984–92 and 1989–97. The end-points of the former are relatively high unemployment years just after recessions (mid-year unemployment was 7.5 percent in 1984 and 7.7 percent in 1992); the more recent period is defined by business cycle peak years (5.2 percent unemployment in 1989 and 4.9 percent in 1997). In Section IV below, we supplement our examination of wage and hours change by occupation for these two recent periods with one that reports wage and employment change between 1970 and 1994. This is useful not only because it adds a decade and a half but also because it measures demand shifts by employment rather than hours and it employs differ-ent dates. These differences provide a further check on the robustness of our results for the recent periods. The longer term data is defined for three periods: 1970–79 (mid-year unemployment rates of 5.0 and 5.7), 1979–86 (5.7 and 7.0), and 1986–94 (7.0 and 6.1).[8]

A unique characteristic of this study is our use of alternative measures of "skill." We use two conventional *indirect* measures of worker skill: the mean wage for the job and the percentage of the employed workforce in the job with more than a high school degree (% > HS). The former presumes that workers in the job will tend to be paid their marginal product, which in turn should closely reflect the skills and other work-related traits of the typical worker employed in the job. The educational attainment measure is also indirect, since its use presumes that across the job structure more years of schooling are closely associated with higher levels of work-relevant skills, and hence higher productivity, for which the employee is actually paid.

These two measures may not adequately capture differences in the skills valued by employers; educational attainment measures are suspect since they do not capture a variety of workplace relevant skills, and the relative wage is unreliable because with imperfect information, limited worker mobility, and at least some role for social norms and institutions, most labor markets may not look much like the textbook model. Thus, motor skills are particularly important for some highly paid professionals (physicians, athletes) as well as many poorly paid blue-collar jobs and are not closely linked to years of schooling. Social interaction skills and emotional intelligence are central to good managerial performance (Goleman 1998). These are traits only loosely linked to years of educational attainment. Best-practice computer programmers and engineers are typically not paid nearly as much as investment bankers and corporate lawyers although years of schooling may be similar. Indeed, even relatively well-paid full-time child care workers tend to earn less than the least well-paid truck drivers, despite higher years of schooling. It seems fair to say that educational attainment and relative wages are, at best, quite rough proxies for job skill requirements.

We therefore supplement these with two "direct" measures of workplace skill. The first is a measure of cognitive skill requirements ("Factor 1," a measure of what Miller et al. 1980, term "substantive complexity"), which consists of scores on the primary factor in a factor analysis of more than forty measures of work-related skills and traits from the *Dictionary of Occupational Titles* of the U.S. Department of Labor.[9] The underlying skill measures reflect thousands of workplace interviews conducted between 1967 and 1974. Although the DOT-based measure is dated, a recent revision, based on interviews conducted in

1989 for occupations in selected high-growth, high-tech industries produced remarkably similar skill scores.[10]

Our second direct measure is the average of three indices of workplace literacy for those 16 and older (prose literacy, document literacy, and quantitative literacy) from the National Adult Literacy Survey (NALS) produced by the National Center for Education Statistics.[11] The literacy measures are based on large-scale national surveys conducted in 1992. Occupation scores are the mean of the scores for each individual in the occupation.

Table 2.1 presents simple correlations among these four skill measures, relative hours change and relative wage change. The two panels in the top half of the table present results weighted by hours worked for 1984–92 and 1989–97. The bottom two panels present the unweighted results. The four skill measures are highly correlated but far from identical. Surprisingly, Factor1, derived from shopfloor interviews between 1966 and 1974, is more highly correlated with the 1992 wage measure than NALS, our functional literacy measure that dates from the same year (e.g., in the weighted correlation, Factor1 and Wage92 have a coefficient of .81, compared to a NALS and Wage92 coefficient of .72). On the other hand, NALS and %>HS are nearly perfectly correlated (.91). Prefiguring results presented below, the last two rows of each panel in Table 2.1 show the correlations between skill measures and wage and hours change. Although statistically significant, the coefficients for wage change and the various skill measures are modest: .47 for %>HS and .38 for NALS in the first period; and .26 and .22 respectively in the second. These results show a substantial decline in the size of the coefficient between the 1980s and 1990s, the reverse of what we would expect on the basis of the skill-biased technological change hypothesis.

Finally, we began this project with the assumption that greater occupation (and industry) detail would provide a clearer picture of the kinds of jobs experiencing wage and employment growth and decline. It is possible, however, that at finer levels of occupation detail, workers doing similar work may get allocated to the wrong occupations. In other words, disaggregation may increase error in the data. A test for within- vs. between-group variation (anova) offers a simple way to determine whether greater disaggregation produces more meaningful (homogeneous) groups: within-job share of wage variance should decline as the level of detail increases. Table 2.2 presents results for four levels of occupation aggregation for 1984, 1989, 1992, and 1997. The results show that disaggregation is clearly associated with less within-group varia-

Table 2.1

Correlations Between Different Skill Measures

Panel A: Total Workers, 1984–92 (weighted by total weekly hours, 1992)

Variable[a]	Wage92	%>HS	NALS	Factor	Relative wage change[b]	Relative hours change[b]
Wage92	1.000					
%>HS	0.748	1.000				
	0.00					
NALS	0.719	0.910	1.000			
	0.00	*0.00*				
Factor	0.812	0.768	0.780	1.000		
	0.00	*0.00*	*0.00*			
Relative	0.244	0.469	0.378	0.237	1.000	
wage change	*0.00*	*0.00*	*0.00*	*0.00*		
Relative	0.180	0.296	0.271	0.168	0.102	1.000
hours change	*0.00*	*0.00*	*0.00*	*0.00*	*0.04*	

Panel B: Total Workers, 1989–97 (weighted by total weekly hours, 1997)

Variable[a]	Wage97	%>HS	NALS	Factor	Relative wage change[b]	Relative hours change[b]
Wage97	1.000					
%>HS	0.789	1.000				
	0.00					
NALS	0.738	0.916	1.000			
	0.00	*0.00*				
Factor	0.832	0.786	0.792	1.000		
	0.00	*0.00*	*0.00*			
Relative	0.059	0.261	0.220	0.103	1.000	
wage change	*0.24*	*0.00*	*0.00*	*0.04*		
Relative	0.233	0.299	0.287	0.247	−0.057	1.000
hours change	*0.00*	*0.00*	*0.00*	*0.00*	*0.26*	

Source: Current Population Survey, Outgoing Rotation Group data.
Notes:
[a] The level of significance is indicated in italics below correlation coefficient.
[b] Relative wage and hour changes are measured as the annual percentage change in the occupation wage (hour) relative to the economy-wide average, weighted by total weekly hours in the end year of period change.

tion for both male and female workers and for each of the four years. At least concerning wages, then, more detailed occupations are more homogeneous. Interestingly, however, the share of total wage variance that occurs within occupations grows substantially over time, particularly between 1992 and 1997.[12]

Table 2.2

Within-Group Share of Wage Variance by Level of Occupational Detail

	1 Digit	2 Digit	3 Digit	Modified 3 Digit
Panel A: All Workers, 1984–97				
1984	60.8	55.7	52.0	50.4
1989	62.7	57.1	53.6	52.2
1992	62.4	57.2	53.8	52.2
1997	71.1	66.2	63.9	61.8
Panel B: Male Workers, 1984–97				
1984	78.1	73.9	69.7	67.6
1989	80.1	74.7	70.5	68.8
1992	76.6	71.7	67.5	65.5
1997	88.7	84.3	81.0	79.1
Panel C: Female Workers, 1984–97				
1984	27.1	25.5	23.6	23.2
1989	32.5	29.8	27.9	27.4
1992	38.3	35.4	33.4	32.8
1997	43.4	40.8	38.8	38.2

IV. Results: Patterns of Hours and Wage Growth

In this section we examine patterns of hours and wage growth at varying levels of occupation and industry detail for 7–9 year periods between 1970 and 1997. We begin with two periods for which we are able to use 1980 occupation classifications with the MORG (merged outgoing rotation group) data, 1984–92 and 1989–97. We examine hours and wage change for four alternative levels of job aggregation for these two periods: one-digit occupation groups (13 occupations), two-digit occupation groups (44 occupations), three-digit occupations (392 occupations), and modified three-digit occupations (450 occupations).[13] In the second part of this section, we examine changes in employment (rather than hours) and do so with a consistent set of detailed (three-digit) occupations for a much longer time frame, 1970 to 1994. The latter are subdivided into three periods, 1970–79, 1979–86, and 1986–94.

Hours and Wage Change, 1984–97

Large Occupation Groups (one-digit)

Table 2.3 presents weighted regression estimates of relative wage change on relative hours growth for male, female, and all workers, using four

Table 2.3

Regression Results by Level of Aggregation

Panel A: One-Digit Major Occupation

		1984–92			1989–97		
		Coeff.	S.E.	Adj. R^2	Coeff.	S.E.	Adj. R^2
Total	Wtd.	0.219 ***	0.090	0.290	0.194 ***	0.081	0.282
(n=13)	Unwtd.	0.062	0.131	−0.069	0.053	0.180	−0.082
Male	Wtd.	0.186	0.112	0.127	0.352 ***	0.109	0.441
(n=13)	Unwtd.	−0.221	0.125	0.149	0.651 ***	0.226	0.377
Female	Wtd.	0.153 ***	0.055	0.359	0.131 ***	0.052	0.307
(n=13)	Unwtd.	0.126	0.066	0.183	0.009	0.111	−0.090

Panel B: Two–Digit Occupation Groups

		1984–92			1989–97		
		Coeff.	S.E.	Adj. R^2	Coeff.	S.E.	Adj. R^2
Total	Wtd.	0.091	0.052	0.045	0.086 **	0.045	0.060
(n=43)	Unwtd.	0.120 **	0.058	0.070	0.024	0.049	−0.018
Male	Wtd.	0.061	0.054	0.006	0.121 **	0.057	0.079
(n=43)	Unwtd.	0.071	0.062	0.007	0.089	0.063	0.024
Female	Wtd.	0.081 ***	0.035	0.092	0.063 **	0.032	0.066
(n=43)	Unwtd.	0.097 **	0.046	0.076	−0.048	0.074	−0.014

Panel C: Three–Digit Occupation Groups

		1984–92			1989–97		
		Coeff.	S.E.	Adj. R^2	Coeff.	S.E.	Adj. R^2
Total	Wtd.	0.022 **	0.011	0.008	−0.011	0.010	0.001
(n=392)	Unwtd.	0.036 ***	0.014	0.014	−0.001	0.014	−0.003
Male	Wtd.	0.002	0.011	−0.003	0.002	0.015	−0.003
(n=358)	Unwtd.	0.015	0.015	0.000	−0.004	0.018	−0.003
Female	Wtd.	0.018	0.011	0.007	−0.016	0.009	0.008
(n=258)	Unwtd.	0.018	0.015	0.002	−0.016	0.012	0.003

Panel D: Modified Three–Digit Occupation Groups[a]

		1984–92			1989–97		
		Coeff.	S.E.	Adj. R^2	Coeff.	S.E.	Adj. R^2
Total	Wtd.	0.024 ***	0.007	0.024	−0.012	0.010	0.001
(n=450)	Unwtd.	0.025 ***	0.010	0.013	−0.008	0.014	−0.002
Male	Wtd.	0.003	0.011	−0.002	0.014	0.014	−0.002
(n=406)	Unwtd.	0.002	0.015	−0.002	−0.011	0.017	−0.002
Female	Wtd.	0.013	0.008	0.006	−0.014 *	0.009	0.005
(n=282)	Unwtd.	0.013	0.010	0.002	−0.013	0.012	0.001

Source: Authors' analysis of Current Population Survey outgoing rotation group data.

Notes: Relative wage and hour changes are measured as the annual percentage change in the occupation wage (hour) relative to the economy–wide average, weighted by total weekly hours in the end year of period change.

*** indicates significance at 1 percent level, ** at 5 percent, and * at 10 percent.

[a] Includes the six largest occupations broken down into 2–15 individual occupation groups.

levels of disaggregation of occupation groupings.[14] We begin with the most aggregated (and therefore most heterogeneous) Census occupation categories. The first column in Panel A shows the results for total, male, and female workers at the one-digit level (thirteen large occupation groups). The positive coefficient in both time periods and for all groups (total, male, female) is consistent with the conventional view that skill-biased demand shifts have led to a (positive) association between wage and employment growth across occupations, as diagramed in Figure 2.2. However, it is only the weighted results that are consistently strong; for the tests across occupations treated equally (not weighted by employment size), the results are strongly positive only for males in the 1989–97 period. The weighted results show about the same relationship between hours change and wage change across occupations for men and women in the 1984–92 period: a 10 percent increase in hours worked (relative to the economy average) was associated with a 1.8 percent increase in wages (relative to the average) for men and a 1.5 percent increase for women. For the 1989–97 period, this association strengthened considerably for men (to a 3.5 percent increase) and fell slightly (to a 1.3 percent increase) for women.

A closer look at where the occupation groups fall around the estimated upward sloping line is instructive. Figures 2.5 and 2.6 present scatter plots for relative hours and wage change for the thirteen large occupation groups for the 1984–92 and 1989–97 time periods, respectively. For each quadrant, we report total weekly hours worked in the occupation groups in the final year of the period, the percentage of all weekly hours worked, the number of occupation groups located in the quadrant, and the percentage of total hours worked in the quadrant by employees with more than a high school degree.

On each figure we draw an unweighted regression line on the scatterplot. This line shows little slope in either period, an impression confirmed by the negligible size of the regression statistics (for example, for 1984–92 the coefficient is .06, with a t-statistic of .47 and an adjusted R^2 of .07). Figures 2.5 and 2.6 suggest that the positive correlation between hours and wage change at this most aggregated level is driven by the performance of the large Professional/Specialty occupation group, which experienced positive hours growth and increasing real earnings.

Figure 2.5 generally supports the conventional view on the skill bias of labor demand changes in the first period under consideration (1984–92):

Figure 2.5 **Wage Change versus Hours Change, 1–Digit Level, 1984–1992**

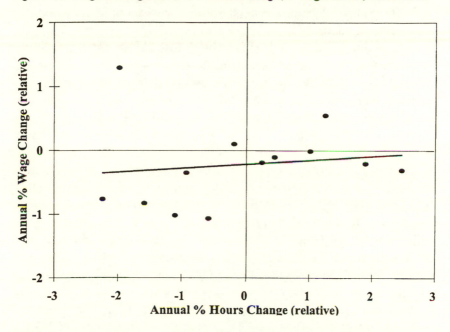

Figure 2.6 **Wage Change versus Hours Change, 1–Digit Level, 1989–1997**

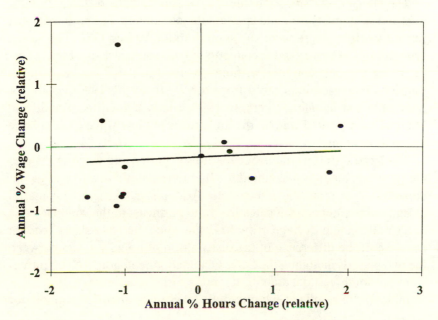

the occupations with the highest wage and hours growth clearly employed the most educated workers. Some 92 percent of hours worked in
the northeast quadrant in the first period were by those with more than
a high school degree; this compares with just 26 percent in the southwest quadrant. In the more recent period (1989–97, Figure 2.6), the gap
between the skill level in northeast quadrant (high wage and hours
growth) and southwest quadrant (low wage and hours growth) narrows: 78 percent of hours worked in the northeast and 39 percent in
the southwest quadrants were by workers with more than a high
school degree.

Perhaps the most striking result at the one-digit level is that occupation groups are not clearly concentrated in the northeast quadrant (characterized by relatively high hours and wage growth) and southwest
quadrant (characterized by relatively low hours and wage growth) in
either period, as would be the case if wage and hours changes were
mainly the result of demand shifts (as diagramed in Figures 2.1 and 2.2
above). Indeed, 56 percent of total weekly hours in 1992 were worked
in occupations in which relative hours and wage growth had opposite
signs in the 1984–92 period (that is, they appear in the northwest and
southeast quadrants of Figure 2.5). This drops to 31 percent in 1997 for
the 1989–97 period.

The same job classification title may be substantially different in earnings and skill levels for male and female job holders. For both male and
female workers, there were substantial hours worked in the low wage
growth/high hours growth occupations (the southeast quadrant). Furthermore, the concentration of hours worked in these southeast quadrant jobs increased noticeably from the 1980s to the 1990s, again for
both male and female workers. In 1997, nearly two-fifths of male and
female hours worked were in the high hours but low wage growth large
occupation groups.

The large shift toward the occupations experiencing declining wages
and growing hours is accounted for by modest shifts in a few large occupations. For men, the Executives, Administrative, and Managerial
Occupations category relocates from the northeast to the southeast due
to a small decline in wage growth. For women, just two shifts account
for most of the difference in the distribution of hours worked between
the two periods including the Sales Occupations category (which moves
from the southwest quadrant to the northeast quadrant).

In sum, the results at the one-digit level offer qualified support for the conventional prediction that wage and hours growth are correlated, a prediction that is consistent with the view that the last two decades have been characterized by extensive skill-biased demand shifts. Further, the stronger results in the more recent period (1989–97) for men in Table 2.3 are consistent with the view that skill-biased demand shifts have accelerated, as would be expected if computerization and globalization are the main sources of the shifts. On the other hand, nearly two-fifths of all hours worked for both men and women in the 1989–97 period were in occupations characterized by relatively high hours growth but lower than average wage growth (the southeast quadrant).

Clearly, a major problem with the one-digit classifications is the "lumpiness" of the data. Small changes in hours or wage growth can have substantial impacts on the summary statistics for each quadrant. The results should be more meaningful at the more narrowly defined two-digit level.

Two-Digit Occupations

Panel B of Table 2.3 presents the regression estimates of relative wage change on relative hours change for forty-four two-digit Census occupations groups. Both periods (1984–92 and 1989–97) show a positive but much weaker association than was found in the one-digit sample. For all workers, the results are similar for both periods: coefficients of .091 and .086, significant at just the 10 percent level, with adjusted R-squared values of only .05 to .06. The strongest results for men appear in the weighted test for the most recent period, but here the coefficient is only one-third its size in the more aggregated data for men, and the equation accounts for under 8 percent of the variation in wage growth, compared to 44 percent in one-digit data. For female workers, the more disaggregated results are strongest in the weighted equation for the early period, but the coefficient is half the size of its counterpart in the estimate for the one-digit sample and the adjusted R^2 is just one-quarter its size in the more aggregated sample. Thus, we find only a hint of a meaningful positive association between relative hours and wage growth in the two-digit data.

While the overall statistical relationship is weak, in some respects a pattern is discernable when we consider wage and hours growth in particular occupations (for reasons of space, we do not present scatterplots at the two- and three-digit levels; we return to them below, however, in our discussion of the most disaggregated modified 3–digit results). In both periods, blue-collar occupations in the goods industries are clearly concentrated in the southwest quadrant—occupations with declines in both relative wages and relative hours. Also consistent with the conventional view, several professional occupation groups experienced positive relative wage and hours change. Most prominent among these are Health Diagnosing Occupations (doctors and dentists); Health Assessment and Treating Occupations; Teachers, except College; Other Professional Specialty Occupations; and Health Technologists. Interestingly, in both periods, managers (Other Executives, Administrators and Managers) and a large supervisory occupation (Supervisors, Sales) experienced relatively high hours growth but low wage growth. Joining them in 1989–97 were two other relatively skilled occupations: Management Related Occupations and Engineers. These results do not seem particularly supportive of Gordon's supervisory burden explanation of earnings inequality growth.

We do, however, find that employees in the occupations with the fastest growing hours and wages have the greatest educational attainment, particularly in the most recent (1989–97) period: of the workers in occupations experiencing positive growth in relative hours and wage, 91 percent had more than a high school degree. This is compared to 81 percent in the 1984–92 period. Of the workers experiencing positive hours growth and relative wage declines in the more recent period, the proportion with greater than high school falls to 68 percent and for workers in occupations with declines in relative wages and hours the figure was just 38 percent. The evidence both across occupations in the later period and across periods for the high wage and hours growth jobs is consistent with the conventional skill-biased demand shift account.

Finally, among the occupation groups with relatively slow hours growth and stagnant or rising relative wages were two moderately skilled, primarily female, administrative support occupation groups (Secretaries; Financial Records and Processing Occupations), and three extremely low-wage groups (Private Household Service Occupations; Food Service Occupations; and Farm Workers and Related Occupations). The mean wages of these last three job groups in 1992 were $5.53, $5.52, and $6.44 (1997 dollars). We speculate that the minimum wage hikes that began in 1989 may help account for their relatively large proportional wage increases. The increase in the number of occupation groups and hours worked in the second period accounted for by occupations experiencing rising relative wages and declining relative hours (from four to eight occupation groups; from 6.7 percent to 12 percent of total hours worked) is consistent with this possibility.

As in the case of one-digit occupations, a significant percentage of all hours worked were in occupations experiencing relative wage declines along with relative hours growth. As with the more highly aggregated data, lumpiness may partly explain this result. Still the overall picture at this level of detail is that a substantial share of hours worked are in the off-diagonal quadrants, with neither positive nor negative relative wage and hours growth jobs; thus, we find that 70 percent of all hours worked in two-digit occupation groups with greater than average hours growth were also in occupation groups with lower than average wage growth.

Relating the observed pattern of wage and hours growth to the level of skills also produces a surprising result. While the expected pattern of wage levels and educational attainment shares are strongly supported for females, they are not for male workers. For men in both periods, among the occupation groups that experienced relatively high wage growth, the "skill" level (greater than high school shares) and real wage levels are similar in both slow and fast growing occupations. Indeed, in the most recent period, male workers in occupation groups with high hours growth but relatively low wage growth had the highest wages and the highest educational attainment. At the two-digit level, the pattern of relative wage change, hours change, and skill levels does not correspond well with the stylized prediction that appears in Figure 2.2.

Three-Digit Occupations

At the three-digit level we retain 392 of the 501 total Census occupations, which should raise considerably the within-group homogeneity of tasks and skill requirements compared to that of occupation groupings at the one- or two-digit level.[15] Given this greater precision, it is striking that the statistical association between relative wage and hours change is even weaker here. As the regression results shown for all workers in Panel C of Table 2.3 indicate the weighted coefficients decline from .08/.09 in the two periods with two-digit data, to −01/.02 in the three-digit data. With one exception, hours change in each of the equations in Panel C accounts for less than one percent of the variation in relative wage change. The reason for the poor statistical fit is readily apparent from the fact that nearly half of the occupations had opposite signs on the wage and hours change measures; that is, they fall in the northwest or southeast quadrants of Figure 2.2. Further, the relationship between hours growth and wage growth appears to weaken over time. While the coefficient on hours growth for all workers is small but positive for the 1984–92 period (.022, t-statistic of 2.01), it becomes negative for the 1989–97 period. Again, a rising share of occupations that fall far from the diagonal of Figure 2.2 helps explain this weakening of an already quite weak statistical relationship.

Northeast quadrant jobs. In both periods, occupations with high wage and hours growth were the most skilled while those experiencing relative declines in wages and hours were the least skilled. This result is consistent with the skill-biased demand shift account. But there is some ambiguity. The ten largest occupations experiencing relative wage and hours growth in the 1984–92 period accounted for about half of all hours worked in 1992. The largest four of these high wage and hours growth occupations were Elementary School Teachers, Registered Nurses, Nurses Aides and Orderlies, and Miscellaneous Administrative Support workers. These are low-to-moderate wage jobs requiring relatively high social ("people") skills. They are also heavily female: 86 percent of the hours worked in these four occupations were by women in 1992. Among the other top ten occupations experiencing positive relative wage and hours growth were social workers and general office supervisors. At least for these six large occupations, it would be surprising to find that technology- or trade-driven skill-biased technological change explains their experience. With the exception of Nurses Aides and Orderlies, our NALS, DOT, and educational attainment measures indicate that these largest jobs with high relative wage and hours growth in 1984–92 required above average cognitive skills. Nor, it should be noted, does this mix of occupations appear supportive of the bureaucratic burden account.

A quite different set of jobs experienced both high wage and high hours growth in the later period, 1989–97. But among the ten largest occupations, only Computer Systems Analysts and Computer Programmers appear to fit the skill-biased demand shift prototype. Note that in the 1984–92 period, Computer Programmers had high wage growth but relatively slow hours growth and Computer Systems Analysts experienced lower than average wage growth. So even for these two information technology occupations, the relative hours and wage growth evidence is ambiguous for the decade and a half since 1984.

It is striking that four of the ten largest occupations in the high wage and hours growth group required very low skills. In these four jobs, less than half of the hours worked in 1997 were by workers with more than a high school degree. In two of these occupations (Cooks; Maids and Housemen), less than one-quarter had more than a high school degree. Their experience of relatively high wage growth again suggests that the legislated increases in the minimum wage over this period may have played a substantial role. If so, it does not appear to have greatly harmed the rate of hours growth for these occupations.

Southwest quadrant jobs. On the other hand, as predicted by both skill mismatch and bureaucratic burden explanations, many of the largest jobs with lower than average hours and wage growth were blue-collar positions requiring low cognitive skills. Still, the data present us with a more complex portrait, since the wage and hours performance of three higher skilled white-collar occupations appear tied to that of their lower-skill, blue-collar counterparts in the same industries: Sales Representatives (manufacturing, mining, and wholesale) and Supervisors in production occupations experienced relative declines in hours and wages in both 1984–92 and 1989–97. While again not supportive of a central role for supervisors in the growth in wage inequality, these results are consistent with Galbraith's industry-level findings (1998).

Further, demand is not just shifting against workers in heavy industrial sectors. Several low- to moderately-skilled white-collar jobs also saw relative hours and wage declines in both periods. In 1984–92, these jobs include Cashiers and Accountants/Auditors, and in 1989–97, Secretaries, Other Financial Officers, and General Office Clerks. This indicates that skill-biased technological change may be having its greatest impact in the office by reducing staffing requirements for moderately skilled administrative support workers.

"Off-Diagonal" quadrant jobs. The ambiguous nature of the evidence regarding skill-biased demand shifts at the detailed occupation level is underlined by examining the types of jobs located "off the diagonal": those for which relative hours growth and relative wage growth were inversely related. A wide variety of jobs appear in the northwest quadrant (relatively high wage growth but lower than average hours growth). In both periods, for example, Automobile Mechanics and Secondary School Teachers are among the largest ten jobs for men in the sample.

However, these two large occupations appear at opposite ends of the skill spectrum. Auto Mechanics have a NALS score of 263 and only 32 percent possessed more than a high school degree in 1992. Secondary School Teachers, on the other hand, have a NALS score of 326 and 99 percent hold more than a high school diploma. For female workers, we also find Secondary School Teachers in this quadrant in both periods, along with a number of much lower skill occupations, such as Child Care Workers and a variety of Sales Worker occupations. In the 1989–97 period, five of the ten largest northeast quadrant jobs for women paid between $5.72 and $7.55 an hour on average. The rising wages and declining employment experienced in these jobs may reflect the combined effects of a rising minimum wage and computerization in the stores and offices.

We also find it difficult to generalize about the jobs in the southeast quadrant—those with relatively high hours growth and below average wage growth. For men, seven of the ten largest jobs in 1984–92 and six of the ten largest in 1989–97 are relatively low-skill (with, say, less than a 300 NALS score). The two largest southeast quadrant jobs in 1984–92 were Truck Drivers and Supervisors & Proprietors, Sales. For 1989–97, the two largest were Managers, n.e.c., and Laborers, excl. Construction (in the next section we subdivide three of these—Truck Drivers, Supervisors, and Managers—by industry). For female workers, Supervisors & Proprietors and Nurse's Aides, Orderlies and Attendants were two of the largest four jobs in this high hours growth, low wage growth quadrant.

As a result of this diversity in skill requirements across occupations both between and within the hours and wage change quadrants, we find no statistical association at the three-digit level between relative wage change and hours change. Panel C of Table 2.3 shows that this holds for both unweighted and weighted (by occupation size as measured by hours worked) tests in both time periods for both males and females. Indeed, if there is any relationship for female workers in the 1989–97 period, it is negative: higher wage growth is associated with relatively low hours growth.

Three-Digit Occupations Subdivided by Industrial Sector

While the three-digit classifications offer considerable occupational detail, there remain some extremely large occupational groupings. For example, there were 232 million hours worked by Managers, n.e.c., in

1992, or over 6 percent of the economy-wide total. Not only does this Manager occupation dwarf all but a few of the other (391) detailed occupations, it is extremely heterogeneous. The retail and personal services/recreation sectors accounted for over 25 percent of this category in 1992, and both were growing at well above average rates in both the 1984–92 and 1989–97 periods. Yet the average wages of these two low-wage manager groups ($12.07 and $14.12) were similar to that of the best paid group of truck drivers ($12.47), despite the fact that the latter had much lower average educational attainment. In contrast, other managers included under the Managers, n.e.c. umbrella included those in Finance, Insurance and Real Estate, who earned about twice as much on average ($25.33) in 1992. While only 18 percent of these high-wage managers had just a high school degree or less in that year, 47 percent of Retail Managers and 78 percent of high-wage Truck Drivers had no more than a high school degree.

Because of this heterogeneity, we subdivided six of the largest occupations by industry sector. We subdivided the largest occupation, Managers, n.e.c., into fifteen sector groups. The next five largest occupations (Secretaries; Supervisors, Sales; Cashiers; Janitors and Cleaners; and Truck Drivers) were disaggregated into two or three large sector groups based on 1989 average sector wage levels. By subdividing these large three-digit occupations we boost the number of occupations to 450.

Scatterplots of wage and hours change for the 450 occupations for each of the two periods are shown in Figures 2.7 and 2.8. These seeming "clouds" of data points illustrate a number of important points. First, there is no clear direct relation between demand growth (hours change) and wage changes, and any hint of such a relation in the first period disappears in the more recent period. The estimated unweighted regression line drawn in the figures shows a slight positive slope in the first period and then a slight negative slope in the second period. In the first period, 43 percent of hours worked were in occupations which experienced opposite changes in hours and wages. In the second period, more than half of the hours worked (52 percent) could be characterized this way. This deterioration of the relation between hours and wage growth confirms what had been found in the analysis of the more aggregated data.

Second, the relation between demand growth and wage growth is statistically weaker at the more disaggregated level. Compare, for example, the slope of the unweighted regression lines in the analysis of the one-digit data with that at the modified three-digit level (Figures 2.5

Figure 2.7 **Wage Change versus Hours Change, Modified 3–Digit Level, 1984–1992**

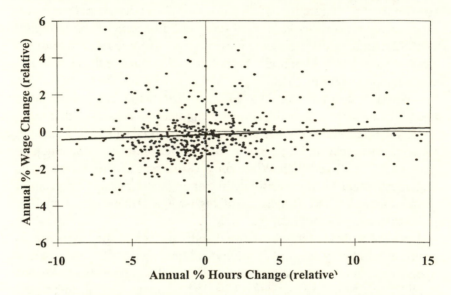

and 2.6 compared to 2.7 and 2.8). The weighted results shown in Panel D of Table 2.3 for total workers confirm this result: the small but highly significant coefficient for 1984–92 becomes negative and insignificant for 1989–97. Once again, if the skill mismatch story has strong empirical support, we would have expected that more detailed and homogeneous occupational groupings would bring more, not less, precision to the relation between hours and wage growth.

A third point relating to the scatterplots is that jobs experiencing positive wage and hours growth show much higher skill levels, on average, than jobs that suffered wage and hours declines. Among those in jobs with positive wage and hours growth in the second period (1989–97), 63 percent possessed greater than high school education, while only 43 percent of those with hours and wage declines had more than a high school education. While this would seem to support the skill mismatch theory, the picture is once again clouded by the nature of these jobs.

The jobs that have shown large and persistent wage and hours growth since 1984 tend to require relatively high skill levels, but are not generally "high-tech" (e.g., strongly engineering or computer related) or high-level supervisory jobs. Table 2.4 shows the modified three-digit occupations that experience *both* high wage and hours growth (.5 per-

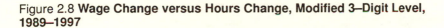

Figure 2.8 **Wage Change versus Hours Change, Modified 3–Digit Level, 1989–1997**

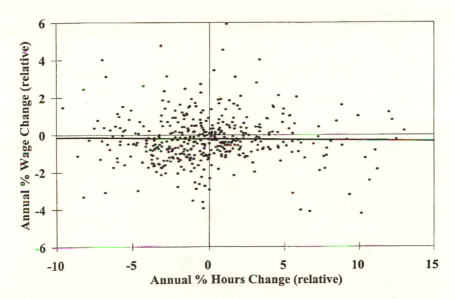

cent or above) in *both* periods. Of the seventeen jobs that met these criteria, eleven were professionals in the health and education sectors. Three others have only low to moderate skill (NALS) scores. The only high-skill, high-tech job on the list (outside the health sector) is Mechanical Engineering Technicians, a fairly small occupation (498,000 average hours worked per week, compared to 67 million for Elementary Teachers). Nor do high-level managers (supervisors) figure prominently in this list.

If we consider only the 1990s, the ten largest high wage and hours growth jobs were Cashiers, Elementary School Teachers, Cooks, Computer Systems Analysts and Scientists, Managers (Retail), Receptionists, Social Workers, Computer Programmers, Guards and Police (except public service), and Data-Entry Keyers. While two computer-related jobs requiring at least moderate skills made this list, so did four very low skill jobs (Cooks, Cashiers, Receptionists, and Data-Entry Keyers). One managerial occupation also makes the list, but is neither a high-wage nor high-skill job. Again, we find little support for either the skill mismatch or bureaucratic burden explanation.

In the 1990s, we find more managers in the southeast quadrant, in which jobs show relatively low wage growth but high employment

Table 2.4

Occupations with Large[a] Wage and Hours Growth in Both Periods
(modified 3-digit)

Occupation	Wage change		Hours change		Skill (NALS)	Weekly hours[b]
	1984–92	1989–97	1984–92	1989–97	1992	1992
Teachers, elementary	0.63	0.95	3.24	2.03	322.5	67,200,000
Physicians	3.06	1.07	3.91	4.96	333.5	12,800,000
Teachers, special education	1.53	1.47	5.26	4.17	317.9	10,500,000
Kitchen workers, food prep	0.50	1.24	5.98	8.90	250.5	6,833,528
Pharmacists	1.50	2.00	3.37	2.43	328.9	6,253,545
Sales workers: radio, TV	1.74	1.83	1.04	1.09	303.3	5,909,862
Radiologic technicians	1.35	0.74	2.59	1.39	311.7	4,953,473
Physical therapists	2.86	2.85	6.77	2.12	346.8	3,529,518
Therapists, n.e.c.	1.69	0.61	6.69	3.46	315.3	2,507,109
Speech therapists	3.06	0.73	3.18	4.60	327.5	2,418,274
Occupational therapists	5.01	1.53	9.21	4.13	349.4	1,543,331
Authors	0.68	1.31	13.65	18.26	336.9	1,374,235
Veterinarians	2.35	1.63	3.64	2.04	350.3	804,724
Actuaries	1.77	1.38	3.69	1.57	351.5	719,161
Dancers	1.71	1.96	5.90	5.25	294.9	570,139
Mech. engineering techs.	2.36	0.79	0.67	6.97	335.5	498,008
Medical science teachers	0.83	4.93	2.26	1.62	360.1	337,516

Notes:
[a] Wage and hours change figures are annual percentage changes. Our criterion for "large" is >= .5%.
[b] Average hours worked per week.

growth. The largest, ranked by size, were Supervisors and Proprietors, Sales Occupations, Registered Nurses, Managers (Manufacturing), and Accountants. While these are no doubt relatively high-skill jobs, they are not particularly associated with technological change. Two of the five fit Gordon's "bureaucrats" who contribute to the supervisory burden. But, again, these are relatively *low* wage growth occupations in this recent period.

The conclusions from the scatterplots are reflected in the weighted regression estimates presented in Panel D of Table 2.3. Separate tests by gender also produce no evidence of a positive relationship between wage and hours change.

The lack of a clear relationship between employment and wage growth is also evident in Figures 2.9 and 2.10, which show relative wage growth

Figure 2.9 **Wage Growth by Hours Growth Decile, 1984–1992**

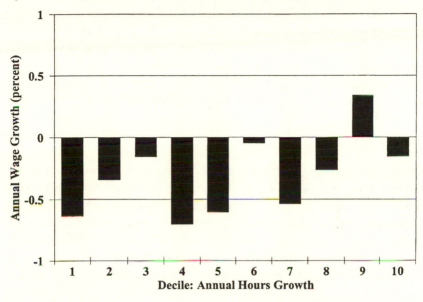

Figure 2.10 **Wage Growth by Hours Growth Decile, 1989–1997**

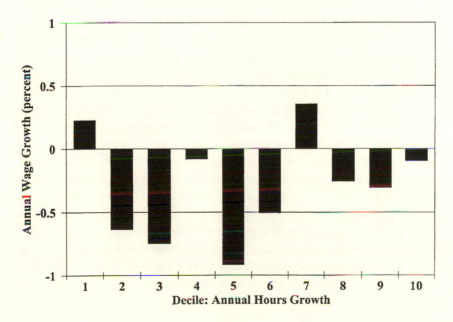

by deciles of employment growth, again measured by growth in relative hours. In the 1984–92 period, the largest relative wage declines were experienced by workers in the first, fourth, and fifth deciles; the ninth decile was the only one showing positive average wage gains. In the later period, the first and seventh decile had positive wage growth. But there is no apparent pattern to the bars: wage growth shows no systematic link to hours growth across disaggregated occupations.

Wage Change and Skill Levels

The single variable equations presented above account for hardly any of the variation in relative wage change. It may be that with a more adequate specification, hours growth would show the expected positive relationship with wage growth. Numerous studies have documented a rising return to skill, as measured by years of schooling. While the explanation remains controversial, it is clear that higher-skilled occupations have experienced higher wage growth (Gittleman 1994; Pryor and Schaffer 1997). But has this relationship strengthened, as we would expect if skill-biased demand shifts have been the main source of growing wage inequality? Here we consider in more detail the role of skill in the wage and hours dynamics analyzed above. We focus mainly on the NALS score, the average of three indices of workplace literacy—prose literacy, document literacy, and quantitative literacy—from the National Adult Literacy Survey. We use only the most disaggregated breakdown of occupations, the three-digit and modified three-digit levels.

Table 2.5 presents results of simple OLS tests that relate wage growth to hours growth and skill levels, the latter measured by the share of workers in a job with greater than a high school degree, by the DOT Factor 1 measure and by the average functional literacy of workers employed in each occupation (NALS). In every test reported here, the skill measure is positively and significantly related to wage change across jobs. While hours growth alone accounted for virtually none of the variation in wage growth in Table 2.3 (R^2 less than 1 percent), the addition of skill measures in Table 2.5 results in equations that account (with one exception) for 3–29 percent of the variation in wage growth across detailed occupations.

Note, however, that the association between wage growth and the skill level of occupations declines noticeably from the 1980s (1984–92) to the 1990s (1989–97) for both men and women. The regression coefficients on the skill variables and the coefficient of variation for the

Table 2.5

Regression Results: Effects of Skill on Wage Growth

	Greater-than-high-school		"Factor 1"		NALS score	
	Hours growth	%>HS	Hours growth	Factor 1	Hours growth	NALS
Panel A: 1984–92						
Total	−0.01	1.70***	0.01	0.24***	−0.0002	0.011***
(N=392)	(0.01)	(0.17)	(0.01)	(0.05)	(0.01)	(0.001)
	Adj. R^2	0.217	Adj. R^2	0.055	Adj. R^2	0.139
Males	−0.02**	1.38***	0.00	0.36***	−0.01	0.010***
(N=358)	(0.01)	(0.15)	(0.01)	(0.05)	(0.01)	(0.001)
	Adj. R^2	0.181	Adj. R^2	0.122	Adj. R^2	0.133
Females	−0.01	2.11***	−0.003	0.45***	−0.01	0.014***
(N=258)	(0.01)	(0.21)	(0.01)	(0.07)	(0.01)	(0.001)
	Adj. R^2	0.291	Adj. R^2	0.151	Adj. R^2	0.181
Panel B: 1989–97						
Total	−0.03***	0.95***	−0.02	0.12***	−0.03	0.007***
(N=392)	(0.01)	(0.16)	(0.01)	(0.05)	(0.01)	(0.001)
	Adj. R^2	0.083	Adj. R^2	0.013	Adj. R^2	0.059
Males	−0.02	0.97***	−0.01	0.21***	−0.02	0.008***
(N=358)	0.01	(0.18)	(0.01)	(0.06)	(0.01)	(0.001)
	Adj. R^2	0.071	Adj. R^2	0.033	Adj. R^2	0.061
Females	−0.03***	0.90***	−0.02	0.19***	−0.02	0.006***
(N=258)	0.01	(0.19)	(0.01)	(0.06)	(0.01)	(0.001)
	Adj. R^2	0.082	Adj. R^2	0.044	Adj. R^2	0.055

Notes: *** indicates significance at 1 percent level, ** at 5 percent, and * at 10 percent.

equation all decline markedly between these two periods for each of the eight tests presented. For all workers with NALS as the skill measure, the coefficient drops from .011 to .007, with a decline in the R^2 from 14 to 6 percent. The magnitude of the decline for male workers is similar, and much larger for female workers. If computerization and globalization are the main sources of a demand shift we would have expected the reverse to hold, since both developments have characterized the 1990s at least as much as (and probably more than) the 1980s, and because it takes time for firms to adjust to structural changes of this sort.

Within the supply/demand model, demand shifts may be manifested in a variety of combinations of hours and wage change depending upon the elasticity of supply. If demand shifts are as skill-biased as the literature claims, then there should be a strong statistical relationship between occupation skill levels and the sum of hours and wage change. We present the results of this exercise in Figures 2.11 and 2.12 for 448 modified three-digit occupations. The trendline is upward sloping, as predicted. But the slope is modest, with the NALS measure accounting for 6.5 percent of the variation in hours + wage change in the first period, and 5.8 percent in the second. In sum, if this is a measure of the demand shift, we find a modestly positive statistical association of skill levels with it, but no evidence of strengthening over time.

The conventional view on the positive correlation between employment and wage growth finds weak and, over time, weakening support at the level of detailed occupations. And yet skill level is clearly and positively associated with both wage and hours growth, patterns that are consistent with the conventional view. How can we reconcile these patterns? The answer must be that some high-skill occupations are experiencing relatively rapid growth in hours and some are enjoying relatively large wage increases, but fewer occupations are experiencing both. For example, we find that many managerial and service occupations show high relative hours growth but low relative wage growth. In addition to Retail Managers, which made the list just described, supervisory jobs located in the southeast quadrant in the 1990s include Managers, Medicine and Health; Securities and Financial Services Sales; Administration and Official, Public Administration; Managers, Education and Social Services; Managers, Transportation; and Managers, Related Occupations, n.e.c. These are high-skill jobs as measured by NALS, but have been experiencing declining relative wages. Once again, we find little support at the detailed occupation level for either the skill mismatch or the supervisory burden explanations.

Employment and Wage Growth, 1970–94

As a check for the robustness of the results reported above and to better assess the change in the association between wage change, employment growth, and skill levels over time, we conducted similar analyses with data from the March Current Population Survey (CPS). In these tests we employ an alternative measure of the hourly wage. We also use a measure of employment (rather than hours) for different years covering a longer time span (1970, 1979, 1986, and 1994).

Although our measure of earnings remains the hourly wage and it is derived from the same underlying source (the CPS), it is constructed

Figure 2.11 **Wage Plus Hours Change versus NALS Score, 1984–1992**

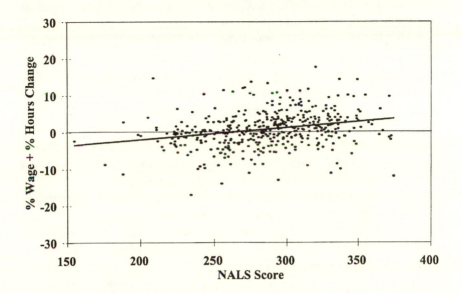

Figure 2.12 **Wage Plus Hours Change versus NALS Score, 1989–1997**

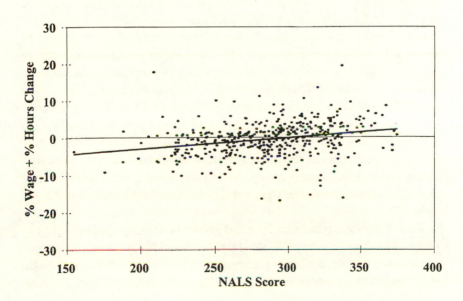

differently. The results presented above were based on the CPS Outgoing Rotation Groups (ORG) data, in which the hourly wage is taken
directly from survey respondents if they were paid by the hour; for sala-
ried workers, the hourly wage was derived from weekly earnings in the
previous week (adjusted by usual hours per week). On the other hand, in
the March CPS data used here, the hourly wage must be derived from
estimates by respondents of their annual earnings in the previous year,
which can then be adjusted to an hourly figure using usual weeks and
hours per week. Bernstein and Mishel (1997) argue that the hourly wage
estimates from the ORG data are superior. Nevertheless, these March
CPS data are widely used in earnings studies and their availability in a
form that allows for comparison before and after the substantial changes
in occupation definitions in the 1980 Census offer us an opportunity to
check the robustness of the results presented above over a much longer
time period. Excluding the smallest occupations, 441 occupations are
included in the first two periods (1970–79 and 1979–86) and 447 in the
most recent period (1986–94).

Results for the simple weighted regression of percentage wage change
on percentage employment change and skill level (the overall NALS
score) for the three subperiods are presented in Table 2.6. Like most of
the coefficients on hours growth in Table 2.5, the top row shows that in
the first two periods (1970–79 and 1979–86), employment growth was
negatively or only weakly positively related to wage change, whether or
not the NALS skill measure was included. Consistent with the skill-
biased demand shift account, the coefficient on NALS is far higher in
the 1980s and 1990s than in the 1970s. But only in the most recent
period do we find the predicted statistically significant positive relationship between employment and wage change. And even here, in the
1986–94 period, when computerization should have had its greatest
impact on the wage structure, the explanatory power of our simple skill-
biased demand shift model of wage change is negligible. Only a tiny
share (1–2 percent) of the variation in wage change across these 447
occupations is accounted for by our measures of employment change
and skill levels, even less than for the results shown in Table 2.5 for
1989–97.

For 1970–79, neither employment growth nor skill level helps to explain wage change. The problem is that in the 1970s we count 186 occupations with relatively high employment growth but low wage growth.
In 1979, these occupations accounted for 43 percent of total employ-

Table 2.6

Regression Results: Wage Change on Hours Change and Skill Level
(Pryor/Schaffer 3-digit occupations)

Variable coefficient (standard error)	Period 1: 1970–1979 (N=441)		Period 2: 1979–1986 (N=441)		Period 3: 1986–1994 (N=447)	
	Model 1	Model 2	Model 1	Model 2	Model 1	Model 2
Employment growth	−0.047** (−0.02)	−0.052** (−0.02)	0.002 (0.003)	−0.0013 (0.003)	0.068*** (0.028)	0.053* (0.028)
NALS		0.002 (0.002)		0.0114*** (0.0025)		0.0095*** (0.0036)
Adjusted R²	0.011	0.010	0.001	0.047	0.011	0.024

Notes: * indicates coefficient significant at the 10 percent level, ** at 5 percent, ***
at 1 percent.
Regressions are weighted by total occupational employment in the last year of
each period.

ment. Equally notable, these low wage growth jobs had the same average score on functional literacy (292) as the 73 occupations that experienced relatively high growth in hours and wages.

For the 1979–86 period, the functional literacy score in high wage and employment growth jobs is substantially higher (304) than the scores for jobs in the other three quadrants (280–85), consistent with the conventional view. Still, over half of all workers were employed in occupations that appear "off the diagonal"—that is, in the northwest and southeast quadrants in Figure 2.2. The results in the middle panel of Table 2.6 indicate that there was a positive association between wage change and skill levels, but not between wage change and employment growth, in the early- to mid-1980s; the coefficient on employment change is small and insignificant in both models. The addition of the NALS skill measure increases the explanatory power of the equation from zero to almost five percent. While this improvement is substantial, these models, like those presented in Table 2.5, appear to provide scant support for the skill-biased demand shift hypothesis.

For the most recent 1986–94 period, both employment change and skill level measures are positive and statistically significant, but (as noted above) the explanatory power of the equations is minimal. Again, behind this poor performance are jobs that are located in the off-diagonal quadrants. The scatter plots of employment growth and the March CPS hourly wage look similar to those that appear in Figures 2.5 through 2.8 (which, again, relied on hours growth and a more direct measure of hourly wages with different years as end points). The average functional literacy (NALS) scores in the occupations experiencing relatively high wage growth and slow employment growth (the northeast quadrant) and for occupations experiencing slow wage growth and relatively large hours growth (the southeast quadrant) are nearly the same as the mean NALS scores for occupations with relatively high hours and wage growth (the northeast quadrant): 287 and 292 compared to 299.

As we found with the ORG data, the monthly CPS data indicate that a large share of the workforce, ranging from 28 to 40 percent, is employed in occupations that show strong employment growth but declining relative wages. In the 1986–94 period, the largest of these were Supervisors and Proprietors, Sales Occupations; Truck Drivers; Janitors and Cleaners; Nursing Aides, Orderlies and Attendants; Cooks; and Stock Handlers and Baggers. The poor wage performance of these service sector jobs is unlikely to be much affected by foreign trade or the outsourcing of production to low-wage foreign countries. On the other hand, if technological change (computerization) accounts for the slow wage growth of these high employment growth jobs, it may be due to *deskilling*, which has the effect of increasing the supply of workers available to firms—a very different skill-biased technological change explanation for recent relative wage trends.

V. Conclusion

Earnings inequality increased substantially between the late 1970s and the late 1990s. It is widely accepted that the rising gap between the best and worst paid workers reflects a growing payoff to skill as the workplace is transformed by computerization and the competitive pressures of globalization. In this view, the "best" jobs have grown fastest, leading to rapid wage increases as employers try to fill positions, while declining demand for the worst jobs has led to collapsing wages, as too many low-skill workers chase too few jobs. If this skill-biased demand shift explanation can account for much of the growth in inequality, we should observe a fairly tight statistical fit between changes in employment and changes in wages: the highest (lowest) skill jobs should show both the highest (lowest) hours/employment growth and the highest (lowest) wage growth. The strength of this fit should improve with our ability to measure the skill of a job. This requires both a good measure of skill and narrowly defined (homogeneous in skill) job classifications. And finally, as both computerization and globalization advance, in the absence of substantial compensating supply shifts, skill-biased demand shifts should produce a strengthening of the association between skill requirements, employment growth, and wage growth across jobs over time.

On balance, at the occupation level the skill-biased demand shift explanation is not strongly supported by our results, which can be summed up in three main points. First, consistent with the conventional wisdom, jobs that have experienced both high (low) wage and high (low) hours growth tend to show, *as a group*, the highest (lowest) skill levels. However, for detailed occupations we can generalize only about the *low* wage and hours growth occupations, which for both male and female workers clearly require the least skills, at least as conventionally measured. Outside of this "southwest quadrant," the picture is much less clear. *For both males and females, high wage and hours growth occupations reflect a mix of low, middle, and high skill requirements.* Indeed, by far the most hours worked in the high wage and employment growth jobs through the mid-1990s have been by education and health service sector professionals. These are jobs whose credentialing (medical licensing, advanced degrees, teaching certificates) typically shelters them from the virulent wage competition that has afflicted much of the workforce. This finding is not strongly supportive of either the conventional computer-driven demand shift story or Gordon's bureaucratic burden account.

Our second finding further complicates the story. Workers are by no means limited or even concentrated in these two conventional categories—the high skilled jobs with high wage and hours growth and the low skilled jobs with low or declining wage and hours growth. Rather, we find that *a large share of total hours worked (and employment) occurs in jobs with relatively high hours growth but low wage growth (the southeast quadrant)*. Together with the range of skill levels required in the high wage and employment growth jobs, this "off-diagonal" result explains our failure to find any statistical relationship between wage change and hours change across occupations.

Interestingly, the relationship between hours and wage change appears to depend on the level of occupational aggregation, but in a way that is just the reverse of what we would have expected. That is, we find a modest positive statistical relationship between relative wage growth and relative hours growth at the most aggregated classification level (thirteen one-digit large occupation groups), even less at the two-digit (forty-four occupation groups), and none at the three-digit (390 occupations) and modified three-digit (450 occupation/industry cells) levels. This result holds for each time period, for both data sets, and for both male and female workers.

Our third principal finding relates to the link between wage change and skill. If skill-biased technological change (computerization) and competitive pressures from globalization and deregulation account for a demand shift against low-skill workers, we would expect the wage change/skill relationship to strengthen over time. We find no evidence that this has occurred. If anything, we find a weakening of this relationship for total, male, and female workers. Nor do we find that the relationship between the sum of hours and wage change (a possible measure of demand shift) and skill levels is either particularly strong (about 6 percent of the variation in this sum) or growing stronger. Like our previous finding, a modest relationship in the 1980s appears no stronger in the 1990s.

Together, these results appear to offer little support for either the skill-biased demand shift or the supervisory burden accounts of the growth in U.S. earnings inequality. But while higher-level private sector managers do not seem to account for the widening wage gap, we do find some provisional support for Gordon's "low-road" hypothesis. Occupation hours and earnings trends do suggest that institutional changes—the declining value of the minimum wage, declining union density and power, and rising shares of irregular (contingent) employment—have been pivotal in the wage collapse experienced by many non-supervisory workers.

We find that low-skilled blue-collar jobs in goods producing industries appear to have played a major role in the earnings collapse; these jobs are heavily concentrated in the low wage and employment growth quadrant. We suspect that trade and outsourcing patterns, de-unionization and deregulation have all played substantial roles in the declining wages and employment of workers in this part of the job structure. On the other hand, many low-skill blue-collar jobs in the service industries show high hours growth but have experienced relatively slow wage growth, suggesting a combination of supply-side (immigration) and institutional (declining value of the minimum wage in the 1980s) factors. We find some middle level office worker jobs located in the slow hours growth but relatively high wage growth jobs, a result that may be explained in part by computerization and, after 1989, by increases in the minimum wage. While a variety of jobs have been characterized by both high wage and high hours growth over the last two decades, education and health sector professionals dominate, particularly when measured by total hours worked.

Our portrait, then, is not supportive of simple explanations. But it is consistent with the view that the undermining of traditional labor market institutions has exposed non-supervisory workers to more virulent wage competition, while at the same time many of those that have done relatively well have been skilled professionals (particularly teachers, physicians, and related health professionals) who are often sheltered from wage competition by labor market institutions that have remained in place: credentials, licenses, and protective internal labor markets. The dominance of the simple textbook model almost certainly biases economists toward simple demand/supply explanations of wages. But as Gordon argued, important changes in relative earnings reflect shifts in the balance of power between workers and employers, and this power can stem at least as much from labor market institutions, public policy choices, and management strategy as from shifts in labor demand and supply. The trends we have reported support this more complex view.

The critical research task that remains is to better disentangle the roles of demand, supply, and institutional factors in the explanation of labor market outcomes at the detailed occupation level. More specifically, we need to do a better job of measuring the effects of the institutional shifts caused by management's offensive against labor—what Gordon termed the "low-road" hypothesis—on earnings inequality. Which non-supervisory jobs have been strongly impacted by computerization, de-unionization, deregulation, outsourcing, trade patterns, changes in the value of the minimum wage, and immigration? Further progress on this front would surely have been at the top of David Gordon's research agenda had he had the opportunity.

Notes

This is a revised version of Howell et al. (1999), a report to the Rockefeller Foundation, printed with permission from the Center for Economic Policy Analysis. We thank Maury Gittleman, Michel Juillard, Jared Bernstein, John Schmitt, and Larry Mishel for their comments and advice and Fred Pryor for sharing data with us. We also thank Friedrich Huebler, Margaret Duncan, and Josh Bivens for their research assistance. This work began under a project funded by the MacArthur Foundation and we thank both the Rockefeller and MacArthur foundations for their generous support.

1. Earnings of the typical ninetieth percentile (high wage) male worker were 4.49 times higher than that of the tenth percentile worker in 1979. This figure rose to 5.31 in 1989 and 5.66 in 1996, reflecting mainly a real wage collapse for those at the bottom of the wage distribution. But even those in the middle of the distribution have done poorly in absolute terms: the real earnings of the median (fiftieth percentile) male worker fell steadily from $14.50 in 1979 to $12.62 in 1996. Among women, the trend has been similar but inequality levels have been lower (3.64 in 1979, 4.74 in 1989, and 5.1 in 1996) and, significantly, this increase has stemmed largely from gains at the top of the distribution (Bernstein and Mishel 1997, table 6).

2. It should be noted, however, that the measurement of changes in relative supplies of skill is problematic, due both to the problem of measurement of skill and the difficulty of identifying the relevant labor market; new transportation and communications technologies have facilitated a speedup in the globalization of production, dramatically increasing the effective supply of low-skill labor (Rodrik 1997; Howell 1997, 1999).

3. Gordon's approach in *Fat and Mean* follows closely his earlier macroeconomic work on the social model for productivity growth (Weisskopf, Bowles, and Gordon 1983).

4. The power of supervisors in the wage squeeze process rises as the corporate ladder is ascended. In a hierarchical and adversarial labor relations system, "you need supervisors to supervise the supervisors . . . and higher-level managers to watch the lower-level managers. A pyramid takes shape in which every level of supervision from the bottom on up is essential to the operations of the entire enterprise" (Gordon 1996, 40).

5. Some work in this direction has been carried out by Howell (1995), Howell and Wieler (1998), and Carnevale and Rose (1998).

6. According to Freeman and Katz (1994), "In the 1980s, the increased use of microcomputers and computer-based technologies shifted demand toward more educated workers. . . . Whether because of computerization or other causes, the pace of relative demand shifts favoring more skilled workers accelerated within sectors." Similarly, Bound and Johnson (1995) write, "Our suspicion is that a secular shift in production functions in favor of workers with relatively high intellectual as opposed to manual ability—a process that accelerated during the 1980s because of computers—is responsible, in concert with the slowdown of the growth in the relative supply of skilled labor, for most of the wage phenomena that have been observed."

7. Demand shifts strongly biased toward the most skilled that dominated supply shifts will produce both higher wages and higher employment levels for skilled compared to less skilled workers. The exception is in the case of perfectly inelastic demand curves, under which only wage changes favoring the most skilled will be observed.

8. The data for this longer term analysis were generously provided by Frederick Pryor and David Schaffer. These data are the basis for much of the empirical work

presented in Pryor and Schaffer (1997). They use a five-stage iteration program developed at the Bureau of Labor Statistics to adjust the allocation of individuals to occupations to reflect the 1970–80 occupation revisions. We received mean hourly wages and employment for three-digit occupations for both total and prime age workers for the four years cited in the text. The obvious disadvantage is that we are limited to the wage and employment measures created by another project.

9. We thank Maury Gittleman for providing the factor scores for the 1980 Census occupation classifications.

10. Personal correspondence with Patricia Simpson, Institute of Human Resources and Industrial Relations, Loyola University.

11. The NALS scores were downloaded from the National Center for Education Statistics http://nces.ed.gov/NADLITS/data.html.

12. We will explore the reasons for this upward trend in within-occupation variation in a forthcoming paper.

13. The Census defines 501 three-digit occupations. We omitted 102 because of small numbers of observations. Only occupations with at least ten observations in both periods were retained. Six large three-digit occupations are subdivided by industry to create the "modified three-digit" set of occupations.

14. Estimates using unweighted occupation groups generated similar results and, while not reported here, are available from the authors on request.

15. Jobs with very small numbers of workers in the sample were excluded. But because the excluded occupations are so small there is little loss in coverage. For example, at the one-digit level we count 3,852 million hours worked in 1992, which compares to 3,848 million hours worked in the same year in our 392 three-digit occupations—a loss of just 4 million hours, or just .01 percent of the total.

References

Berman, Eli, John Bound, and Zvi Griliches. 1994. "Changes in Demand for Skilled Labor within U.S. Manufacturing Industries: Evidence from the Annual Survey of Manufacturing." *Quarterly Journal of Economics* 109, no. 2 (May): 367–397.

Bernstein, Jared, and Lawrence Mishel. 1997. "Has Wage Inequality Stopped Growing?" *Monthly Labor Review* 120, no. 12 (December): 3–16.

Blank, Rebecca. 1994. "The Employment Strategy: Public Policies to Increase Work and Earnings." In *Confronting Poverty: Prescriptions for Change*, ed. S. Danziger, G.D. Sandefur, and D.H. Weinberg. New York: Russell Sage Foundation.

Bluestone, Barry, and Bennett Harrison. 1982. *The Deindustrialization of America*. New York: Basic Books.

Bound, John, and George Johnson. 1995. "What Are the Causes of Rising Wage Inequality in the United States?" *Federal Reserve Bank of New York Economic Policy Review* 1, no. 1 (January): 9–17.

Carnevale, Anthony P., and Stephen J. Rose. 1998. *Education For What? The New Office Economy: Technical Report*. Princeton: Education Testing Service.

Freeman, Richard B., and Lawrence Katz. 1994. "Rising Wage Inequality: The United States vs. Other Advanced Countries." In *Working Under Different Rules*, ed. Richard B. Freeman. New York: Russell Sage Foundation.

Galbraith, James. 1998. *Created Unequal: The Crisis in American Pay.* New York: Free Press.

Gittleman, Maury. 1994. "Earnings in the 1980s: An Occupational Perspective." *Monthly Labor Review* 117, no. 7 (July): 16–27.

Gittleman, Maury, and David R. Howell. 1995. "Changes in the Structure and Quality of Jobs in the United States: Effects by Race and Gender." *Industrial and Labor Relations Review* 48, no. 3 (April): 420–440.

Goleman, Daniel. 1998. *Working with Emotional Intelligence.* New York: Bantam Books.

Gordon, David M. 1996. *Fat and Mean: The Corporate Squeeze of Working Americans and the Myth of Managerial "Downsizing."* New York: Free Press.

Gottschalk, Peter. 1997. "Inequality, Income Growth, and Mobility: The Basic Facts." *Journal of Economic Perspectives* 11, no. 2 (Spring): 21–40.

Gottschalk, Peter, and Timothy M. Smeeding. 1997. "Cross-National Comparisons of Earnings and Income Inequality." *Journal of Economic Literature* 35, no. 2 (June): 633–687.

Glyn, Andrew, and Wiemer Salverda. 1998. "Employment Inequalities." Conference on Policies for Low-Wage Employment and Social Exclusion in Europe. University of Groningen. Mimeo.

Howell, David R. 1995. "Collapsing Wages and Rising Inequality: Has Computerization Shifted the Demand for Skills?" *Challenge* 38, no. 1 (Jan.–Feb.): 27–35.

Howell, David R., and Edward N. Wolff. 1991. "Trends in the Growth and Distribution of Skills in the U.S. Workplace, 1960–85." *Industrial and Labor Relations Review* 44, no. 3 (April): 486–502.

Howell, David R., and Susan S. Wieler. 1998. "Skill-Biased Demand Shifts and the Wage Collapse in the United States: A Critical Perspective." *Eastern Economic Journal* 24, no. 3 (Summer): 343–366.

Howell, David R., Ellen Houston, and William Milberg. 1999. "Demand Shifts and Earnings Inequality: Wage and Hours Growth by Occupation in the U.S. 1970–97." New York: New School for Social Research, Center for Economic Policy Analysis. Mimeo.

Levy, Frank. 1998. *The New Dollars and Dreams: American Incomes and Economic Change.* New York: Russell Sage Foundation.

Levy, Frank, and Richard J. Murnane. 1992. "U.S. Earnings Levels and Earnings Inequality: A Review of Recent Trends and Proposed Explanations." *Journal of Economic Literature* 30, no. 3 (September): 1333–1381.

Machin, Stephen, Annette Ryan, and John Van Reenen. 1996. "Technology and Changes in Skill Structure: Evidence from an International Panel of Industries." London: Center for Economic Performance. Discussion Paper no. 4.

Mishel, Lawrence, Jared Bernstein, and John Schmitt. 1999. *The State of Working America. 1998–99.* Ithaca: Cornell University Press.

Moss, Philip. 1998. "Earnings Inequality and the Quality of Jobs: The Status of Current Research and Proposals for an Expanded Research Agenda." Annandale on Hudson, NY: The Jerome Levy Economics Institute of Bard College. Mimeo.

Miller, Ann R., Donald J. Treiman, Pamela S. Cain, and Patricia A. Roos. 1980. *Work, Jobs and Occupations: A Critical Review of the Dictionary of Occupational Titles.* Washington, DC: National Academy Press.

Pryor, Frederic L. 1999. *Who's Not Working and Why? Employment, Cognitive Skills, Wages, and the Changing U.S. Labor Market*. New York: Cambridge University Press.

Pryor, Frederic L., and David Schaffer. 1997. "Wages and the University Educated: A Paradox Resolved." *Monthly Labor Review* 120, no. 7 (July): 3–14.

Rodrik, Dani. 1997. *Has Globalization Gone Too Far?* Washington, DC: Institute For International Economics.

Snower, Dennis J. 1998. "Causes of Changing Earnings Inequality." Conference on Income Inequality: Issues and Policy Options. Federal Reserve Bank of Kansas City. Mimeo.

Webster, David John. 1998. "Wage Analysis Computations." In *The State of Working America 1998–99*, ed. Lawrence Mishel, Jared Bernstein, and John Schmitt. Armonk, NY: M.E. Sharpe.

Weisskopf, Thomas, Samual Bowles, and David Gordon. 1983. "Heart and Minds: A Social Model of U.S. Productivity Growth." *Brookings Paper on Economic Activity* 2: 381–450.

3

Juliet B. Schor

VOLUNTARY DOWNSHIFTING IN THE 1990S

I. Introduction

In his final book, *Fat and Mean: The Corporate Squeeze of Working Americans and the Myth of Managerial "Downsizing,"* David Gordon (1996) argued that the conventional wisdom on corporate strategies had gotten it wrong: corporations were not humanizing work, delayering through downsizing, or shifting to a regime of cooperative employment relations. Rather, they had become more obsessed with control and less respectful of workers. At the same time, they were cutting wages and driving their employees harder by requiring longer hours of work, monitored and disciplined by a growing (and unproductive) army of managers and supervisors. Instead of adopting an enlightened, humanistic twenty-first century attitude, as many commentators claim, corporations have been heading back to the nineteenth century.

In many ways, Gordon's analysis is compatible with and sheds light on voluntary "downshifting," a phenomenon in which individuals choose to reduce their working hours (and generally, in consequence, their income and consumption levels) in the pursuit of nonmaterial goals such as leisure time, better family relationships, and reduced stress. The argument is that as employers push workers harder, and reduce wages, what is known as the "employment rent" (commonly referred to in the heterodox literature as the "cost of job loss") declines. The employment rent reflects the benefits that an individual derives as a result of holding a current job, relative to her status if she lost that job and had to search for another one; both mainstream and heterodox economists have linked this concept to a wide variety of labor market outcomes, ranging from productivity to employee turnover to strike frequency.[1] A reduction in the employment rent resulting from more intense supervision and a decline in the quality of work life would be expected to result in an increase in outward job mobility. The often-modest material benefits of paid work, combined with a perceived increase in the nonmaterial and emotional costs imposed on workers in the "fat and mean" labor hierarchy, could conceivably inspire greater exit from the labor market altogether.[2] Indeed, contingent on workers possessing both alternative means of supporting themselves materially, and building a cultural space within which this withdrawal of labor supply is considered a legitimate response to the pressures of the commodified labor market, downshifting could become an increasingly common form of resistance to the dictates of private employers.

From my qualitative research, I find that although not all downshifters can be described as "refugees" from fat and mean employers, a significant number do fit this description. They describe their former jobs as too demanding. A trend that was first identified among fast-track high-earning professionals[3] has expanded to include large numbers of middle-class individuals and significant numbers of people with low incomes. In this context, I believe downshifting is a predictable response to the model of production described in *Fat and Mean*. This chapter provides some preliminary analysis of downshifting, its differing forms, and its potential significance in future labor market developments.

II. Downshifting in the 1990s

Beginning in the early 1990s, stories about a social trend which came to be known as "downshifting" began appearing in the popular press. *Time* magazine ran a cover story on "The Simple Life," profiling yuppies who were opting out of the fast-track urban life, moving to smaller cities and taking on less demanding careers. Journalist Amy Saltzman published a book on the phenomenon (Saltzman 1991), and the Trends Research Institute in Rhinebeck, New York, declared that "voluntary simplicity" had become one of the "Top Ten Trends" in the nation. A steady stream of articles on the topic appeared throughout the first half of the decade. In 1995, upon the occasion of a pilot survey of the results presented here, yet another round of stories about how Americans were jumping out of the "corporate rat race" made its way into the nation's major media. The press remained fascinated by this phenomenon. (For popular accounts, see Marks 1995; Healy 1996. Books include Elgin 1993; Dominguez and Robin 1992; Andrews 1997; Blix and Heitmiller 1997; Luhrs 1997. See also Segal 1996. A case study of the voluntary simplicity movement can be found in Blanchard 1994. For a related analysis of the rise of post-materialist values, see Inglehart 1977, 1990.)

Perhaps surprisingly, all this media coverage has not generated much academic research aimed at validating or disproving the existence or importance of downshifting. In this essay I report on a telephone survey designed to ascertain some basic parameters about the downshifting phenomenon.[4] Thus, the present effort is a descriptive one, whose purpose is to stimulate interest in downshifting as a worthy and important topic for further investigation.

III. Defining Downshifting

What is downshifting? One consequence of the absence of a scholarly literature on the topic is that there is no established definition of this trend. The following types of downshifts are possible:

1. Income downshift: a reduction in annual income.
2. Spending downshift: a reduction in annual spending.
3. Hours downshift: a reduction in hours worked.
4. Pace of life downshift: a reduction in daily pace of life.
5. Geographic downshift: a move to a smaller, slower-paced locale.

Furthermore, "downshifts," as I will refer to the trend, can be primarily caused by a voluntary decision on the part of the individual or can be triggered by an adverse and unwanted labor market event, such as the loss of a job or a reduction in pay. (I term these "involuntary" downshifts; this chapter mainly discusses voluntary downshifting, and therefore the shorthand "downshifting" is used to refer to the voluntary type.) Downshifts can also be temporary (e.g., a few years of labor force withdrawal upon the birth of a child) or permanent (e.g., no attempt to return to the pre-downshift state).

Finally, we can also think about downshifting in terms of actual versus potential income, hours and spending states. The standard conceptualization is of a downward deviation from an established labor market or earnings path. Indeed, this is the essence of the term "downshift" (i.e., to shift downward). In addition, one might also want to consider individuals who forgo their potential path of earnings in favor of a lower trajectory, because it offers more free time, more meaning, less pressure, or other benefits. Thus, individuals who follow a labor market trajectory that is below their potential trajectory might be thought of not as *down*shifters but as income forgoers. Examples might include college graduates who opt for low-paid service sector jobs in order to pursue non-market interests, or MBAs who opt for public service or family life instead of following the usual corporate trajectory. However, while it is conceptually challenging and interesting, this essay does not address the phenomenon of income forgoers.

IV. Telephone Survey Results

As a first step toward ascertaining whether "downshifting" represents a significant social trend, or is merely confined to a small number of East Coast "yuppies," I conducted two national, random sample telephone surveys. The first, a pilot study, took place in February of 1995. It was conducted by the Harwood Group. The second, a longer survey devoted exclusively to downshifting, was conducted in November of 1996 through EDK Associates, a New York survey research firm. Both polls had 800 respondents.

To identify downshifters, the following definitional choices were made. We focused in the first instance on income downshift (i.e., on reductions in annual income). We differentiated between voluntary and involuntary downshifts, and defined a downshift as a change that occurred over the last five years. (The five-year period seemed appropriate because the trend had been first identified at the beginning of the 1990s, and the pilot study took place in 1995.) The basic downshifting question was the following:

> In the last five years, have you *voluntarily* made a long-term change in your life which has resulted in your making less money—other than taking a regularly scheduled retirement? (Examples of these changes include switching to a lower paying job, reducing your work hours, a career change, or quitting work to stay at home.)

Basic Results

In the February 1995 pilot study, the fraction of the sample that answered this question affirmatively was 28 percent. This number was sufficiently high to arouse suspicion of a response bias. The pilot study was carried out both during a weekday evening and a Friday evening.

Table 3.1

Voluntary Downshifting

Question: In the last five years, have you *voluntarily* made a long term change in your life which has resulted in your making less money—other than taking a regularly scheduled retirement? (Examples of these changes include switching to a lower-paying job, reducing your work hours, a career change, or quitting work to stay at home.)

	(%)		(%)
Yes	19	No	81

Question: Do you think your lifestyle change will be permanent or just temporary?

Permanent	55	Temporary	44
Don't know/refused	1		

One possible source of bias was that downshifters are more likely to be home on weekday evenings because of their lower working hours and reduced incomes. In order to minimize this potential bias, the November 1996 survey was conducted on a Sunday evening. (The assumption was that Sunday evening is the night for which the propensity to be out of the home would be most equal between downshifters and non-downshifters.) As expected, the fraction of the workforce responding positively to the above question fell to 19 percent, a number more in line with ex ante expectations. Of the 19 percent identified in 1996, 55 percent of these reported that their lifestyle change was permanent, while 44 percent reported it to be temporary (see Table 3.1). Thus, about 10 percent of adults reported that they had undertaken a permanent lifestyle change, clearly a quite significant trend.

Demographic Characteristics of the Voluntary Downshifter Population

Table 3.2 provides a summary of the basic characteristics of the voluntary downshifter population, as compared to the nondownshifter majority of the sample. The first finding is that downshifters are not significantly more likely to be women than men. This is somewhat surprising because of the higher propensity of women to withdraw from the labor force to care for children. There is also a popular sense that downshifting is more prevalent among women. A number of possible explanations suggest themselves. First, some of this gender parity likely results from couples downshifting together. Second, male and female interpretations or honesty about how "voluntary" and "involuntary" the change has been may differ, such that males who have been involuntarily downshifted are more likely to report their shift as voluntary, thereby inflating the voluntary downshifter category. Finally, the popular perception may simply be wrong: perhaps men and women may be equally likely to downshift by choice.

Table 3.2 also provides the age distribution of voluntary downshifting. Here we can see that the propensity to downshift is greatest in the 30–39 age category, where the difference between the downshifting fraction and the non-downshifter segment is 13 percent. Downshifting is also over-represented in the two adjacent age categories (20–29 and 40–49). Downshifting is least likely to occur in the youngest and two oldest groups. (Partly this is an artifact of the definition—regular retirements are excluded.)

Regarding other characteristics of downshifters, again contrary to some of the popular perception, downshifting is not only a trend for the college-educated. While downshifting does occur slightly disproportionately among those with college educations and above, more than 20 percent of those with only a high school degree report that they have voluntarily downshifted. The propensity to downshift is greater among the various categories of nonmarrieds, and marrieds are much less likely to downshift. The propensity to downshift is slightly higher among ethnic minorities such as African Americans and Latinos/as than it is among whites. (This was an unexpected finding in view of the media's near-total attention to white downshifters.) Finally, we note that parents with children at home are more likely to be downshifters, as one might expect if time constraints were a central element in the decision to downshift (see below).

As indicated in Table 3.3, we find that ex post incomes of downshifters are heavily weighted to lower income categories and that the stereotype of downshifters as an affluent group is quite inaccurate. For example, 23 percent of voluntary downshifters (as compared to only 10 percent of nondownshifters) had household incomes of less than $10,000 per year, and 35 percent were in the $10,000–$25,000 category (compared to 25 percent of the nondownshifter population). Here we find that the income reductions downshifters undergo are quite substantial. For example, only 7 percent had ex ante incomes of below $10,000, while 22 percent have ex post incomes at that level. A total of 55 percent of downshifters

Table 3.2

Characteristics of Voluntary and Nonvoluntary Downshifters

	Voluntary downshifters (%)	Nonvoluntary downshifters (%)
Gender composition		
Male	48	50
Female	52	50
Age distribution		
18–19	3	3
20–29	18	15
30–39	34	21
40–49	27	22
50–64	15	17
> 64	4	22
Educational attainment		
Some high school	8	8
High school diploma	2	32
Some college	30	27
Four-year college degree	25	19
Post-graduate degree	14	12
Other	1	1
Marital status		
Married	54	63
Single, never married	24	21
Divorced, separated, or widowed	19	15
Living with partner	3	1
Racial composition		
White	85	87
African American	9	7
Latino/a	4	2
Asian	0	1
Other	2	3
Presence of children		
None	53	65
1	17	14
2	20	13
3	8	7
4 or more	3	2

had ex ante incomes of \$35,000 or below, while 71 percent of them earned that amount ex post. At the top of the income ladder, 11 percent of downshifters had ex ante incomes of \$75,000 or more, while fewer than 5 percent were in that category ex post.

Types of Downshifting and Attitudes Toward Downshifting

While this survey screened for income downshifters, it also asked about hours and spending downshifts (see Table 3.4). In general, these forms

Table 3.3

Pre-Downshift and 1996 Incomes of Downshifters and Nondownshifters

Annual Household income	Voluntary downshifters pre-downshift income (%)	Voluntary downshifters 1996 income (%)	Nondownshifters 1996 income (%)
< $10,000	7	23	10
$10–$25,000	30	35	25
$25–$35,000	18	13	20
$35–$50,000	17	16	21
$50–$75,000	7	9	14
$75–$100,000	6	2	5
> $100,000	5	2	5
Don't know/refused	11	0	0

Table 3.4

Hours and Spending Reductions Among Voluntary Downshifters

Hours of Work Before and After Downshifting

Weekly Hours	Pre-downshift (%)	Post-downshift (%)
<30	7	48
31–40	40	31
41–50	24	14
>50	28	7

Spending Reductions After Downshifting

Question: "How has your overall spending changed since the lifestyle change?" (%)

Spending reduced slightly, by about 10 percent	21
Spending reduced by a fair amount, by about 25 percent	29
Spending cut in half	18
Spending reduced by more than half	13
Spending has not fallen	16
Don't know	3

of downshifting are highly correlated, as one might expect given the ex ante income distribution of downshifters (whose incomes are heavily dependent on labor income). The extent of hours reduction among downshifters is substantial. Before the change, 52 percent of the sample averaged 41 or more hours per week, but after the change only 21 percent did. After the change, nearly half (48 percent) worked fewer than 30 hours per week, of whom 30 percent were not working at all, and 18 percent worked between 10 and 30 hours. Downshifters also had high levels of spending

Table 3.5

Types of and Reasons for Downshifting

Voluntary Downshifters by Type of Downshift

Question: "Which of the following best describes the lifestyle change you made?" (%)

Changed to a lower paying job	29
Reduced work hours	12
Quit working outside the home	16
Changed careers and went back to school	17
Started own business	10
Reduced the number of jobs held	2
Refused a promotion	1
Other	12

Primary and Second Reason for Downshifting Among Voluntary Downshifters

	Primary reason (%)	Secondary reason (%)
Wanted more time, less stress, and more balance in life	31	18
Wanted to spend more time caring for children	18	10
No longer interested in material success	5	7
Succeeding in today's economy is too difficult	5	8
Wanted a more meaningful life	15	14
Wanted a less materialistic lifestyle	3	9
Other	23	29

reductions. Only 16 percent were not spending downshifters; 31 percent reduced their spending by one-half or more; 29 percent reduced their spending by a quarter; and 21 percent reduced by only about 10 percent. Thus, the median level of spending reduction was quite high, with spending typically falling by between one-quarter and one-half.

Types of and Reasons for Downshifting

In terms of the form of downshifting, the sample was distributed among five main types of changes, with 12 percent choosing the "other" category (see Table 3.5). A full 30 percent changed to a lower paying job, 12 percent reduced their working hours, 16 percent stopped working for pay, 17 percent changed careers and/or went back to school, and 10 percent started their own businesses.

The most common reasons downshifters identified were to reduce stress, achieve "balance," and gain time. Asked to choose their primary and secondary motivations for downshifting, nearly half chose this option.

In my qualitative research, the theme that many downshifters were "refugees" from corporate America was recurrent, although my interviews over-represented this group.[5] Here are some of the kinds of descriptions my interviewees gave:

- "My job was quite stressful, and I felt that I was missing most of life for the sake of a good salary"(former researcher at a chemical company who earned about $40,000 a year).
- "I simply was too stressed out. I had pushed myself beyond my limits. I started to burn out. And the classic burnout syndrome, forgetting everything and not being able to do the things that you normally could do, being depressed and all that" (a former DEC employee).
- "It was like being in an unhappy marriage. [The job] paid the bills" (a sales employee in a building supply company).
- "I was coming home physically and mentally exhausted. . . . My quote for the last year was 'they could pay me a hundred thousand dollars and I wouldn't be here'" (a clinical nurse).
- "It took me until I was 40 years old to really deal with the fact that I didn't like my work and I've spent a long time doing it. . . . It was a demanding job. I worked all the time" (a college registrar).

How do downshifters feel about the changes they have made? Their post-downshift attitudes reveal that for the majority, more money would be nice, but is less important than the quality of life gains from downshifting (see Table 3.6). About one-third report difficulty adjusting to their lower incomes—the "hardship" and "unhappy" categories sum to 34 percent, although only 15 percent of the total seem to regret the change. Finally, while most of the population seems not to be familiar with the term "downshifter," voluntary downshifters were much more likely to report that it fit them. And while the entire nation reports that money and material goods are less important to them now than they were in the past, voluntary downshifters are much more likely to feel this way.

V. Conclusion

The findings of this telephone survey are consistent with the claims that downshifting is an important social trend. Furthermore, its basic moti-

Table 3.6

Attitudes Toward Downshifting

Post-Downshift Attitudes Among Voluntary Downshifters (%)

I'm happy about the change, and I don't miss the income very much.	28
I'm happy about the change, but I miss the extra income.	35
Losing the income was a real hardship, but I'm still happy about the change.	19
I'm unhappy about the change.	15

Attitudes to the Term "Downshifter"

Question: "How well would you say the term 'downshifter' applies to you?"

	Voluntary downshifter (%)	Nonvoluntary downshifter (%)
Extremely well	14	2
Somewhat well	16	6
Not well	28	41
I am not familiar with this term	43	51

Changing Attitudes to Materialism

Question: "I feel that money and material goods are less important to me now than they were in the past."

	Voluntary downshifter (%)	Nonvoluntary downshifter (%)
Strongly agree	29	19
Agree	38	41
Disagree	29	32
Strongly disagree	5	9

vational and attitudinal dimensions are consistent with the popular accounts. For example, downshifters have laid strong emphasis on time and balance, and demonstrate a less materialistic orientation than non-downshifters. Where accounts of downshifting in the popular media have been most inaccurate is in their failure to include low income, noncollege educated, and non-Caucasian profiles in their stories. Downshifting appears to be a far more demographically diverse and wide-ranging phenomenon than has been previously recognized. It is a phenomenon that appears to deserve much more research, and that may well have important implications for our understanding of labor supply behavior, life cycle dynamics, and the changing nature of the American labor market.

Because downshifting is rooted in fundamental dissatisfactions of workers with the conditions of their working lives, it should be of particular interest to heterodox economists—in the tradition of David Gordon —seeking to better understand the consequences of modern labor market institutions for workers, and to highlight the possibilities for worker resistance to those institutions. Obviously the forms of worker resistance will continue to evolve in the wake of broader economic, political, and cultural developments. With his long-term interest in labor supply issues, David Gordon realized better than most that this resistance will manifest itself in flexible and surprising ways, even within the most pro-employer of institutional regimes. Downshifting might not initially seem like an especially "radical" act in comparison with more traditional forms of collective action by workers. But the statements and views of downshifters suggest that—for many—it is an act of resistance nonetheless, and to some degree their actions will place pressure on employers to improve the quality of work life in their establishments. To the extent that workers are materially and culturally capable of partially or fully withdrawing from paid employment, then the employer's task becomes even harder—and the implicit bargaining power of workers is enhanced accordingly. In this context, then, the phenomenon of downshifting embodies a mentality of opposition to the dictates of the profit-maximizing, cost-minimizing employment relationship.

Notes

I would like to thank Harald van der Werff for research assistance. For financial support, I am indebted to the Merck Family Fund, the PEW Global Stewardship Initiative, and the John S. Guggenheim Foundation. I would also like to thank Ethel Klein of EDK Associates, who graciously fielded the downshifter poll, and the Harwood Group for their fielding of the pilot survey.

1. Existing measures of the cost of job loss are relatively narrow, expressed solely in monetary terms and focusing on unemployment duration and the level of income-replacing social welfare benefits. These measures thus miss many of the quality-of-life issues discussed in this chapter.

2. While one might naturally turn to quit rates as an indicator of downshifting, they are of limited usefulness because the proximate (and "official") causes of even voluntary downshifts can be early retirements, buyouts, involuntary layoff, or firing for cause.

3. Saltzman (1991).

4. For more details on the methodology employed in the survey results reported here, see Schor (1998).

5. Such "refugees" are over-represented in my interviews. Interviewees were

found through nonrandom methods, which targeted voluntary quitters and the unemployed, as well as individuals who had undertaken large income downshifts. About
half of the interviewees were contacted through a workshop entitled "How to Live
Well on Practically Nothing," given at a Boston area unemployment center special-
izing in white collar employees, and screened for their suitability as voluntary
downshifters. The other half were individuals living in Seattle who had some con-
tact with foundations, newsletters, or study circles associated with the voluntary
simplicity movement. Perhaps because I screened for large downshifts, the inter-
viewee population exaggerates the demographic features identified in the telephone
poll. It heavily over-represents women, singles, people without children or with
grown children, individuals with college or post-graduate education, and those whose
ex ante income exceeded $35,000 per year. Furthermore, I also believe women are
more likely to quit jobs in the face of high levels of workplace stress. (The above
quotes are all from women.)

References

Andrews, Cecile. 1997. *The Circle of Simplicity: Return to the Good Life*. New
     York: HarperCollins.
Blanchard, Elisa A. 1994. "Beyond Consumer Culture: A Study of Revaluation and
     Voluntary Action." Unpublished thesis, Tufts University.
Blix, Jacqueline, and David Heitmiller. 1997. *Getting a Life: Real Lives Trans-
     formed by Your Money or Your Life*. New York: Viking Penguin.
Dominguez, Joe, and Vicki Robin. 1992. *Your Money or Your Life*. New York: Pen-
     guin Books.
Elgin, Duane. 1993. *Voluntary Simplicity: Toward a Way of Life That Is Outwardly
     Simple, Inwardly Rich*. New York: William Morrow.
Gordon, David M. 1996. *Fat and Mean: The Corporate Squeeze of Working Ameri-
     cans and the Myth of Managerial "Downsizing."* New York: Free Press.
Healy, Melissa. 1996. "To Some, Money Now Counts for Less." *Los Angeles Times*,
     December 24.
Hochschild, Arlie Russell. 1997. *The Time Bind: When Work Becomes Home and
     Home Becomes Work*. San Francisco: Henry Holt.
Hugick, Larry, and Jennifer Leonard. 1991. "Job Dissatisfaction Grows; 'Moon-
     lighting' on the Rise." Gallup Poll News Service, September 2.
Inglehart, Ronald. 1977. *The Silent Revolution*. Princeton: Princeton University Press.
———. 1990. *Culture Shift*. Princeton: Princeton University Press.
Luhrs, Janet. 1997. *The Simple Living Guide*. New York: Broadway Books.
McKenna, Elizabeth Perle. 1997. *When Work Doesn't Work Anymore: Women, Work
     and Identity*. New York: Delacorte.
Marks, John. 1995. "Time Out." *U.S. News and World Report*, December 11.
Mishel, Larry, Jared Bernstein, and Larry Schmitt. 1999. *The State of Working
     America 1998–99*. Ithaca: Cornell University Press.
Saltzman, Amy. 1991. *Downshifting: Reinventing Success on a Slower Track*. New
     York: HarperCollins.

Schor, Juliet B. 1992. *The Overworked American: The Unexpected Decline of Leisure*. New York: Basic Books.

———. 1998. *The Overspent American: Upscaling, Downshifting and the New Consumerism*. New York: Basic Books.

Schor, Juliet B., and Samuel Bowles. 1987. "The Cost of Job Loss and the Incidence of Strikes." *Review of Economics and Statistics* 69, no. 4 (November): 584–592.

Segal, Jerome M. 1996. "The Politics of Simplicity." *Tikkun* 11, no. 4 (July/August): 20–25.

4

Samuel Bowles and Herbert Gintis

THE FUTURE OF EGALITARIAN POLITICS

> *A man ought to be a friend to his friend and repay gift with gift. People should meet smiles with smiles and lies with treachery.*
> —From *The Edda*, a thirteenth-century collection of Norse epic verse

I. Egalitarianism on Its Own

David Gordon's professional life began at the zenith of a golden age of egalitarianism and like so many of us, he was swept up in the confidence of its moral claims and the apparently ineluctable force of the historical circumstances propelling it. But radical egalitarianism today is the orphan of a defunct socialism. The unruly and abandoned child of the liberal enlightenment had been taken in by socialism in the mid-nineteenth century. Protected and overshadowed by its new foster parent, radical egalitarianism was relieved of the burden of arguing its own case. As socialism's foster child, equality would be the by-product of an unprecedented post-capitalist order, not something to be defended morally and promoted politically on its own terms in the world as it is.

It thus fell to reformists, be they laborist, social democratic, Euro-communist, or New Deal, to make capitalism livable for workers and the less well off, a task they accomplished with remarkable success in the advanced economies. But in the process the egalitarian project was purged of its utopian yearnings for a world of equal freedom and dignity, and narrowed to the pursuit of a more equal distribution of goods. Over the years even this project has encountered increasingly effective resistance and experienced major political reversals.

Is egalitarianism passé? We think not. The welfare state is in trouble not because selfishness is rampant (it is not), but because many egalitarian programs no longer evoke, and sometimes now offend, deeply held notions of fairness, encompassing both reciprocity and generosity, but stopping far short of unconditional altruism toward the less well off. Recasting egalitarianism to tap these sentiments should be high on the agenda of those who worry about the human toll being taken by poverty, inequality, and insecurity in the United States and in the world.

The U.S. public remains deeply committed to helping those in need. In 1991 an ABC/WP poll found that twice as many were "willing to pay higher taxes" to "reduce poverty" as were opposed. In 1995 61 percent expressed willingness to pay more taxes to "provide job training and public service jobs for people on welfare so that they can get off welfare" (Weaver et al. 1995). Almost three-quarters of those surveyed by *Time* magazine in 1991 agreed (more than half of them "completely") with the statement: "The government should guarantee every citizen enough to eat and a place to sleep."

Many, however, think that policies to pursue these objectives are either ineffective or unfair. In a 1995 CBS/NYT survey, for example, 89 percent supported a mandated work requirement for those on welfare. It is thus not surprising that egalitarian programs have been cut even as increases in measured inequality of before tax and transfer income have taken place. For the most part voters have responded with approval rather than resistance.

Egalitarians now defend their programs on moral and empirical grounds that many, even among the less well off, find uncompelling. In the face of a hostile public, many egalitarians have become soured on what they consider to be a selfish electorate that identifies with materialistic middle-class values and is indifferent to the plight of the less fortunate.

We believe this pessimism is fundamentally misdirected. It misunderstands not only the reasons for opposition to egalitarian programs, but the powerful sentiments supporting them. It is not self-interest that opposes the welfare state, nor is it unconditional generosity that supports it. We will show that there is a solid foundation for cooperation and sharing in two basic human motives, which we term *strong reciprocity* and *basic needs generosity*; that hostility to contemporary forms of egalitarianism is not evidence against that deep foundation, but evidence for it; and that new egalitarian initiatives are fully compatible with that foundation.

Understanding the predicament of egalitarian politics today thus requires a reconsideration of *Homo economicus*, the unremittingly selfish prototype whose asocial propensities have provided the starting point for deliberations on constitutions and policies from Thomas Hobbes to the current debate on welfare reform. We do not wish to replace the textbook *Homo*, however, with a cardboard-cutout altruist, an equally one-dimensional actor unconditionally willing to make personally costly contributions to others. While these motives are much admired by many advocates of the welfare state, we doubt that unconditional altruism explains its success, nor does its absence explain our current malaise. In experiments and surveys people are not stingy, but their generosity is conditional. Moreover, they distinguish among the goods and services to be distributed, favoring those which meet basic needs, and among the recipients themselves, favoring those thought to be "deserving."

Strong reciprocity, along with basic needs generosity, not unconditional altruism, better explains the motivations that undergird egalitarian politics. By strong reciprocity we mean a propensity to cooperate and share with others similarly disposed, even at personal cost, and a willingness to punish those who violate cooperative and other social norms, even when punishing is personally costly. We call a person acting this way *Homo reciprocans*. *Homo reciprocans* cares about the well-being of others and about the processes determining outcomes—whether they are fair, for example, or violate a social norm. He differs in this from the self-regarding and outcome oriented *Homo economicus*. We see *Homo reciprocans* at work in Chicago's neighborhoods in a recent study (Sampson et al. 1997) that documented a widespread willingness to intervene with co-residents to discourage truancy, public disorders, and antisocial behaviors, as well as the dramatic impact of this "collective efficacy" on community safety and amenities.

Homo reciprocans is not committed to the abstract goal of equal outcomes, but rather to a rough balancing out of burdens and rewards. In earlier times—when, for example, an individual's conventional claim on material resources was conditioned by noble birth or divine origin—what counted as "balancing out" might entail highly unequal comfort and wealth. But, as we will see, in the absence of specific counter-claims, modern forms of reciprocity often take equal division as a reference point.

We do not wish to banish *Homo economicus*, however. The evidence we introduce shows that a substantial fraction of individuals consistently follow self-regarding precepts. Moreover most individuals appear to draw upon a repertoire of contrasting behaviors: whether one acts selfishly or generously depends as much on the situation as the person. The fact that *Homo economicus* is alive and well (if often in the minority) is good news, not bad, as people often rely on asocial individualism to undermine socially harmful forms of collusion ranging from price-fixing to ethnic violence. Pure altruists also doubtless exist and make important contributions to social life. In short, egalitarian policymaking, no less than the grand projects of constitutional design, risks irrelevance if policymakers ignore the irreducible heterogeneity of human motivations. The problem of institutional design is not, as the classical economists thought, that selfish individuals be induced to interact in ways producing desirable aggregate outcomes, but rather that a mix of motives—selfish, reciprocal, altruistic, and spiteful—interact in ways that prevent the selfish from exploiting the generous and hence unraveling cooperation when it is beneficial.

The strong reciprocity of *Homo reciprocans* goes considerably beyond those cooperative behaviors that can be fully accounted for in terms of the self-regarding, outcome oriented motives that are the defining characteristics of *Homo economicus*. We call these self-interested forms of cooperation weak "reciprocity." Examples include market exchange and cooperation enforced by tit-for-tat behavior—what biologists call "reciprocal altruism." Such actions are costly to the giver but in fact are self-interested because they involve future repayment. Strong reciprocity, like the biologists' concept of altruism, imposes costs on *Homo reciprocans* without prospect of repayment. Yet unlike the vernacular usage of altruism, it is neither unconditional nor necessarily motivated by good will toward the recipient.

Students of cultural and biological evolution have long wondered how individually costly but socially beneficial traits, such as altruism, might evolve in competition with genetically and economically rewarded selfish traits. Like altruism toward strangers, strong reciprocity thus represents an evolutionary puzzle, one that we will seek to unravel. But first we will show that *Homo reciprocans* is indeed among the *dramatis personae* in today's political arena, and most likely has been for the last hundred thousand years.

II. The Legacy of a Hundred Thousand Years of Sharing

Other than unconditional altruism, there are two distinct reasons why people might support egalitarian policies. First, many egalitarian programs are forms of social insurance that will be supported even by those who believe they will probably pay in more than their expected claims over a lifetime. Included among these are unemployment and health insurance, and more broadly, the various social programs that soften the blows during the rocky periods that people experience in the course of their lives. Even the securely rich support amelioration of the conditions of the poor on prudential grounds. The insurance motive is consistent with conventional notions of self-interest, considering that people are broadly prudent and risk-averse.

The second reason for support of egalitarian programs, by contrast, is not fundamentally self-regarding: egalitarianism is often based on a commitment to what we have termed *strong reciprocity*.[1] It will come as no surprise that people are considerably more generous than the model in economics textbooks allows. More remarkable, however, is that they are equally unselfish in seeking to punish, often at great cost to themselves, those who have done harm to them and others. Programs designed to tap these other-regarding motives may succeed where others that offend underlying motivational structures have been abandoned.

Both historical and contemporary experimental evidence support this position. Consider first the historical evidence. In his *Injustice: The Social Bases of Obedience and Revolt*, Barrington Moore, Jr. (1978), sought to discern if there might be common motivational bases—"general conceptions of unfair and unjust behavior" (p. 21)—for the moral outrage fueling struggles for justice that have recurred throughout human history. The moral code may conceal, he concludes from his wide-ranging investigation,

> a general ground plan, a conception of what social relationships ought to be. It is a conception that by no means excludes hierarchy and authority, where exceptional qualities and defects can be the source of enormous admiration and awe. At the same time, it is one where services and favors, trust and affection, in the course of mutual exchanges, are ideally expected to find some rough balancing out. (1978, 509)

Moore termed the general ground plan he uncovered "the concept of reciprocity—or better, mutual obligation, a term that does not imply equality of burdens or obligations" (p. 506). In like manner James Scott (1976) analyzed agrarian revolts, identifying violations of the "norm of reciprocity" as one of the essential triggers of insurrectionary motivations. We do not think that Scott's or Moore's assessments are idiosyncratic.

One is tempted to consider strong reciprocity a late arrival in social evolution, possibly one whose provenance is to be found in Enlightenment individualism, or later in the era of liberal democratic or socialist societies—a set of beliefs whose reproduction is secured by the deliberate inculcation of modern concepts of distributive justice through schooling and other intentional means. However, this account does not square with overwhelming evidence of the distant etiology of strong reciprocity.

Christopher Boehm, a primatologist at the University of Southern California, concluded on the basis of an encyclopedic survey that

> with the advent of anatomically modern humans who continued to live in small groups and had not yet domesticated plants and animals, it is very likely that all human societies practiced egalitarian behavior and that most of the time they did so very successfully. One main conclusion, then, is that intentional leveling linked to an egalitarian ethos is an immediate and probably an extremely widespread cause of human societies' failing to develop authoritative or coercive leadership. (1993, 226)

Anthropologist Bruce Knauft of Emory University adds:

> In all ethnographically known simple societies, cooperative sharing of provisions is extended to mates, offspring, and many others within the band. . . . Archeological evidence suggests that widespread networks facilitating diffuse access to and transfer of resources and information have been pronounced at least since the Upper Paleolithic. . . . The strong internalization of a sharing ethic is in many respects the *sine qua non* of culture in these societies. (1991, 393, 395)

Far from a mere moment in the history of anatomically modern humans, the period described by Knauft and Boehm spans something like 100,000 years before the present to the advent and spread of agriculture 12,000 years ago, or perhaps 90 percent of the time we have existed on the planet.

One group of contemporary foragers, the Aché of Eastern Paraguay, have been particularly closely studied, and the amounts and nutritional values of food acquired and consumed by members of the group measured (Kaplan et al. 1984). Sharing is so widespread, the researchers found, that on average three-quarters of what anyone eats was acquired by someone outside the consumer's nuclear family, and even more remarkable, in the case of meat and honey (the main goods foraged by men), women, children, and adult siblings of the acquirer receive no more from their husbands, fathers, and brothers respectively than would be expected by chance, and men eat from their own kills a good deal *less* than would be expected by chance. The Aché are probably unusually egalitarian, and there is evidence that hunting prowess is rewarded, if not with more food, then with enhanced social esteem and increased mating success. Nevertheless it is typical in foraging societies that families with less successful hunters, and indeed those unable to hunt, are nonetheless adequately provisioned by the group.

The resulting egalitarian distribution of resources is not the unintended by-product of an ecological or other constraint; rather it is deliberately sought. Using data from forty-eight simple societies, Boehm concluded that "these societies may be considered to be intentional communities, groups of people that make up their minds about the amount of hierarchy they wish to live with and then see to it that the program is followed" (1993, 239). He found evidence that potentially arrogant members of the group were constrained by public opinion, criticism and ridicule, disobedience, ostracism, and assassination.

It seems likely, then, that most of human history has been characterized by what James Woodburn (1982, 431) calls "politically assertive egalitarianism." The modern welfare state is thus but an example of a ubiquitous social form. Sharing institutions, from families to extended gift giving, to barn raisings and tithing, to egalitarian division rules for the catch of the hunt, have cropped up in human history with such regularity and under such diverse circumstances that one is tempted to place them among Talcott Parsons's (1964) *evolutionary universals*: social institutions that confer such extensive benefits upon their users that they regularly reappear in the course of history in otherwise diverse societies.

Karl Polanyi's (1957) account of the reaction to the human costs of nineteenth-century laissez-faire capitalism and the eventual emergence of modern protections of the weak from the vicissitudes of the market, as well as the sharing of the national product, records just one of thousands of cases of the independent emergence of institutions of this type. The evolutionary viability of sharing institutions and of the motivations that support them counsels against those who have written off egalitarianism as an idea whose time has come and gone.[2]

Our suggestion that these distantly originating behaviors may be important influences on contemporary behavior is not an ethical endorsement of them or the societies from which they originated—indeed some of the baser human motives, such as the desire for revenge, are examples of strong reciprocity. Rather it is a hypothesis that if true has significant bearing on present-day egalitarianism, because it can help us understand the pattern of public approval and disapproval of welfare state initiatives. Is it true?

III. *Homo Reciprocans*

An impressive body of experimental evidence, much of it deployed in the first instance to validate the model of the selfish purveyor of market rationality, *Homo economicus*, in fact has served to undermine this model. In its place this body of evidence suggests a new *persona*. A convenient starting point in tracing the birth of *Homo reciprocans* is a tournament involving differing strategies of the play in the prisoner's dilemma game undertaken two decades ago by Robert Axelrod at the University of Michigan.[3] The prisoner's dilemma requires each of two players to choose simultaneously one of two actions, "cooperate" or "defect." The payoffs are such that both players do better by cooperating than by defecting, but whatever one player does, the other player does better by defecting (for example, the payoff to mutual cooperation is 10 for each, the payoff to mutual defecting is 5 for each, but the payoff to defecting when the other player cooperates is 15 for the defector and 0 for the cooperator). The iterated prisoner's dilemma is simply repeated play of the well-known game with "winners" being those with high cumulative scores over however many rounds are played.

Axelrod asked a number of game theorists, economists, political scientists, sociologists, and psychologists to submit computer programs giving complete strategies for playing the game, successive rounds of which were repeated with the same partner. Each program was pitted against every other program, as well as itself and a program that randomly chose to cooperate and defect. Surprisingly, the winner among the fourteen strategies submitted was the simplest, called "tit-for-tat" (submitted by game theorist Anatol Rappoport). Tit-for-tat cooperates on the first round, and then does whatever its partner did on the previous round.

Following up on this result, Axelrod held a second tournament in which a larger number of participants, including the original contributors, were told of the success of tit-for-tat and asked to submit another program for playing the iterated prisoner's dilemma. Knowing that tit-for-tat was the strategy to beat did not help the players: once again Rappoport submitted tit-for-tat, and once again, it won.

Speculating on the strong showing of tit-for-tat, Axelrod noted that this strategy for cooperation has three attributes that are essential for successful cooperation. The first is that tit-for-tat is *nice*: it begins by cooperating, and it is never the first to defect. Second, tit-for-tat is *punishing*: it retaliates relentlessly against defection. Finally, tit-for-tat is *forgiving*: as soon as a defecting partner returns to cooperating, tit-for-tat returns to cooperating.

Homo economicus would readily embrace tit-for-tat, of course, at least if there were enough other tit-for-tatters around and there were a reasonable chance that one would interact repeatedly with the same person. Under these conditions tit-for-tat will be the self-interested strategy to follow, and thus is an example of reciprocal altruism rather than strong reciprocity. But for reasons that will become clear immediately, we think that the ubiquity of tit-for-tat sentiments among people (rather than computer programs) is more aptly explained by strong reciprocity motives that violate the tenets of economic man.

There have been many experiments with human subjects involving the iterated prisoner's dilemma. If Axelrod's tournaments show that nice guys finish first, the experiments reveal that there are lots of nice guys, even among the economics majors who show up for experimental games.

1. The simplest, but still quite revealing, laboratory experiment is the "dictator game," in which one of two players, the "proposer," is given a sum of money (typically 10), is asked to choose any part of the sum to give to the second player (the two players are mutually anonymous), and is permitted to keep the rest. *Homo economicus* gives nothing in this situation, whereas in actual experimental situations, a majority of proposers give positive amounts, typically ranging from 20 to 60 percent of the total (Forsythe et al. 1994).[4]

2. The commonly observed rejection of substantial positive offers in what are called ultimatum games is our second piece of experimental evidence. Experimental protocols differ, but the general structure of the ultimatum game is simple. Subjects are paired; one is the responder, the other the proposer. The proposer is provisionally awarded an amount ("the pie"—typically 10) to be divided between proposer and responder. The proposer offers a certain portion of the pie to the responder. If the responder accepts, the responder gets the proposed portion, and the proposer keeps the rest. If the responder rejects the offer, both get noth-

ing.[5] In experiments conducted in the United States, Slovakia, Japan, Israel, Slovenia, Germany, Russia, and Indonesia the vast majority of proposers offer between 40 and 50 of the pie, and offers lower than 30 of the pie are often rejected (Fehr and Schmidt 1999). These results have occurred in experiments with stakes as high as three months' earnings (Cameron 1995).

When asked why they offer more than one cent, proposers commonly say that they are afraid that respondents will consider low offers unfair and reject them as a way to punish proposers' unwillingness to share. When respondents reject offers, they give virtually the same reasons for their actions. The proposers' actions might be explained by selfishness but the respondents' cannot. Because these behaviors occur in single-shot interactions and on the last round of multi-round interactions, they cannot be accounted for by the responder's attempt to modify subsequent behavior of the proposer. Punishment per se is the most likely motive. As evidence for this interpretation, we note that the rejection of positive offers is substantially less when the game is altered so that rejection does not punish the proposer (Abbink et al. 1996). Moreover, the fact that offers generated by a computer rather than another person are significantly less likely to be rejected suggests that those rejecting low offers at a cost to themselves are reacting to violations of fairness norms rather than simply rejecting disadvantageous offers (Blount 1995). See also Bolton and Zwick (1995) and Suleiman (1996). Thus the ultimatum game experiments provide evidence for our view that strong reciprocity is a common motivation.

3. More directly analogous to strong reciprocity in groups, however, are findings in what are called n-player public goods experiments. The following is a common variant. Ten players are given 1 in each of 10 rounds. On each round, each player can contribute any portion of the 1 (anonymously) to a "common pool." The experimenter divides the amount in the common pool by two, and gives *each* player that much money. If all ten players are cooperative, on each round each puts 1 in the pool, the experimenter divides the 10 in the pool by two, and gives each player 5. After ten rounds of this, each subject has 50. By being selfish, however, each player can do better as long as the others are cooperating. By keeping the 1, the player ends up with "his" 10, plus receives 45 as his share of the pool, for a total of 55. If all behave this way, however, each receives only 10. Thus this is an "iterated prisoner's dilemma" in which self-regarding players contribute nothing.

In fact, however, only a small fraction of players contribute nothing to the common pool. Rather, in the early stages of the game, people generally contribute half their money to the pool. In the later stages of the game, contributions decay until at the end, they are contributing very little. Proponents of the *Homo economicus* model initially suggested that the reason for decay of public contribution is that participants really do not understand the game at first, and as they begin to learn it, they begin to realize the superiority of the free-riding strategy. However, there is considerable evidence that this interpretation is incorrect. For instance, James Andreoni (1988) finds that when the whole process is repeated with the same subjects, the initial levels of cooperation are restored, but once again cooperation decays as the game progresses.

Andreoni (1995), an economist at the University of Wisconsin, suggests a *Homo reciprocans* explanation for the decay of cooperation: public-spirited contributors want to retaliate against free-riders and the only way available to them in the game is by not contributing themselves. Indeed, if players are permitted to retaliate directly against noncontributors, but at a cost to themselves, as in the experiments of Ernst Fehr and Simon Gächter (forthcoming), economists at the University of Zürich, they do so. In this situation, contributions rise in subsequent rounds to near the maximal level. Moreover, punishment levels are undiminished in the final rounds, suggesting that disciplining norm violators is an end in itself and hence will be exhibited even when there is no prospect of modifying the subsequent behavior of the shirker or potential future shirkers.

Such experiments show that agents are willing to incur a cost to punish those whom they perceive to have treated them, or a group to which they belong, badly.[6] Also, in everyday life, we see people consumed with the desire for revenge against those who have harmed them or their families, even where no material gain can be expected (Nisbett and Cohen 1996; Boehm 1984).

Moreover, strong reciprocity coexists with simple generosity and compassion in many, perhaps most people. Evidence for this comes not only from dictator games, as we have seen, but also from an ingenious set of experiments devised by political scientists Norm Frohlich and Joe Oppenheimer (1992). Twenty-eight groups of subjects engaged in individual work tasks and decided on a principle of redistribution within the group of the rewards associated with successful performance of the tasks.

At the conclusion of the experiment, the experimenters distributed cash rewards to the subjects according to their productivity and the rules of redistribution selected by the group, so the stakes were real. As the subjects decided on the redistribution rule before knowing how well they would perform on the task, the experiment would seem to elicit the subjects' abstract notions of just reward, a kind of experimental instance of the Rawlsian veil of ignorance.

By far the most popular principle of distribution was a minimal floor to be granted to every member of the group irrespective of the individual's productivity in the task. Subjects elected to finance the floor by a tax on the individual earnings of the more productive members. High levels of support for the floor principle were expressed by the high productivity (and hence highly taxed) members, and their level of satisfaction with the floor principle increased with repeated play. Of course the rules selected by the group reflect reciprocity as well as generosity, as the principle of individual reward proportional to productivity was only modified, not annulled, by the tax. When these rules were imposed on the groups by the experimenters rather than chosen by the groups, the floor principle remained popular, but less so.

These results show clearly that people are not generally the self-interested actors of traditional economics, since they value treating others fairly, and will incur personal costs to do so. Nor are people the unconditional altruists of utopian thought, since they want to hurt free-riders and other norm-violators. These experiments also show that strong reciprocity is not simply a mechanism for norm enforcement, but also often includes a powerful concept of *fairness* or *sharing*—the notion that all else equal, there should be a rough balance of rights and obligations in social exchange. Proposers in the dictator game treat sharing as a good in itself, and respondents in the ultimatum game retaliate not against the violation of norms in the abstract, but against norms of equal sharing in particular.

A remarkable aspect of these experiments—and one very germane to our concern with egalitarian policy—is the degree to which behaviors are affected by the experimentally contrived social relationship between players. Communication among participants prior to the game, or experimental conditions that reduce the subjective "social distance" among participants, lead to higher and more sustained levels of generosity and cooperation.[7] For example, fraternity brothers at UCLA were asked to rank outcomes in a prisoner's dilemma situation given that they were interacting with a fellow fraternity brother, a member of another (un-named) fraternity, a nonfraternity student at UCLA, a student from USC, and an officer from the UCLA Police Department. They showed a strong preference for mutual cooperation over defection against one's partner when playing with fraternity brothers, with the rankings reversing with increasing social distance—they were as willing to exploit the USC students as the UCLA police! (Kollock 1997).

People care about whom they give to: Eckel and Grossman (1997) found that proposers in a dictator game gave more when the recipient was "the Red Cross" rather than another experimental subject. Finally, when the right to be proposer in the ultimatum game is earned by being a winner in a trivia quiz rather than by lot, proposers offered less, and respondents accepted lower offers (Hoffman et al. 1994). It appears that minor manipulations of the social context of interactions may support significant behavioral differences.

In all of the experiments a significant fraction of subjects (about a quarter, typically) conform to the self-interested preferences of *Homo economicus*, and it is often the self-serving behavior of this minority that, when it goes unpunished, unravels initial generosity and cooperation. These experiments also indicate that strong reciprocity spans all the societies studied, though in somewhat varying strength and content.[8]

The following five generalizations sum up the relevance of these experiments to the problem of designing and sustaining programs to promote economic security and eliminate poverty. First, people exhibit significant levels of generosity, even toward strangers. Second, people share more of what they acquire by chance rather than what they acquire by personal effort. Third, people contribute to public goods and cooperate to collective endeavors, and consider it unfair to free-ride on the contributions and efforts of others. Fourth, people punish free-riders at substantial costs to themselves, even when they cannot reasonably expect future personal gain therefrom.

It would not be difficult to design a system of income security and economic opportunity that would tap rather than offend the motivations expressed in these first four generalizations. Such a system would be generous toward the poor, rewarding those who perform socially valued work and who seek to improve their chances of engaging in such work, as well as to those who are poor through accidents not of their own making, such as illness and job displacement.

The fifth, however, is more troublesome: each of these aspects of

EGALITARIAN POLITICS   93

reciprocity is more salient, the less is the perceived social distance among the participants. This last generalization may help explain why inequalities are so readily sustained even among apparently generous publics. Economic inequality—particularly when overlaid with racial, ethnic, language, and other differences—increases the social distance that then undermines the motivational basis for reaching out to those in need. Indeed, surveys consistently reveal that the support for those in need is stronger in societies whose before tax and transfer incomes are more equal.

The experimental evidence, casual observation of everyday life, ethnographic and paleoanthropological accounts of hunter-gatherer foraging bands from the late paleolithic to the present, and historical narratives of collective struggles have combined to convince us that strong reciprocity is a powerful and ubiquitous motive. But we hesitate to revise *Homo economicus* by elevating the individually costly sharing and punishment of norm violators characteristic of *Homo reciprocans* to a privileged place in the repertoire of human behaviors until we have addressed the evolutionary puzzle posed at the outset. In short, we are more prone to believe and to generalize from the experimental and historical evidence we have introduced if we can explain how strong reciprocity motives might have evolved despite the costs these motives seemingly impose on those bearing them.

We have elaborated our attempt to resolve this puzzle in a recent technical paper and we are continuing to explore the issue with a research team of experimentalists, ethnographers, and others (Bowles and Gintis 1998a). Our reasoning is that strong reciprocity supports the adherence to norms within groups, and some of these norms—requiring work toward common ends, sharing, and monogamy, for example—are beneficial to most group members. Where reciprocity motives embrace the individually costly enforcement of these group-beneficial norms, strong reciprocity may evolve because *Homo reciprocans* will be disproportionately likely to be in groups that have effective norm adherence, and hence to enjoy the group benefits of these norms. By contrast, where reciprocity motivates the individually costly enforcement of norms that on average confer little benefit on group members, or inflict group costs, of course reciprocity is unlikely to evolve.

Strong reciprocity thus allows groups to engage in common practices without the resort to costly and often ineffective hierarchical authority, and thereby vastly increases the repertoire of social experiments capable of diffusing through cultural and genetic competition. The relevant traits may be transmitted genetically and proliferate under the influence of natural selection, or they may be transmitted culturally through learning from elders and age mates and proliferate because successful groups tend to absorb failing groups, or to be emulated by them. We think it likely that both genetic and cultural transmission is involved. The 100,000 years in which anatomically modern humans lived primarily in foraging bands constitutes a sufficiently long time period, and a favorable social and physical ecology, for the evolution of the combination of norm enforcement and sharing that we term strong reciprocity.

IV. Strong Reciprocity and the Revolt Against Welfare

This model of *Homo reciprocans* supports our optimism concerning the political viability of egalitarian policies. Like Petr Kropotkin (1989 [1903]) almost a century ago, we find compelling evidence—both evolutionary and contemporary—for the force of human behavioral predispositions to act both generously and reciprocally rather than self-interestedly in many social situations. While most egalitarians have failed to appreciate the practical importance of these predispositions in policy matters, their salience was not missed by the conservative economist and philosopher Frederick Hayek:

> [W]anting to do good to known people will not achieve the most for the community, but only the observation of its abstract and seemingly purposeless rules. . . . [T]he long submerged innate instincts have again surged to the top. [The] demand for a just distribution . . . is thus strictly an atavism, based on primordial emotions. And it is these widely prevalent feelings to which prophets, [and] moral philosophers . . . appeal by their plans for the deliberate creation of a new type of society. (1978, 18, 20)

But while strong reciprocity may support egalitarianism, it may also help explain the rising tide of opposition to welfare state policies in the advanced market economies in the past decades. Specifically, in light of the experimental regularities outlined above, we suspect the following to be true as well: egalitarian policies that reward people independent of whether and how much they contribute to society are considered unfair and are not supported, even if the intended recipients are otherwise worthy of support, and even if the incidence of noncontribution in the target population is rather low. This would explain the opposition to many welfare measures for the poor, particularly since such measures are thought to have promoted various social pathologies. At the same time it explains the continuing support for social security and medicare in the United States, since the public perception is that the recipients are "deserving" and the policies do not support what are considered antisocial behaviors. The public goods experiments are also consistent with the notion that tax resistance by the nonwealthy may stem from their perception that the well-to-do are not paying their fair share.

These inferences from the experimental evidence find some confirmation in survey and focus group data. Opposition to egalitarian policies does not primarily reflect the selfish interests of the economically secure. Indeed, income and social background are very poor predictors of the degree of one's support for either particular programs or egalitarianism in general. Of far greater import is one's views of why the poor are poor, and specifically one's beliefs about the relative importance of effort rather than luck or other circumstances beyond the control of the individual in explaining individual incomes.[9] Christina Fong of Washington University (2000) compared individuals' responses on nationally representative surveys to questions indicating support for increases or decreases in expenditure on welfare with responses to questions about why the poor are poor ("lack of effort by the poor themselves"). In a 1990 sample of the General Social Survey she found that only 18 percent of those citing "lack of effort" thought too little was spent on welfare, while 49 percent responded "too much." By contrast, among those who thought that "lack of effort by the poor themselves" was "not important" in explaining poverty, 44 percent thought that we were spending too little on welfare, and only 28 percent too much. Remarkably, Fong found that the belief that effort is important to "getting ahead in life" has a considerably larger impact on opposition to aid to the poor than one's income, years of schooling, and parents' socioeconomic status *combined*—those whose effort beliefs differed from the average by a standard deviation were more opposed to aid than those whose level of privilege on all three measures was a standard deviation above the mean.

Fong's research confirms earlier studies. In a 1972 sample of white women in Boston the perceived work ethic of the poor was a far better predictor of support for aid to the poor than one's family income, religion, education, and a host of other demographic and social background variables (Williamson 1974). Indeed, in predicting support for such aid,

the addition of a single variable measuring beliefs about work motivation tripled the explanatory power made possible using all of the background variables.

Consistent with our interpretation of these data, support for antipov-
erty expenditures varies with economic conditions. Fong found, for example that statistically controlling for race, schooling, income, religion,
and other variables, the self-employed tend to oppose such policies, and
that much of their opposition is statistically associated with a belief—
no doubt grounded in their experience—that individual effort makes a
difference in getting ahead. Martin Gilens of Yale University found (1999)
that during recessions people are less likely to explain poverty by "lack
of effort by the poor," and more likely to support egalitarian programs.

A more striking fact about the decline in the support for the former
Aid to Families with Dependent Children, Food Stamps, and other means-
tested social support programs in the United States, however, is that
overwhelming majorities oppose the status quo, whatever their income,
race, or personal history with such programs. This pattern of public sen-
timent, we think, can be accounted for in terms of the principle of strong
reciprocity.

We rely mainly on two studies. The first (Farkas and Robinson 1996)
analyzes data collected in late 1995 by Public Agenda, a nonprofit, non-
partisan research organization. The authors conducted eight focus groups
around the country, then did a national survey, involving half-hour interviews, of 1,000 randomly selected Americans, plus a national
oversample of 200 African-Americans. The second, political scientist
Martin Gilens's *Why Americans Hate Welfare* (1999), is an analysis and
review of several polls executed during the 1990s and earlier by various
news organizations.[10]

In the Farkas and Robinson (1996) survey 63 percent of respondents
thought the welfare system should be eliminated or "fundamentally over-
hauled," while another 34 percent thought it should be "adjusted somewhat." Only 3 percent approved of the system as is (p. 9). Even among
respondents from households receiving welfare only 9 percent expressed
basic approval of the system, while 42 percent wanted a fundamental
overhaul and an additional 46 percent wanted some adjustments.

The cost of welfare programs cannot explain this opposition. While
people generally overstate the share of the federal budget devoted to
welfare (p. 9), this cannot account for the observed opposition.[11] Farkas
and Robinson note that

By more than four to one (65 percent to 14 percent), Americans say the most upsetting thing about welfare is that "it encourages people to adopt the wrong lifestyle and values," not that "it costs to much tax money." . . . Of nine possible reforms presented to respondents—ranging from requiring job training to paying surprise visits to make sure recipients deserve benefits—reducing benefits ranked last in popularity. (1996, 9–10)

The cost, apparently, is not the problem. In focus groups, "Participants invariably dismissed arguments about the limited financial costs of welfare in almost derisive terms as irrelevant and beside the point" (1996, 10).

Nor can the perception of fraud account for this opposition. It is true that 64 percent of respondents (and 66 percent of respondents on welfare) believe welfare fraud is a serious problem. However, most do not consider it more serious than in other government programs, and only 35 percent of survey respondents would be more "comfortable with welfare" if fraud were eliminated (1996, 11, 12).

In commenting on this fact Martin Gilens observes that

Politics is often viewed, by élites at least, as a process centered on the question "who gets what." For ordinary Americans, however, politics is more often about "who *deserves* what" and the welfare state is no exception. (1999, 1–2)

In the Farkas and Robinson study, respondents overwhelmingly consider welfare to be unfair to working people and addictive to recipients. By a more than five to one margin (69 percent to 13 percent, and 64 percent to 11 percent for people receiving welfare), respondents say that recipients abuse the system—for instance by not looking for work—rather than actually cheating the system—for example, by collecting multiple benefits (1996). Moreover, 68 percent object (59 percent of welfare recipients) that welfare is "passed on from generation to generation, creating a permanent underclass." In the same vein, 70 percent (71 percent of welfare recipients) say welfare makes it "financially better for people to stay on welfare than to get a job," 57 percent (62 percent of welfare recipients) think welfare encourages "people to be lazy" and 60 percent (64 percent of welfare recipients) say the welfare system "encourages people to have kids out of wedlock" (1996, 14, 15).

But this is beside the point. Whether or not, for example, welfare *causes* out of wedlock births, or fosters an unwillingness to work, citizens object that the system provides financial support for those who undertake these socially disapproved behaviors. Their desire is to bear witness against the behavior and to disassociate themselves from it, whether or not their actions can change it.

This then is the moral opposition to welfare. Many of the objections to the system and many of the ethical judgments of the poor are based on misconceptions, a lack of compassion, and prejudice, fanned by political entrepreneurs of the right. Racial stereotyping and welfare bashing are closely associated. The Farkas and Robinson (1996) survey shows that whites are much more likely than African Americans to attribute negative attributes to welfare recipients, and much more likely to blame an individual's poverty on lack of effort. But even here reciprocity motives are evident. The survey data show, writes Gilens, that:

> For most white Americans, race-based opposition to welfare is not fed by ill-will toward blacks, nor is it based on whites' desire to maintain their economic advantages over African Americans. Instead race-based opposition to welfare stems from the specific perception that, as a group, African Americans are not committed to the work ethic. (1999, 3)

Taking account of the *fact* that many Americans see the current welfare system as a violation of deeply held reciprocity norms does not oblige us to either agree or disagree with these views. Still less does it require that policymakers adopt punitive measures and stingy budgets for the poor. Indeed, the public strongly supports income support measures when asked in ways that make clear the deserving nature of the poor: a 1995 NYT/CBS poll, for instance, found that twice as many agreed as disagreed that "it is the responsibility of the government to take care of people who can't take care of themselves."

Like Frolich and Oppenheimer's experimental subjects, those surveyed by pollsters exhibit what we have termed "basic needs generosity," a virtually unconditional willingness to share with others to assure them of some minimal standard, especially, as the survey data show, when this is implemented through provision of food, basic medical care, housing, and other essential goods. The interplay of basic needs generosity and strong reciprocity, we think, accounts for the salient facts about public opinion concerning welfare.

V. Conclusion

If we are right, egalitarians have misunderstood the revolt against welfare and the resistance to helping the needy, attributing it to selfishness by the electorate rather than the failure of many programs to tap power-ful commitments to fairness and generosity and the fact that some pro-grams appear to violate deeply held reciprocity norms.

There is an obvious objection to our argument. "Morality is socially determined," we hear the reader musing, "so why not transform moral-ity to fit the needs of egalitarian policy rather than tailoring policy to existing morality?" Why not promote a public morality of expanded, virtually unconditional altruism toward people whom the hyper-competitive, hyperindividualist market system have left behind, rather than pandering to the sometimes punitive expressions of strong reci-procity? Have not radical egalitarians, from nineteenth-century aboli-tionists to contemporary feminists, civil libertarians, and welfare state activists, successfully made consciousness-raising a central part of their political practice? What ever happened to the socialist ideal of "from each according to his ability, to each according to his needs"? Why, in short, be trapped by the present in designing a future?

Our answer is that while a strong public morality is important in an egalitarian society, the human mind is not a blank slate that is equally disposed to accept whatever moral rules are presented to it by either dominant élites or egalitarian reformers. Rather, people are predisposed to accept some moral rules; other rules can be imposed upon them with some difficulty; and still others cannot be imposed in any stable manner at all. Egalitarians have been successful in appealing to the more el-evated human motives precisely when they have shown that dominant institutions violate norms of reciprocity, and may be replaced by institu-tions more consistent with these norms. Countless other egalitarian ini-tiatives have failed. We believe that basic needs generosity and strong reciprocity are among those that we are predisposed to accept. Barrington Moore, Jr., in his comparative study of revolution and revolt cited ear-lier, expresses this idea in the following words:

> [A]wareness of social injustice would be impossible if human beings could be made to accept any and all rules. Evidently there are *some* constraints on the making of moral rules and therefore on the possible forms of moral outrage. (1978, 5)

What accounts for our moral predispositions? The answer is some combination of genes and culture. Neither is immutable, but likewise neither is amenable to reconstruction in an arbitrary manner. The cul-tural and the genetic structures that frame our lives and affect our propensity to accept or reject particular moral principles are products of cultural and biological evolution. Moral principles succeed because they have aided those individuals who have used them and those groups in which they have been prevalent. They may well conform to particular philosophical, political, and/or religious logics, but they persist largely because the individuals and social groups that have deployed these moral principles have prevailed, while others that have not have perished or been assimilated.

This is not to say that culture change is always conservative and slow-moving, for we know that this is not the case. Nor is public opinion immune to persuasion, as the meteoric rise of environmental concerns and feminist values over the past three decades attest. Rather it is to say that cultural change, like technical change, is subject to enduring laws and material constraints. The evidence is that among these regularities is the ease with which people assume the behavior of *Homo reciprocans* and the unsustainability of egalitarian programs that violate norms of reciprocity.

Many traditional projects of egalitarians, such as land reform and employee ownership of the workplace, are strongly consistent with reciprocity norms, as they make people the owners not only of the fruits of their labor, but more broadly of the consequences of their actions. The same may be said of more conventional initiatives such as improved educational opportunity and policies to support home ownership—there is good evidence, for example, that home ownership promotes active participation in local politics and a willingness to discipline personally those engaging in antisocial behavior in the neighborhood. An expansion of subsidies designed to promote employment and increase earnings among the poor would tap powerful reciprocity motives, as has been suggested by Columbia University economist Edmund Phelps in his recent book *Rewarding Work* (1997). Similarly, social insurance programs might be reformulated along lines suggested by University of California economist John Roemer (1993) to protect individuals from risks over which they have no control, while not indemnifying people against the results of their own choices, other than providing a minimal floor to living standards. In this manner, for example, families could be protected against regional fluctuations in home values—the main form of wealth for most people—as Yale economist Robert Shiller (1993) has shown. Other forms of insurance could partially protect workers from shifts in demand for their services induced by global economic changes.

If we are correct, an egalitarian society can be built on the basis of these and other policies consistent with strong reciprocity, along with a guarantee of an acceptable minimal living standard consistent with the widely documented motives of basic needs generosity.

David Gordon thought deeply about the unraveling of the egalitarian project that had nurtured our generation of activists and in an important respect made us who we are. We will miss him now as we, in our many different ways, recast the egalitarian projects and rekindle the egalitarian hopes that illuminated his too short, but exemplary, life.

Notes

We would like to thank Ernst Fehr, Nancy Folbre, Elisabeth Wood, and Erik Wright for comments, and the MacArthur Foundation for financial support.

1. Ernst Fehr, whose experimental work is described below, calls this "reciprocal fairness." See Fehr and Gächter (1998).

2. On the structural basis of pro-social norms in a game-theoretic framework, see Bowles and Gintis (1998b). On the relationship of market institutions to the development of culture, see Bowles (1998). On the evolution of strong reciprocity, see Bowles and Gintis (1998a).

3. See Axelrod and Hamilton (1981) and Axelrod (1984) for details and theoretical development.

4. As in other experimental situations, a significant minority (between 25 and 42 percent in the Forsythe et al. experiments) behave self-interestedly and give nothing. Moreover, in a double-anonymous study (Hoffman et al. 1994), in which not even the experimenter knows the behavior of the proposer, the fraction of proposers who gave nothing increased to two-thirds. This accords with our notion that strong reciprocity is a conditional behavior, in this case weakening in the face of high levels of social anonymity.

5. See Güth et al. (1982), Camerer and Thaler (1995), and Roth (1995).

6. See Ostrom et al. (1992) on common pool resources, Fehr et al. (1997) on efficiency wages, and Gächter and Fehr (1999) on public goods. Coleman (1988) develops the parallel point that free riding in social networks can be avoided if network members provide positive rewards for cooperating.

7. For the communication result, see Isaac and Walker (1988), and for the social distance result, see Kollock (1997) and Hoffman et al. (1996).

8. The only known exception to this statement concerns experiments run by the UCLA anthropologist Joe Henrich, a member of our research group who works with the Machiguenga Indians, a famously individualistic indigenous group living in a remote region of the Peruvian Amazon. In the ultimatum game, he found offers to be small, and even small offers were typically accepted. In the public goods game, contributions to the public account were very low. We believe the most likely explanation of this result is a peculiarity of the subjects: their basic social unit consists of closely related kin, with extra-kin social relationships being much weaker than typical even of simple societies.

9. Thomas Piketty (1995) also explores the significance of one's beliefs about the importance of effort but in his model those who believe effort leads to success oppose redistribution not because the poor are undeserving but because the necessary taxes will discourage effort, thus raising the cost of aid.

10. A third study by Weaver et al. (1995), drawing in addition on NORC and General Social Survey data, comes to broadly similar conclusions.

11. As a general rule nonexperts vastly overstate the share of the tax revenues devoted to things of which they disapprove, whether it be foreign aid, welfare, aids research, or military expenditure—the opposition is generally the cause of the exaggeration, not vice versa.

References

Abbink, Klaus, Gary E. Bolton, Abdolkarim Sadrieh, and Fang-Fang Tang. 1996. "Adaptive Learning versus Punishment in Ultimatum Bargaining." University of Bonn. Discussion Paper no. BO–381.

Andreoni, James. 1988. "Why Free Ride? Strategies and Learning in Public Good Experiments." *Journal of Public Economics* 37, no. 3 (December): 291–304.

———. 1995. "Cooperation in Public Goods Experiments: Kindness or Confusion?" *American Economic Review* 85, no. 4 (December): 891–904.

Axelrod, Robert. 1984. *The Evolution of Cooperation.* New York: Basic Books.

Axelrod, Robert, and William D. Hamilton. 1981. "The Evolution of Cooperation." *Science* 211: 1390–1396.

Blount, Sally. 1995. "When Social Outcomes Aren't Fair: The Effect of Causal Attributions on Preferences." *Organizational Behavior & Human Decision Processes* 63, no. 2 (August): 131–144.

Boehm, Christopher. 1984. *Blood Revenge: The Enactment and Management of Conflict in Montenegro and Other Tribal Societies.* Philadelphia: University of Pennsylvania Press.

———. 1993. "Egalitarian Behavior and Reverse Dominance Hierarchy." *Current Anthropology* 34, no. 3 (June): 227–254.

Bolton, Gary E., and Rami Zwick. 1995. "Anonymity versus Punishment in Ultimatum Games." *Games and Economic Behavior* 10, no. 1 (July): 95–121.

Bowles, Samuel. 1998. "Endogenous Preferences: The Cultural Consequences of Markets and Other Economic Institutions." *Journal of Economic Literature* 36, no. 1 (March): 75–111.

Bowles, Samuel, and Herbert Gintis. 1998a. "The Evolution of Strong Reciprocity." Santa Fe Institute, Working Paper 98–08–073E.

———. 1998b. "The Moral Economy of Community: Structured Populations and the Evolution of Prosocial Norms." *Evolution & Human Behavior* 19, no. 1 (January): 3–25.

Camerer, Colin, and Richard Thaler. 1995. "Ultimatums, Dictators, and Manners." *Journal of Economic Perspectives* 9, no. 2 (Spring): 209–219.

Cameron, Lisa. 1995. "Raising the Stakes in the Ultimatum Game: Experimental Evidence from Indonesia." Princeton: Department of Economics, Princeton University. Discussion Paper no. 345.

Coleman, James S. 1988. "Free Riders and Zealots: The Role of Social Networks." *Sociological Theory* 6 (Spring): 52–57.

Eckel, Catherine, and Philip Grossman. 1997. "Chivalry and Solidarity in Ultimatum Games." Blacksburg, VA: Virginia Polytechnic Institute, Working Paper #E92–23, February.

Farkas, Steve, and Jean Robinson. 1996. *The Values We Live By: What Americans Want from Welfare Reform*. New York: Public Agenda.

Fehr, Ernst, and Klaus M. Schmidt. 1999. "A Theory of Fairness, Competition, and Cooperation." *Quarterly Journal of Economics* 114, no. 3 (August): 817–868.

Fehr, Ernst, and Simon Gächter. 1998. "Reciprocity and Economics: The Economic Implications of 'Homo Reciprocans.'" *European Economic Review* 42, no. 3–5 (May): 845–859.

————. Forthcoming. "Cooperation and Punishment." *American Economic Review*.

Fehr, Ernst, Simon Gächter, and Georg Kirchsteiger. 1997. "Reciprocity as a Contract Enforcement Device: Experimental Evidence." *Econometrica* 65, no. 4 (July): 833–860.

Fong, Christina. 2000. "Social Insurance or Conditional Generosity: The Role of Beliefs about Self- and Exogenous-Determination of Incomes in Redistributive Politics." Washington University Department of Political Science. Mimeo.

Forsythe, Robert, Joel Horowitz, N.E. Savin, and Martin Sefton. 1994. "Replicability, Fairness and Pay in Experiments with Simple Bargaining Games." *Games and Economic Behavior* 6, no. 3 (May): 347–369.

Frohlich, Norman, and Joe A. Oppenheimer. 1992. *Choosing Justice: An Experimental Approach to Ethical Theory*. Berkeley: University of California Press.

Gächter, Simon, and Ernst Fehr. 1999. "Collective Action as a Social Exchange." *Journal of Economic Behavior and Organization* 39, no. 4 (August): 341–369.

Gilens, Martin. 1999. *Why Americans Hate Welfare*. Chicago: University of Chicago Press.

Güth, Werner, Rolf Schmittberger, and Bernd Schwarz. 1982. "An Experimental Analysis of Ultimatum Bargaining." *Journal of Economic Behavior and Organization* 3, no. 4 (May): 367–388.

Hayek, Frederick. 1978. *The Three Sources of Human Values*. London: London School of Economics.

Hoffman, Elizabeth, Kevin McCabe, and Vernon L. Smith. 1996. "Social Distance and Other-Regarding Behavior in Dictator Games." *American Economic Review* 86, no. 3 (June): 653–660.

Hoffman, Elizabeth, Kevin McCabe, Keith Shachat, and Vernon L. Smith. 1994. "Preferences, Property Rights, and Anonymity in Bargaining Games." *Games and Economic Behavior* 7, no. 3 (November): 346–380.

Isaac, R. Mark, and James M. Walker. 1988. "Group Size Effects in Public Goods Provision: The Voluntary Contribution Mechanism." *Quarterly Journal of Economics* 103, no. 1 (February): 179–200.

Kaplan, Hillard, Kim Hill, Kristen Hawkes, and Ana Hurtado. 1984. "Food Sharing among Aché Hunter-Gatherers of Eastern Paraguay." *Current Anthropology* 25, no. 1 (February): 113–115.

Knauft, Bruce. 1991. "Violence and Sociality in Human Evolution." *Current Anthropology* 32, no. 4 (August/October): 391–428.

Kollock, Peter. 1997. "Transforming Social Dilemmas: Group Identity and Cooperation." In *Modeling Rational and Moral Agents*, ed. Peter Danielson. Oxford: Oxford University Press.

Kropotkin, Petr. 1989 [1903]. *Mutual Aid: A Factor in Evolution*. New York: Black Rose Books.

Moore, Jr., Barrington. 1978. *Injustice: The Social Bases of Obedience and Revolt*. White Plains: M. E. Sharpe.

Nisbett, Richard E., and Dov Cohen. 1996. *Culture of Honor: The Psychology of Violence in the South*. Boulder, CO: Westview Press.

Ostrom, Elinor, James Walker, and Roy Gardner. 1992. "Covenants with and without a Sword: Self-Governance Is Possible." *American Political Science Review* 86, no. 2 (June): 404–417.

Parsons, Talcott. 1964. "Evolutionary Universals in Society." *American Sociological Review* 29, no. 3 (June): 339–357.

Phelps, Edmund S. 1997. *Rewarding Work: How to Restore Participation and Self-Support to Free Enterprise*. Cambridge: Harvard University Press.

Piketty, Thomas. 1995. "Social Mobility and Redistributive Politics." *Quarterly Journal of Economics* 110, no. 3 (August): 551–584.

Polanyi, Karl. 1957. *The Great Transformation: The Political and Economic Origins of Our Time*. Beacon Hill: Beacon Press.

Roemer, John. 1993. "A Pragmatic Theory of Responsibility for the Egalitarian Planner." *Philosophy and Public Affairs* 22:146–166.

Roth, Alvin. 1995. "Bargaining Experiments." In *The Handbook of Experimental Economics*, ed. John Kagel and Alvin Roth. Princeton: Princeton University Press.

Sampson, Robert J., Stephen W. Raudenbush, and Felton Earls. 1997. "Neighborhoods and Violent Crime: A Multilevel Study of Collective Efficacy." *Science* 277 (August): 918–924.

Scott, James C. 1976. *The Moral Economy of the Peasant: Rebellion and Subsistence in Southeast Asia*. New Haven: Yale University Press.

Shiller, Robert J. 1993. *Macro Markets: Creating Institutions for Managing Society's Largest Economic Risks*. Oxford: Clarendon Press.

Suleiman, Ramzi. 1996. "Expectations and Fairness in a Modified Ultimatum Game." *Journal of Economic Psychology* 17, no. 5 (November): 531–554.

Weaver, R. Kent, Robert Y. Shapiro, and Lawrence R. Jacobs. 1995. "Poll Trends: Welfare." *Public Opinion Quarterly* 59, no. 4 (Winter): 606–627.

Williamson, John B. 1974. "Beliefs about the Motivation of the Poor and Attitudes toward Poverty Policy." *Social Problems* 21, no. 5 (June): 734–747.

Woodburn, James. 1982. "Egalitarian Societies." *Man* 17, no. 3 (September): 431–451.

Part II

Power and the Macroeconomy

5

Thomas I. Palley

CONFLICT, DISTRIBUTION, AND FINANCE IN ALTERNATIVE MACROECONOMIC TRADITIONS

I. Introduction

Power and conflict over the distribution of income are both important features of economic life, and they are features that were of central interest to David Gordon. These features are noticeably absent in both neo-Keynesian and new classical macroeconomics, and this absence has motivated much dissatisfaction with these paradigms. Undoubtedly, it also contributed to Gordon's dissatisfaction with them.

Within both paradigms, "power" is suppressed through the assumption of competitive markets which ensure that all are "powerless." Side-by-side, the effects of income distribution are suppressed either through the representative agent assumption which reduces all agents to a single agent, or through permanent income theory which attributes all agents with identical propensities to consume.

Incorporating the effects of power and income distribution into macroeconomics gives rise to two different projects. The first project concerns construction of substantive microeconomic foundations for these phenomena. Thus, developing a micro-founded treatment of power suggests the adoption of non-cooperative bargaining theory, while developing a micro-founded treatment of the effects of income distribution calls for developing theories of consumption behavior that challenge permanent income theory. The second project concerns the placement of power and income distribution within macro models, and identifying how they affect the macroeconomic process. It is this second question that constitutes the focus of this paper.

The macroeconomic significance of power and income distribution is best revealed through a comparative approach that contrasts the manner in which alternative paradigms describe the macroeconomic process. There are two important implications that follow from such a treatment. First, macroeconomics is ultimately a matter of process analysis, being concerned with causal relations. It is differences in the construction of the underlying causal processes that constitute the primary distinction between competing macroeconomic paradigms. Second, full recognition of the economic effects of power and income distribution gives rise to constructions of the macro process that differ significantly from the conventional neo-Keynesian and new classical constructions. It is this feature that gives intellectual and policy significance to the post-Keynesian macroeconomic project.

In the course of surveying the economic processes contained in the above-mentioned strains of macroeconomic analysis, special attention is given to the work of David Gordon. It is also argued that Gordon's work fits with the modern post-Keynesian tradition. Post-Keynesian thinking has focused on problems of aggregate demand and finance, while David Gordon focused on the problems of production and conflict at work. A fusion of the two gives rise to a general post-Keynesian theory of macroeconomics that rivals that of new classical macroeconomics. It can provide the foundation for a resurgence of progressive macroeconomics, and when combined with the greater plausibility and better explanatory power of the general post-Keynesian theory, it offers hope of a wider progressive intellectual and policy triumph.

II. David Gordon and Post-Keynesian Economics

David Gordon would (and did) deny that his thought was post-Keynesian in character.[1] Given that this paper argues differently, it is appropriate to begin with a few observations on this matter.

A core proposition of post-Keynesian economics is the centrality of aggregate demand in the determination of the level of economic activity. This proposition was clearly evident in Gordon's own macroeconomic work (Gordon 1995a, 1995b) in which the level of aggregate demand interacted with conditions on the supply side to determine the level of capacity utilization and employment. Digging deeper, Gordon's treatment of the components of aggregate demand was also post-Keynesian. Thus, his aggregate consumption function incorporated a Kaleckian (Kalecki 1942) difference in the propensity to consume out of wage and profit income, thereby introducing a channel for income distribution to impact aggregate demand. The investment function was also post-Keynesian with investment spending depending on the rate of capacity utilization, the cost of capital, and the rate of profit.

The monetary dimensions of Gordon's work were weakly developed, but here too he borrowed from post-Keynesian economics through adoption of a horizontalist approach to interest rates (Gordon 1995b). The horizontalist approach (Moore 1988) maintains that interest rates are exogenously set by the central bank. The money supply expands passively at the given interest rate to accommodate any increase in economic activity. Other post-Keynesian accounts of the money supply (Palley 1987, 1994a) provide a richer account of money supply determination in which interest rates may rise with economic activity. The money supply responds positively to increased credit demand via adjustments in the banking system, but the induced accommodation need not be full and interest rates can rise.

A second financial feature emphasized by post-Keynesians is debt, and this feature is completely absent in Gordon's work. That said, it is easy to see how it can be included since it impacts the demand side, and Gordon's demand side was post-Keynesian. The focus on debt derives from the seminal work of Minsky (1982), which has been formalized in a number of business cycle models (Foley 1987; Palley 1994b, 1997a). Debt is initially expansionary as agents spend their borrowings, and this drives the upswing. However, over time the accumulation of debt service burdens acts as an increasing drag on demand, and this triggers the downturn. If prices and nominal wages begin to fall, the accumulated debt burden becomes an even bigger drag on demand, and this undermines the new classical claim that price and wage flexibility can ensure an automatic return to full employment (Palley 1996a, 1999).

A final area of finance emphasized by post-Keynesians but neglected by Gordon is that of finance constraints. Here, the argument is that investment spending may be constrained because of finance constraints operating on the firm. The importance of such constraints has been empirically documented by Fazzari (1988). Once again, because these constraints operate on investment spending and the demand side, they can be seamlessly incorporated into Gordon's macroeconomic framework.

When it comes to the supply side, David Gordon and the post-Keynesians worked on different issues. The post-Keynesian focus has been schizophrenic. One side has addressed the question of the significance of aggregate demand for firms' supply decisions, while another side has addressed the abstract notions of the production function and capital. Gordon's focus was on the historical and sociological situatedness of production. These are big differences. However, the questions raised by post-Keynesians are germane to Gordon's theoretical work, while Gordon's theoretical work is fully consistent with the post-Keynesian vision of the supply side.

With regard to firms' production decisions, many post-Keynesians have been willing to use the standard neo-classical production function apparatus and impose demand constraints on individual firms. This analysis is in the spirit of Barro and Grossman (1971) and Malinvaud (1977).[2] Others (Davidson 1983) have sought to abandon the marginal product of labor curve as having anything to do with the labor demand schedule, and have argued for replacing the aggregate production function apparatus with Keynes' (1936) aggregate Z-supply function. However, microeconomic excavation of the Z-supply function suggests that it is a reduced form that embodies the aggregate production function so that the marginal product of labor remains present, albeit in the background. Palley (1997b) presents a model of Keynes' Z-supply function that distinguishes between aggregate demand and aggregate supply, but has aggregate supply depend on firms' expectations of aggregate demand. This treatment incorporates a production function and the marginal product of labor, and is consistent with Keynes' Z-supply schedule outlined in *The General Theory* which openly made reference to these features. In this framework, firms' expectations of aggregate demand replace the demand constraints of the Barro and Grossman (1971) framework.

A more heterodox group of post-Keynesians (see, for example, Lavoie 1992) has abandoned both diminishing returns to labor and the notion of continuity in the production function regarding choice of the labor–capital mix. In their macro models, an aggregate production function still exists, but it is of the fixed coefficient type. Analytically, the purpose is to provide a framework of constant average costs that can generate a simple mark-up pricing rule. This goal can also be reached by adoption of an institutionalist perspective in which information is complex, incomplete, and costly to acquire and process (Cyert and March 1963). Under these conditions, firms may adopt simple pricing rules of thumb which take the form of a mark-up over normal average costs. In this framework, the standard production function remains intact yet the firm is still led to mark-up pricing behavior.[3] This illustrates how different microeconomic reasonings can lead to the same macroeconomic representation.

Another implication of the fixed coefficients approach is that the neo-classical marginal productivity theory of income distribution can no longer apply. This is because choice over capital–labor mix is not continuous so that marginal products are not well defined. A new theory of income distribution is needed. For many post-Keynesians this has led to adoption of the Kaldor (1955–56) and Pasinetti (1961–62) approach which emphasizes the demand side of the economy, but for others (the author included) this approach is unsatisfactory because it provides no role for conflict in labor markets.

Finally, a more subversive post-Keynesian criticism that also has its origins in the excavation of the supply side is the Cambridge (U.K.) capital critique. This critique maintains that it is impossible to aggregate capital, and therefore impossible to construct an aggregate production function. Without an aggregate notion of capital, it is also impossible to talk of a marginal product of capital, and once again marginal productivity theory cannot provide a coherent theory of the return to capital and income distribution. However, the capital critique also destroys the notion of an aggregate fixed coefficients production function since that also relies on the notion of an aggregate capital input. Thus, the fixed coefficients critique and the Cambridge (U.K.) capital critique both destroy the marginal productivity theory of income distribution, but they in turn stand at odds with each other.

David Gordon's own theory of the supply side is represented in his profitability function (Gordon 1995a, 1995b). In many regards, this function is a theoretical black box that implicitly incorporates both the production decisions of the firm and the outcome of the wage struggle in labor markets. Gordon openly discusses an aggregate capital stock which implies that he rejected the Cambridge capital critique and accepted the possibility of an aggregate production function. Standard microeconomic analysis of the firm shows that the profit function embeds the firm's production function. Gordon's own profitability function is continuous and differentiable, and employment can vary despite the fixity of capital. This implies that inside the black box of his profitability function there is a neo-classical styled aggregate production function, which places Gordon in the same camp as those post-Keynesians that have been willing to use the neo-classical production function apparatus.

Gordon's major contribution was to historically and sociologically situate production. This is the foundation of his social structures of accumulation argument (see for example Gordon et al. 1987). However, because the profitability function is a black box that is never derived from microeconomic foundations, its theoretical workings are hard to ascertain. The microeconomic logic appears to rest on contested exchange theory (Bowles and Gintis 1990; Bowles 1985), which in turn belongs to the wider efficiency wage paradigm. Contested exchange theory emphasizes issues of ownership and control, with different structures of ownership and control inducing different provision of worker effort and requiring different levels of firm monitoring of workers.

Contested exchange–efficiency wage theory substantively enriches the aggregate production function, adding worker effort and firm monitoring costs as variables. This is a significant improvement upon the standard production function used by post-Keynesians. However, that said, post-Keynesians have willingly embraced efficiency wage theory as is evident by regular articles on this subject published in the *Journal of Post Keynesian Economics*, the flagship post-Keynesian journal. Moreover, post-Keynesians have themselves had a long-standing interest in the sociological foundations of the firm as evidenced by Eichner's (1976) work on the megacorp and Penrose's (1959) work on the theory of the firm. Thus, though the particular focus of Gordon's work differed from that of the post-Keynesians, it is fully consistent in spirit. At the same time, the supply side work of the post-Keynesians is relevant for Gordon's own theoretical framework.

In sum, David Gordon and the post-Keynesians shared a broadly similar underlying vision of how modern capitalist economies work, and they also shared a common theoretical architecture (both on the demand side and the supply side) for describing that vision. It is for this reason that one can say that David Gordon's work fits within the modern post-Keynesian tradition.

Finally, there is one last reason why David Gordon distanced himself from post-Keynesians, especially from American post-Keynesians. One of Gordon's greatest strengths was as an empirical economist, and he had an unquestioning faith in the ability of econometric analysis to distinguish truth from error. However, a group of American post-Keynesians, principally associated with Paul Davidson, assert that the real world is non-ergodic.[4] By this is meant that economic events are not governed by knowable probability distributions, and that economic life partakes of historical uniqueness. This matter is of importance for the question of expectation formation in a fundamentally uncertain world. It also implies that the assumptions underlying econometric theory do not hold in the real world. The American post-Keynesian non-ergodicity critique therefore diminishes the credibility of econometrics. On this issue there was no room for compromise, and when combined with a clash of personalities, it led David Gordon to unnecessarily overstate the divide between his work and that of the post-Keynesians. Both sides contributed to this division, and all lost as a consequence. It is time to close that divide.

III. Competing Constructions of the Macroeconomic Process

Since *The General Theory* (Keynes 1936), systems of simultaneous equations have constituted the major language of macroeconomics. Behind these systems of equations lie implicit descriptions of the economic process, and aspects of this process are expressed in the functional arguments, patterns of inter-dependence across equations, and equilibrium conditions.

The new micro-foundations approach to macroeconomics seeks to provide a microeconomic grounding for the behavioral equations in these systems of simultaneous equations. In principle, the micro-foundations methodology is consistent with Marxian, Keynesian, and classical macroeconomics. It is not a willingness to incorporate micro-foundations that distinguishes the paradigms. Rather, it is differences in the representation of the causal economic processes that are contained in the various systems of equations. This section briefly outlines the analytic contours of four traditions in macroeconomics.

The Classical Macro Process

Figure 5.1 describes the economic process embodied in the new classical approach to macroeconomics (see Sargent 1979, Chapter 1). Table 5.1 defines the variables. The classical process is marked by a unidirectional line of causation running from labor markets to goods markets, and on to the financial sector. The classical model's economic logic is as follows. The labor market determines employment and real wages, with labor market outcomes being determined in a perfectly competitive market through the interaction of the forces of labor supply and demand. Labor demand depends upon the existing capital stock and the productivity of labor, which in turn depends upon the production tech-

Figure 5.1 **The Classical Approach to the Macroeconomic Process**

nology. Labor supply depends on household wealth and preferences over leisure and consumption. Given the level of employment determined in labor markets, firms' production technology then determines output. It is in this sense that economic activity depends upon the "triplets"— tastes, technology, and endowments. Money is irrelevant, and this is the basis of the classical "dichotomy" between a real general equilibrium and an overlaying nominal representation.

Given this level of output, the goods market is cleared by interest rate adjustment. This clearing process rests on the loanable funds theory of interest rates, which has interest rates adjusting such that real loan demand (for both consumption and investment) equals income saved. Adjustment of the interest rate therefore clears the goods market, and it is interest rate adjustment that validates Say's Law.[5]

Lastly, given the level of interest rates, the financial sector determines the price level. Financial market equilibrium is achieved by price level adjustment which ensures that the demand for real money balances equals the supply of real money balances. The demand for real money balances depends upon the level of income and interest rates, which have already been determined in the labor and loanable funds markets. Price level adjustment ensures sufficient real money balances, given the existing nominal money stock. This concludes the classical macro process. The important feature is that there are no feedbacks between markets, and it is in this sense that the flow of causation is unidirectional.[6]

Within the classical macroeconomic process, power and income distribution are absent. Labor markets are characterized by perfect competition, which means that both labor and firms have "no power." Economically, this means that they are both price takers: this is different from the assumption of "equal power." In the loanable funds market, which ensures balance between demand and supply for goods, income distribution is also absent. Permanent income theory ensures that all households have the same marginal propensity to consume, independent of their level of income. The fungibility of money income means

Table 5.1

Definition of Variables

N	employment
y	output
w	real wage
i	nominal interest rate
m	mark-up
P	profits
K	capital stock
AD	aggregate demand
I	investment
C	consumption
D	firms' debt
E	firms' equity

that the distribution of income between profits and wages doesn't matter.

Can power and income distribution be introduced? The answer is yes. If workers are given power through trade unions, then union preferences over wages and employment, in combination with firms' labor demand schedules determine the level of employment and output. Thereafter, the economic process in the goods market and financial sector is as before. Given a downward sloping labor demand schedule, workers can only gain higher wages at the expense of lower employment.[7] Thus, introducing unions gives rise to reduced output and unemployment.

The effects of income distribution can also be introduced by dropping permanent income theory. If household spending is governed by conventional Keynesian consumption theory, and profit income is concentrated amongst higher income households, then the marginal propensity to save out of profits will be larger than that out of wages. The distribution of income will therefore affect saving, which in turn affects interest rates in the loanable funds market. However, it has no impact on the level of employment. An increased wage share increases consumption, and this raises interest rates and lowers investment spending. Thus, more equal income distribution is bad for capital accumulation and growth. This is the economic logic behind "trickle down" theory.

In sum, adoption of the classical macroeconomic model leads to a characterization of the economic process whereby increased worker power reduces employment and output. A more equal distribution of income raises interest rates, lowers investment, and reduces capital accumulation and growth.

The Neo-Keynesian Macro Process

Figure 5.2 illustrates the neo-Keynesian macro process, as typified by the ISLM model (Hicks 1937). Now there is an interdependence between the goods market and the financial sector, and they jointly determine the level of output and interest rates. This interdependence is captured by the lower causal arrow running from the goods market to the financial sector, and by the upper causal arrow running from the financial sector to the goods market. The level of aggregate demand (AD) determines the level of income, which in turn influences the demand for financial assets. The latter then influences interest rates, which feed back and influence AD.

Once the goods market and financial sector have jointly determined the level of output, firms' production technology determines the level of employment and real wages (equal to the marginal product of labor) consistent with this level of output. Thus, in the neo-Keynesian macroeconomic process the direction of causality is the exact opposite of the classical macroeconomic process, and runs from the goods market to the labor market.

The neo-Keynesian construction of the macro process posits that goods market conditions determine real wages and employment. AD determines employment which in turn determines marginal costs, and changes in marginal cost are passed on in the form of price changes. Given exogenous nominal wages, the real wage is determined by the price level which in turn is determined by the marginal cost of output. This neo-Keynesian process is the reverse of the classical process in which employment and real wages are determined in labor markets independently of goods market conditions.

An important implication of the neo-Keynesian description of the macro process is that workers' actions in labor markets are economically irrelevant for the determination of real wages and employment. This is because the existence of unemployment means that employment outcomes are off the labor supply schedule, and it is the labor supply schedule that describes workers' actions. Instead, firms' production technology and production level decisions are all that matter for employment and real wages. The actions and decisions of workers, as embodied in the labor supply function, are of no consequence. This contrasts with the classical process which has workers actively involved in the determination of employment and real wages through their labor supply de-

Figure 5.2 **The Neo-Keynesian Approach to the Macroeconomic Process**

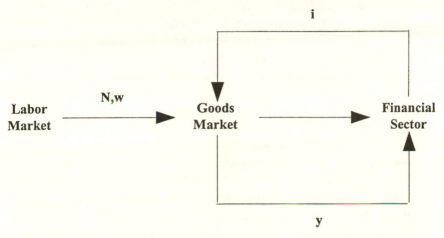

cisions. Paradoxically, the classical model gives a stronger role to workers than does the neo-Keynesian model.

Though the neo-Keynesian model is weak regarding the treatment of worker power, it does a much better job regarding the effects of income distribution. These can be incorporated readily within the neo-Keynesian model, thereby linking it to the Kaleckian tradition in macroeconomics. If the propensity to consume out of wage income exceeds that out of profit income, a shift in distribution toward wage income will raise aggregate demand, output, employment, and interest rates. In the ISLM model, this corresponds to a rightward movement of the IS curve.[8]

Incorporating AD effects of income distribution within the neo-Keynesian macro model raises questions about the determination of income distribution. The neo-Keynesian model, as did Keynes (1936), relies on perfectly competitive marginal productivity theory to resolve the problem of income distribution. Real wages are determined by reference to the exogenously given marginal product of labor schedule, and this excludes social considerations of power. Opening income distribution to social influences therefore requires a departure from perfectly competitive marginal product theory.

One channel for accomplishing this is the introduction of imperfect competition and mark-up pricing in goods markets (Palley 1991–1992). Prices are then determined as follows:

(1) $$P = [1 + m]W/f_N$$

where P = price, m = mark-up, W = nominal wage, and f_N = marginal product of labor (MPL). The effect of introducing imperfect competition is to replace the marginal product of labor (MPL) schedule with a mark-up adjusted MPL schedule. Increases in the mark-up shift this schedule down and reduce real wages for every level of employment. Variations in the mark-up now affect real wages, and the mark-up becomes a point of entry for influencing the distribution of income. In neo-classical constructions of imperfect competition, the mark-up is determined by reference to the elasticity of product demand, which in turn depends on consumer preferences. In the left Keynesian construction of the macroeconomic process (see below) it is the outcome of business–labor conflict.

A second channel for allowing social considerations to influence employment and real wages is efficiency wage theory (Palley 1996b). In this case, the productivity of workers depends on their effort. For a given level of real aggregate demand, the level of effort determines the needed level of employment. Firms also have an incentive to pay efficiency wages to elicit an optimal amount of effort. If the amount of effort provided depends on the perceived fairness of the wage, this provides an avenue for social considerations to influence wages and employment since these perceptions are socially influenced.

A third channel whereby social influences can affect income distribution is by endogenizing technology. This channel has been emphasized by Bowles and Gintis (1990) in their "contested exchange" paradigm, and it was also emphasized by David Gordon in his book, *Fat and Mean* (1996). Firms choose technology with a view to maximizing profits. Two important implications follow from this. First, there is a potential conflict between productive efficiency (defined as the most output for a given amount of input) and income distribution. This is because firms may choose productively inefficient technologies that reduce the size of the pie, if such technologies increase the absolute size of the slice going to profits. Second, the allocation of control regarding choice of technology now matters for income distribution, and since control is socially determined, this means that social influences again matter.

Finally, it is worth noting that the neo-Keynesian construction of the macro process is incompatible with the traditional neo-classical model of trade unions. According to the neo-classical union model, unions maximize a strictly concave objective function defined over employment and real wages, and choose a unique optimal level of employment. This construction is consistent with the classical macro process in which the labor market determines employment, real wages, and the level of output. However, it is inconsistent with the neo-Keynesian macro process in which output and employment are determined in the goods market by the forces of aggregate demand. Unions have no direct control over the level of aggregate demand, and according to Keynesian theory they therefore cannot determine the level of employment.

The above observation highlights the need for a new Keynesian theory of unions. Incorporating unions into the neo-Keynesian macro process requires abandoning the assumption that they can directly determine the level of employment. Instead, unions can determine a real wage–employment schedule (i.e., a wage curve such as that empirically estimated by Blanchflower and Oswald 1990; Blanchflower 1994) which replaces the marginal product of labor schedule. This wage curve serves as a surrogate labor demand schedule, and where the economy settles on this surrogate demand curve depends on the state of aggregate demand. The specific determination of this wage curve then allows considerations of labor market power to enter the neo-Keynesian model.[9]

The Classical Marxist Process

Figure 5.3 provides a "schematic" representation of the classical Marxist process. Labor market outcomes, which include the wage rate, the level of labor intensity, and the size of the reserve army, determine the rate of profit. These labor market outcomes depend on structural conditions including the political consciousness of the working class and the nature of technology. The rate of profit then determines investment spending and the rate of capital accumulation. The rate of profit also determines the rate of interest. The level of investment spending feeds back to affect the rate of profit through its impact on the level of the capital stock. It is this loop that lies behind Marxist theories of crisis predicated on the falling rate of profit resulting from increased capital intensity of production. Finally, investment spending and capital accumulation may also impact the nature of technology, thereby impacting outcomes in the labor market.

The classical Marxist macro process informed much of David Gordon's work in the 1970s, and it also informed his notion of the social structure of accumulation (or SSA, Gordon 1978). The SSA approach

Figure 5.3 **The Classical Marxian Macroeconomic Process**

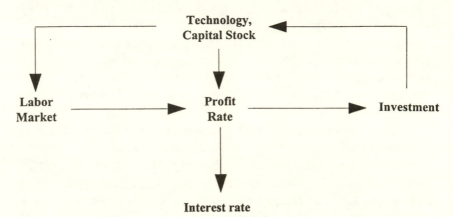

seeks to historically and sociologically situate the institutional arrangements governing the particulars of production and labor markets, and
their effect on profit rates and growth. Bowles and Gintis' (1990) contested exchange paradigm was also initially developed with an eye to
the classical Marxist perspective. Though using neo-classical
microeconomic methods, it provides an economic account of the role of
ownership and control over technology choice in determining income
distribution and profitability.

There are a number of noticeable features in the above rendering of
the classical Marxist process. First, the classical Marxist process has a
longer time horizon in mind given its focus on capital accumulation.
This contrasts with the new classical and neo-Keynesian approaches
which are strictly short run in focus and take the capital stock as given.

Second, the classical Marxist process has some similarities with the
new classical process in the sense that at any moment in time with given
technologies, labor market outcomes are primitive. Thus, causation flows
"out" of the labor market and the supply side of the economy into the
rest of the economy. This contrasts with the neo-Keynesian process in
which aggregate demand determines economic activity and labor market outcomes are a residual.

A third feature of the classical Marxist process is that profit rates,
which are determined in the real economy, determine the interest rate.
Thus, finance is very much super-structural, and this may explain why
so little attention has been paid to financial issues by SSA proponents.

Lastly, considerations of aggregate demand are absent from the classical Marxist process. This is a contentious claim, since theories of under-consumption are also part of heterodox economics. However, these latter theories have a strong Keynesian dimension to them. The Marxist notion of over-accumulation is not an aggregate demand phenomenon. Instead, it is a supply-side phenomenon that rests on excessive capital deepening.[10]

The evolution of the profit rate is central to classical Marxist accounts of the economy. The profit rate is the ratio of the level of profits to the capital stock, P/K. Classical Marxists have a tendency to focus on the denominator, K. An alternative approach is to focus on the numerator, P. This is the spirit of the Kaleckian approach in which investment spending by capitalists determines the level of profits. This identification of an investment spending–profit relationship introduces aggregate demand back into the model, and opens the possibility for a link between the economics of Keynes and Marxist dynamics of accumulation. This link is explored in the next section.

The Kaleckian Process

Figure 5.4 shows the Kaleckian construction of the macro process. This description of the economic process developed largely out of the Cambridge (U.K.) post-Keynesian school of economic thought associated with Robinson, Kaldor, Kalecki, and Goodwin. In his early work on macroeconomics David Gordon (1978) focused primarily on concerns suggested by the above classical Marxist approach. However, his later work had more of a short run focus (Gordon 1995a, 1995b) and effectively adopted a Kaleckian process.

The key feature about the Kaleckian framework is the looping process linking goods markets and labor markets. Goods markets are Keynesian in construction, in that the level of output depends on the level of AD. However, the level of AD depends upon the functional distribution of income owing to differential propensities to consume out of wage and profit income. This is the Kaleckian contribution to the short run Keynesian model, and it serves to embed income distribution in the model.

The level of output, in conjunction with the production technology, affects the level of employment in labor markets. The level of employment then positively affects the level of wages, which in turn affects AD

Figure 5.4 **The Kaleckian Approach to the Macroeconomic Process**

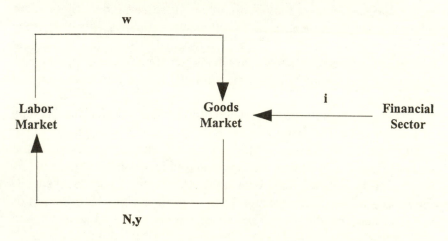

and goods markets. One theoretical mechanism for this labor market channel is the real wage Phillips curve which dates back to Goodwin's (1967) classic work on the cyclical accumulation process. An alternative mechanism involves labor market bargaining, and this mechanism has been explored in a short run macro model by Palley (1998).

The Kaleckian mechanism emphasizes the effect of labor markets on real wages and consumption demands. However, the level of real wages also affects profitability since there is an isomorphism between changes in real wages and changes in the profit rate holding the capital stock and the level of employment constant. This isomorphism opens a second channel whereby labor market outcomes affect profitability, thereby affecting investment spending, aggregate demand, and goods markets. This channel has been explored by Bhaduri and Marglin (1990), and it links with Cambridge (U.K.) post-Keynesianism which has long emphasized that profit rates matter for investment spending. Thus, we can define a variable that is the ratio of the profit rate and the interest rate given by

(2) $$q = [P/K]/i.$$

Investment is positively related to q.[11] Changes in the wage bargain that raise real wages will therefore tend to depress P and q, resulting in lower investment spending. Whether output expands depends on whether the wage–consumption effect dominates the profit–investment effect.

The link between wages and profit rates also ties back to the question of the mark-up and imperfect competition in macroeconomics. Neo-classical treatments of imperfect competition treat the mark-up in terms of the elasticity of product demand and the degree of monopoly power. This is a theme that is echoed in the Kaleckian tradition, but the Kaleckian mark-up can also be seen as determined by labor market outcomes which determine wage and profit shares. Assuming a constant marginal product of labor, and using equation (1), yields expressions for the profit share, wage share, and mark-up given by

(3a) $$s_P = m/[1 + m]$$
(3b) $$s_W = 1/[1 + m]$$
(3c) $$m = s_P/s_W = s_P/[1 - s_P].$$

The mark-up is therefore equal to the ratio of the profit and wage shares, where these shares are influenced by conditions of labor market power.

The channels (consumption and investment spending) whereby real wages and profits affect AD are clear. Less clear is the microeconomic logic whereby goods market activity affects labor market outcomes. The "contested exchange" paradigm, which David Gordon adopted and underlay much of *Fat and Mean* (1996), focuses on the problem of extracting effort from workers. In Gordon's formal macroeconomic work (1995a, 1995b), this effort extraction problem generates the relation between the profit rate and the level of employment. As labor markets tighten, effort extraction becomes more difficult thereby inducing firms to pay higher efficiency wages, and this constrains economic expansion. Gordon sought to identify policies that could relax this constraint. He recognized that the effort extraction problem depended on the nature of firms' organization, and he argued that making corporations more democratic could generate a cooperative response on the part of workers that eased the extraction problem.[12]

An alternative construction of the labor market–real wage nexus is in terms of non-cooperative bargaining theory. Labor market conditions impact the relative bargaining power of workers and firms, with lower unemployment increasing worker bargaining power thereby enabling them to win higher real wages. Just as choice of production technology matters for the effort extraction story, so too it matters in the bargaining power story. In the bargaining framework (Skillman 1988, 1991; Skillman and Ryder 1993), firms choose technologies that increase their bargaining power vis-à-vis workers through such means as making it easier to replace existing "insider" workers with "outsiders."[13]

The effort extraction and bargaining mechanisms are not mutually exclusive, but they are different. David Gordon (1994b, 1996) tended to focus on the problematic of business organization and effort extraction. Cambridge post-Keynesians have tended to emphasize bargaining strength considerations.

A Marxist–Kaleckian Synthesis

Earlier, I alluded to the possibility of a synthesis of the classical Marxist and Kaleckian approaches. Such a synthesis is shown in Figure 5.5. The top half of the figure is identified with the Marxist process shown in Figure 5.3, while the bottom half of the figure is identified with the Kaleckian process shown in Figure 5.4. This figure therefore contains both short and long run concerns, and it has strong affinities with the work of Anwar Shaikh (1989, 1992).

Beginning with the bottom half, aggregate demand (AD) determines the level of output (y) in goods markets, which in turn determines the level of employment (N) in labor markets. This much is Keynesian. Labor market outcomes then determine the relative bargaining strength of workers and firms, which determines real wages (w) and the mark-up (m).[14] Wages and employment then determine consumption spending which feeds into aggregate demand. The mark-up determines the profit rate, which determines investment spending, which in turn feeds into aggregate demand.

This short run Kaleckian construction is linked to the long run Marxist process through investment spending and its effect on the capital stock and technology. The formal expression for the profit rate is

$$(4) \qquad P/K = P/y \cdot y/K = sp/k = m/[1 + m]k$$

where P = level of profits, K = capital stock, y = level of output, and k = capital-output ratio. The addition of an upper loop running from investment to the capital-output ratio to the profit rate then allows for capital stock dynamics to fit in. Capital deepening can then lead to a declining profit rate and a Marxist crisis of accumulation. Additionally, investment can impact technology thereby impacting bargaining power, real wages, and profitability.

Figure 5.5 **A Synthesis of Kaleckian and Classical Marxist Models**

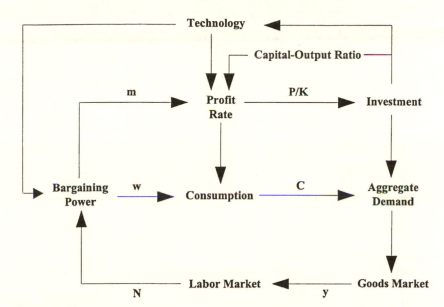

IV. A General Post-Keynesian Synthesis: Finance and the Macroeconomic Process

Both the new classical (Figure 5.1) and neo-Keynesian (Figure 5.2) models have a blind spot regarding power and conflict, whereas the impact of financial markets is under-developed in both the Marxist (Figure 5.3) and Kaleckian (Figure 5.4) models. David Gordon was rightly critical of the deficiencies of the new classical and neo-Keynesian models, but he and other left macro economists have exhibited a blind spot to the weaknesses of their own traditions.

That finance matters for the business cycle is evident in the credit-led U.S. economic expansions of the 1980s and 1990s, and the significance of financial markets has been underscored by the economic crisis that afflicted southeast Asia in 1997. Finance matters for income distribution, the process of capital accumulation, and the distribution of power. It therefore needs to figure as a central component of any plausible economic model.

Figure 5.4 describing the Kaleckian process has interest rates being exogenously set. The fact that interest rates are not set by conditions in

Figure 5.6 **A General Post-Keynesian Approach to the Macroeconomic Process**

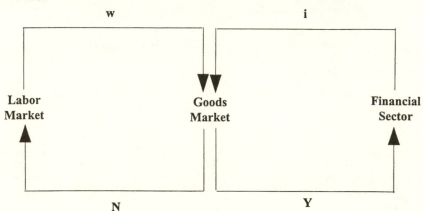

the real economy distinguishes it from the classical Marxist process of Figure 5.3. At issue is the question of whether interest rates are exogenous or endogenous, and if they are endogenous, how are they set.

The assumption of exogenous interest rates can be identified with the post-Keynesian "accommodationist" construction (Pollin 1991) of the endogenous money supply. The limitation of this approach is that it essentially leaves the financial sector out of the economic process, except as an exogenous influence. For this reason it is an unsatisfactory construction of the role of finance in the macroeconomic process.

An alternative is the post-Keynesian structuralist approach to endogenous money (Palley 1987–1988, 1994a), which has both the money supply and interest rates endogenously determined by economic conditions. Such a description allows for feedbacks between the goods market and financial sector.

Figure 5.6 describes a general post-Keynesian construction of the macroeconomic process that allows for feedbacks between the financial and real sectors. It is a synthesis of the neo-Keynesian (Figure 5.2) and Kaleckian (Figure 5.4) processes, and the longer run classical Marxist (Figure 5.3) process also fits within it. The left hand side of Figure 5.6 can be viewed as a simplified presentation of the economic process in Figure 5.5, while the right hand side of Figure 5.6 reflects the neo-Keynesian dimension. The strength of the neo-Keynesian school is its analysis of the interaction between goods markets and the financial sector; the strength of the Kaleckian–classical Marxist school is its identification of the loop between goods markets and labor markets.

Though containing a neo-Keynesian financial sector–real sector feedback loop, the post-Keynesian construction of the specifics of this loop are considerably different. They differ with regard to the endogeneity of the money supply, and they differ with regard to the significance of credit. Thus, for neo-Keynesians the money supply is determined by the money multiplier which depends on portfolio preferences; for post-Keynesians it also depends on bank credit demand.

Table 5.2 provides a detailed decomposition of the channels linking the financial and real sectors. Just as Figure 5.5 can be thought of as a detailed exposition of the left hand loop in Figure 5.6, Table 5.2 can be thought of as a detailed exposition of the right hand loop in Figure 5.6. The bottom half of Table 5.2 shows how developments in goods markets link with the financial sector, while the top half links developments in the financial sector with goods markets.

There are three different ways in which goods markets affect the financial sector. First, changes in income affect the demand for money and other assets, thereby initiating changes in asset prices, interest rates, and quantities of inside assets and liabilities. This channel is the hallmark of the ISLM model, and it has been expanded to a multi-asset context in the work of James Tobin (1969, 1982). Changes in aggregate demand matter if consumption or investment are used to scale money demand (Davidson 1965). In addition to affecting the demand for assets, changes in income also affect the demand for credit. The absence of credit markets in the ISLM model means that this feature has been relatively neglected, and reviving interest in credit has been another major contribution of the post-Keynesian theory of endogenous money.

Goods markets also affect financial markets through changes in the price level. Changes in the price level change the real value of holdings of financial assets and liabilities. Keynes (1936) focused on the effect on the real money supply, and this has also been the focus of ISLM models. Changes in the price level are also intimately connected with real balance wealth and debt burden effects, and they therefore matter for the link between the financial sector and real activity, about which more is said below.

A third channel is the rate of inflation which affects the pattern of asset demands. This channel has been emphasized by Tobin (1965, 1975) with regard to both long run and short run effects. Inflation promotes a portfolio shift toward capital which can increase the steady state capital/

Table 5.2 **Linkages Between Goods Markets and the Financial Sector**

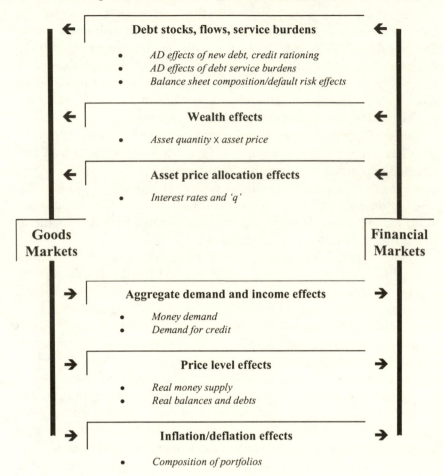

labor ratio; deflation promotes a shift toward money, and this can give rise to prolonged depression by raising real interest rates and lowering investment spending and aggregate demand.

Turning to the upper loop of Table 5.2, there are again three channels. The first channel concerns interest rate and asset price allocation effects, a channel which neo-Keynesian constructions of the macroeconomy emphasize. Changes in asset demands and supplies cause changes in asset prices and interest rates. Given that aggregate demand is interest-sensitive, this causes changes in the level of goods market activity. An emphasis on interest rates is the hallmark of the ISLM model.

Tobin's multi-asset approach (1969, 1982) emphasizes the significance of equity prices and the cost of equity capital for investment spending. This is the foundation of the q theory of investment (Brainard and Tobin 1968; Brainard 1977), and it has both interest rates and asset prices serving to convey the effects of financial sector developments into goods markets.

The second channel whereby the financial sector affects the goods market is through wealth effects, with changes in the value of household net wealth affecting consumption spending. This is the foundation of the Pigou effect whereby lower prices increase the real value of financial wealth, and this argument has been used to support the claim that Keynesian involuntary equilibrium unemployment rests on downwardly rigid prices. The inclusion of a Pigou wealth effect is common to the ISLM model, though one point of contention has been what constitutes net household financial wealth (Barro 1974). Wealth effects also figure prominently in neo-Keynesian analyses of deficit-financed fiscal policy (Blinder and Solow 1973), but there has been relatively little attention paid to the wealth effects of inside debt. By focusing attention on bank lending, the post-Keynesian theory of endogenous money redirects attention toward this concern.

The third channel whereby the financial sector affects the goods market is through inside debt stocks, flows, and service burdens. As noted above, this channel is under-emphasized in ISLM macroeconomics owing to the ISLM's lack of inside credit markets. The macroeconomic contribution of the theory of endogenous money concerns the recognition of the critical significance of this channel. The impact of inside debt stocks has been acknowledged in discussions of the Fisher (1933) debt effect (Tobin 1980; Caskey and Fazzari 1987), which explains why lower prices and nominal wages may actually reduce aggregate demand. This contrasts with the claims of the Pigou wealth effect. Another way in which debt stocks have been examined is through their impact on the composition of firms' balance sheets. Thus, as firms become relatively more indebted, this lowers their credit-worthiness and reduces their ability to borrow to finance investment spending (Franke and Semmler 1989).

Though the macroeconomic effects of "stocks" of inside debt have been examined, less attention has been given to the effects of changing "flows" of inside debt. These flows matter for the determination of aggregate demand, and it is here that the theory of endogenous money makes an original contribution to macroeconomics. This "flow" channel for bank lending has been examined in Palley (1997a). The key innovation is the recognition that bank lending creates purchasing power, and this impacts the level of aggregate demand when borrowers spend their loans. Thereafter, the newly created money balances circulate as part of the circular flow of money income so that aggregate demand is raised as long as the loans remain in circulation.

The fact that bank lending creates new money balances distinguishes such lending from lending effected through bond markets. The latter involves a transfer of money balances from lender to borrower, whereas the former involves the creation of new money balances. For this reason, bank lending is more expansionary than bond market lending. However, both forms of lending give rise to debt service burdens which act to transfer income between debtors and creditors. This highlights how financial markets and interest rates affect the distribution of income, and this impact is becoming increasingly significant as the scale of borrowing rises relative to GDP.

When combined with differential propensities to consume on the part of debtors and creditors, the transfer of income between debtors and creditors can serve as the foundation for a credit-driven explanation of the business cycle. Borrowing is initially expansionary and raises aggregate demand. However, borrowing leaves behind the deflationary footprint of debt service burdens. Over time, the expansionary effect of new borrowing is swamped by debt service burdens, and this initiates the downturn.

A central bank can be added to this post-Keynesian construction of the financial sector, and it can influence the level of interest rates and the behavior of financial intermediaries. Considerations of central banking (i.e., the state) introduces political conflict since different interests will compete to control central bank policy. These issues have been raised by Epstein (1994) who distinguishes between labor, industrial capital, and financial capital. Recognition of the economic significance of political conflict over the setting of economic policy therefore introduces another source of conflict into the post-Keynesian model.

Figure 5.6 represents a fusing together of the neo-Keynesian and post-Keynesian macroeconomic processes. The possibilities for developing such a comprehensive framework are evident in Shaikh (1989, 1992) and Moudud (1998). These papers add debt effects to the Marxist-Kaleckian synthesis described in Figure 5.5. Shaikh focuses on the implications of business debt for capital accumulation, while Moudud focuses on the impact of public deficits and debt for capital accumulation. Both adopt a Kaleckian process in their descriptions of short run real sector behavior, and to this is added the longer run Marxist capital accumulation process described in Figure 5.3.[15] Other forms of financial interaction other than debt are clearly possible.

Finally, Figure 5.6 and Table 5.2 restrict finance to impacting only aggregate demand. Yet finance may also impact the distribution of economic power. In particular, it may be used as a "worker discipline device" that intimidates workers and shifts the distribution of income away from wages. This disciplining effect is captured in Figure 5.7 in which there is a loop linking the financial sector and the labor market. The logic of this loop is that firms use debt to protect revenues from being claimed by workers as wages (Bronars and Deere 1991). Firms can choose to leverage up their balance sheets, and convert residual profit income into pre-committed debt service. Higher debt–equity ratios weaken the financial viability of the firm, and in doing so send a credible threat to workers that the firm may close in the event of labor trouble. Consequently, firms' balance sheet configurations may be chosen with an eye to distributional outcomes, just as are their production technologies. The debt–equity ratio is a means of credibly preempting workers. However, owners of firms also recognize that increasing the debt–equity ratio raises the probability of an encounter with bankruptcy, and if bankruptcy costs are large for owners, this will discourage them from using this instrument of control. Lastly, it should be noted that higher interest rates serve a similar function, since for any given debt–equity ratio, they cause a greater share of revenue to be pre-committed. Thus, monetary policy can also threaten workers, over and above its aggregate demand–employment effect.

This discipline effect of financial markets operates through the supply side of the economy, and therefore marks a departure from the Keynesian tradition which focuses on the impact of financial markets on aggregate demand and goods markets. The above supply side financial market loop links with modern developments in the new classical tradition (as discussed in note 6). These developments emphasize the impact of credit rationing which arises from imperfect information. As a result, firms may be restricted in what they can borrow to fund production, and this lowers output and employment. Financial markets therefore impact both the demand and supply sides of the economy, and this construction is fully consistent with a general post-Keynesian model of the macroeconomic process.

Figure 5.7 **The Post-Keynesian Approach with Finance as a Worker Discipline Device**

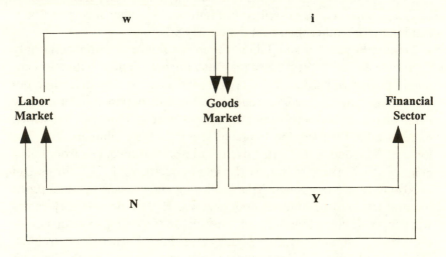

V. Conclusion

To sum up: Power and conflict are largely absent from conventional macroeconomics, a feature which has generated persistent dissatisfaction with mainstream paradigms, be they new classical or neo-Keynesian. The economic significance of power and conflict depends critically on the underlying construction of the macroeconomic process. This paper has explored the implicit macroeconomic process embedded in the new classical, neo-Keynesian, classical Marxist, and Kaleckian post-Keynesian constructions of the economy. Most importantly, it has shown how the neo-Keynesian and Kaleckian or post-Keynesian models can be fused to provide a powerful synthetic model. The Marxist long run process of capital accumulation also fits well within this synthesis. The proposed general post-Keynesian model incorporates both the effects of labor market conflict and financial market activity within a framework in which output is demand-determined. Lastly, it was argued that not only is finance relevant for aggregate demand, but it also serves as a worker discipline device that has distributional implications.

Notes

This chapter was first published as an article in vol. 31, no. 4 (1999) of the *Review of Radical Political Economics*. Permission to print this article is granted by the Union for Radical Political Economics.

1. See for instance Gordon (1994a) in which he claimed his social structuralist macroeconomic model was fundamentally different from the post-Keynesian model.

2. However, while accepting this framework, post-Keynesians reject the claims of Barro and Grossman (1971) and Malinvaud (1977) that price and nominal wage flexibility would automatically restore full employment.

3. The focus on costs of collecting and processing complex information is the focus of the new neo-classical institutionalism. Costs at the margin continue to be all important, but now the focus is marginal costs of information collection and processing and the marginal benefits of additional and improved information.

4. See Davidson (1991).

5. In more complicated models with a wealth effect, the real value of financial wealth can affect goods market allocations and the interest rate, which introduces a feedback loop between the goods market and the financial market (Metzler 1951).

6. Modern new classical models do allow for some feedback from financial markets into the production process and labor markets. These effects operate through credit rationing (Stiglitz and Weiss 1981). Information imperfections result in financial markets restricting the availability of credit to firms, which restricts the amount of employment and production that firms can undertake. The important feature of this feedback is that it operates from financial markets through the supply side. This distinguishes it from the Keynesian tradition which emphasizes demand side effects of financial markets. Both are important.

7. In Nash bargaining models of unions (McDonald and Solow 1981), the wage-employment outcome lies on the contract curve which is positively sloped. An increase in union power can therefore result in an increase in both wages and employment. However, the Nash bargaining model requires that unions directly control the employment decision. This is counter-factual, and therefore renders the model problematic.

8. There are a number of possible ways of including the effect of income distribution on aggregate demand. The first is liquidity constraints: if wage households are liquidity constrained, these households will have a marginal propensity to consume of unity, and shifts in distribution toward wage income will increase consumption demand. The second is life cycle consumption theory: if the young are wage earners and have a higher marginal propensity to consume than the elderly, then an increased wage share will also increase consumption demand. Rule-of-thumb saving behavior is a third channel: in this instance, households may save all profit and interest income, and only consume out of wage income. Suspending the super-rationality of households is a fourth channel. In this case, households may not reduce personal saving to offset saving done by pension funds on their behalf through retained dividends and interest paid to the pension fund.

9. See Palley (1998).

10. The work of Anwar Shaikh (1989, 1992) includes significant demand dimensions and addresses both short and long run aspects of the economic process. Shaikh's work illustrates the contentiousness of the current classificatory schema. It is placed within the Marx–Keynes–Kalecki synthesis that is described later.

11. This statement of q differs from neo-classical q theory (Hayashi 1982) in which the profit rate is identified with the marginal product of capital. It also differs from Brainard (1977) and Brainard and Tobin's (1968) q in which the profit rate is identified with the cost of equity capital, which in turn depends on equity prices.

12. Moreover, it might also lead to higher productivity because firms would be freed from a concern with choosing technologies that were "extractively efficient." Instead, they could choose those technologies that were most "productively efficient."

13. This is subtly different from the contested exchange story. There, firms choose the production technology by balancing "extractive efficiency" against "productive efficiency." In the bargaining story they choose technology by balancing "productive efficiency" against "bargaining strength."

14. Palley (1998) details this process.

15. To the extent that these models generate a falling rate of profit, this would remain an important distinction within a general post-Keynesian synthesis.

References

Barro, Robert J. 1974. "Are Government Bonds Net Wealth?" *Journal of Political Economy* 82, no. 6 (November/December): 1095–1117.

Barro, Robert J., and Herschel Grossman. 1971. "A General Disequilibrium Model of Income and Employment." *American Economic Review* 61, no. 1 (March): 82–93.

Bhaduri, Amit, and Stephen Marglin. 1990. "Unemployment and the Real Wage: The Economic Basis for Contesting Political Ideologies." *Cambridge Journal of Economics* 14, no. 4 (December): 375–93.

Blanchflower, David G. 1994. *The Wage Curve*. Cambridge: MIT Press.

Blanchflower, David G., and Andrew J. Oswald. 1990. "The Wage Curve." *Scandinavian Journal of Economics* 92, no. 2: 215–35.

Blinder, Alan S., and Robert M. Solow. 1973. "Does Fiscal Policy Matter?" *Journal of Public Economics* 2, no. 4 (November): 319–37.

Bowles, Samuel. 1985. "The Production Process in a Competitive Economy: Walrasian, Marxian, and Neo-Hobbesian Models." *American Economic Review* 75, no. 1 (March): 16–36.

Bowles, Samuel, and Herb Gintis. 1990. "Contested Exchange: New Micro Foundations for the Political Economy of Capitalism." *Politics and Society* 18, no. 2 (June): 165–222.

Brainard, William C. 1977. "Asset Markets and the Cost of Capital." In *Economic Progress: Private Values and Public Policy. Essays in Honor of William Fellner*, ed. R. Nelson and Bela Belassa. Amsterdam: North-Holland.

Brainard, William C., and James Tobin. 1968. "Pitfalls in Financial Model Building." *American Economic Review* 58, no. 2 (May): 99–122.

Bronars, Stephen G., and Donald R. Deere. 1991. "The Threat of Unionization, the Use of Debt, and the Preservation of Shareholder Wealth." *Quarterly Journal of Economics* 106, no. 1 (February): 231–54.

Caskey, John, and Steven M. Fazzari. 1987. "Aggregate Demand Contractions with Nominal Debt Commitments: Is Wage Flexibility Stabilizing?" *Economic Inquiry* 25, no. 4 (October): 583–97.

Cyert, Richard M., and James G. March. 1963. *A Behavioral Theory of the Firm*. Englewood Cliffs, NJ: Prentice-Hall.

Davidson, Paul. 1965. "Keynes' Finance Motive." *Oxford Economic Papers* 17, no. 1 (March): 47–65.

————. 1983. "The Marginal Product of Labor Is Not the Demand Curve for Labor and Lucas's Labor Supply Curve Is Not the Supply Curve for Labor in the Real World." *Journal of Post Keynesian Economics* 6, no. 1 (Fall): 105–17.

————. 1991. "Is Probability Theory Relevant for Uncertainty? A Post Keynesian Perspective." *Journal of Economic Perspectives* 5, no. 1 (Winter): 129–43.

Eichner, Alfred S. 1976. *The Megacorp and Oligopoly: Micro Foundations of Macro Dynamics*. Cambridge, UK: Cambridge University Press.

Epstein, Gerald. 1994. "A Political Economy Model of Comparative Central Banking." In *New Perspective in Monetary Macroeconomics: Explorations in the Tradition of Hyman P. Minsky*, ed. Gary Dymski and Robert Pollin. Ann Arbor: University of Michigan Press.

Fazzari, Steven, R., Glenn Hubbard, and Bruce C. Petersen. 1988. "Financing Constraints and Corporate Investment Activity." *Brookings Papers on Economic Activity* 1: 141–95.

Fisher, Irving. 1933. "The Debt-Deflation Theory of Great Depressions." *Econometrica* 1, no. 1 (October): 337–57.

Foley, Duncan. 1987. "Liquidity–Profit Rate Cycles in a Capitalist Economy." *Journal of Economic Behavior and Organization* 8, no. 3 (September): 363–77.

Franke, Reiner, and Willi Semmler. 1989. "Debt Financing of Firms, Stability, and Cycles in a Macroeconomic Growth Model." In *Financial Dynamics and Business Cycles: New Perspectives*, ed. W. Semmler. Armonk, NY: M.E. Sharpe.

Gintis, Herb. 1976. "The Nature of Labor Exchange and the Theory of Capitalist Production." *Review of Radical Political Economics* 8, no. 2 (Summer): 36–54.

Goodwin, R.M. 1967. "A Growth Cycle." In *Socialism, Capitalism and Economic Growth*, ed. C.H. Feinstein. Cambridge: Cambridge University Press.

Gordon, David M. 1978. "Up and Down the Long Roller Coaster." In *U.S. Capitalism in Crisis*. New York: Union for Radical Political Economics.

————. 1994a. "Putting Heterodox Macro to the Test: Comparing Post-Keynesian, Marxian, and Social Structuralist Macroeconometric Models of the Post-War U.S. Economy." In *Competition, Technology, and Money: Classical and Post Keynesian Perspectives*, ed. Mark A. Glick. Aldershot, UK: Edward Elgar.

————. 1994b. "Bosses of Different Stripes: A Cross-National Perspective on Monitoring and Supervision." *American Economic Review* 84, no. 2 (May): 375–79.

————. 1995a. "Growth, Distribution, and the Rules of the Game: Social Structuralist Macro Foundations for a Democratic Economic Policy." In *Macroeconomic Policy after the Conservative Era: Studies in Investment, Saving and Finance*, ed. Gerald Epstein and Herb Gintis. New York: Cambridge University Press.

————. 1995b. "Putting the Horse (Back) before the Cart: Disentangling the Macro Relationship between Investment and Savings." In *Macroeconomic Policy after the Conservative Era: Studies in Investment, Saving and Finance*, eds. Gerald Epstein and Herb Gintis. New York: Cambridge University Press.

————. 1996. *Fat and Mean: The Corporate Squeeze of Working Americans and the Myth of Managerial "Downsizing."* New York: Free Press.

Gordon, David M., Thomas E. Weiskopf, and Samuel Bowles. 1987. "Power, Accumulation, and Crisis: The Rise and Demise of the Postwar Social Structure of Accumulation." In *The Imperiled Economy: Volume 1*, ed. Robert Cherry et al. New York: Union for Radical Political Economics.

Hayashi, Fumio. 1982. "Tobin's Marginal q and Average q: A Neoclassical Interpretation." *Econometrica* 50, no. 1 (January): 213–24.

Hicks, John R. 1937. "Mr. Keynes and the 'Classics': A Suggested Interpretation." *Econometrica* 5, no. 1: 146–59.

Kaldor, Nicholas. 1955–1956. "Alternative Theories of Distribution." *Review of Economic Studies* 23, no. 61: 94–100.

Kalecki, Michal. 1942. "A Theory of Profits." *Economic Journal* 52, no. 2 (June/September): 258–67.

Keynes, John Maynard. 1936. *The General Theory of Employment, Interest and Money*. London: Macmillan.

Lavoie, Marc. 1992. *Foundations of Post-Keynesian Economics*. Aldershot, UK: Edward Elgar.

Malinvaud, Edvin. 1977. *The Theory of Unemployment Reconsidered*. Oxford: Basil Blackwell.

McDonald, Ian, and Robert Solow. 1981. "Wage Bargaining and Employment." *American Economic Review* 71, no. 5 (December): 896–908.

Metzler, Lloyd A. 1951. "Wealth, Saving, and the Rate of Interest." *Journal of Political Economy* 59, no. 2 (April): 93–116.

Minsky, Hyman. 1982. *Can 'It' Happen Again?* Armonk, NY: M.E. Sharpe.

Moore, Basil J. 1988. *Horizontalists and Verticalists: The Macroeconomics of Credit Money*. Cambridge: Cambridge University Press.

Moudud, Jaimie K. 1998. "Finance and the Macroeconomic Process in a Classical Growth and Cycles Model." Annandale on Hudson, NY: The Jerome Levy Economics Institute. Mimeo.

Palley, Thomas I. 1987–1988. "Bank Lending, Discount Window Borrowing, and the Endogenous Money Supply: A Theoretical Framework." *Journal of Post Keynesian Economics* 10, no. 2 (Winter): 282–303.

———. 1991–1992. "Money, Credit and Prices in a Kaldorian Macro Model." *Journal of Post Keynesian Economics* 14, no. 2 (Winter): 183–204.

———. 1994a. "Competing Views of the Money Supply: Theory and Evidence." *Metroeconomica* 45, no. 1 (February): 67–88.

———. 1994b. "Debt, Aggregate Demand and the Business Cycle: An Analysis in the Spirit of Minsky and Kaldor." *Journal of Post Keynesian Economics* 16, no. 3 (Spring): 371–90.

———. 1996a. *Post Keynesian Economics: Debt, Distribution, and the Macro Economy*. New York: St. Martin's Press.

———. 1996b."Efficiency Wage Theory and Keynesian Macroeconomics." New York: New School for Social Research. Mimeo.

———. 1997a. "Endogenous Money and the Business Cycle." *Journal of Economics* 65, no. 2: 133–49.

———. 1997b. "Expectations, the Production Period, and Keynes' Aggregate Supply Schedule." *Manchester School of Economic and Social Studies* 65, no. 3 (June): 295–309.

———. 1998. "Macroeconomics with Conflict and Income Distribution." *Review of Political Economy* 10, no. 3 (July): 329–42.

———. 1999. "General Disequilibrium Analysis with Inside Debt." *Journal of Macroeconomics* 21, no. 4 (Fall): 103–13.

Pasinetti, Luigi. 1961–1962. "Rate of Profit and Income Distribution in Relation to the Rate of Economic Growth." *Review of Economic Studies* 29: 267–79.

Penrose, Edith T. 1959. *The Theory of the Growth of the Firm.* Oxford: Blackwell.

Pollin, Robert. 1991. "Two Theories of Money Supply Endogeneity: Some Empirical Evidence." *Journal of Post Keynesian Economics* 13, no. 3 (Spring): 366–96.

Sargent, Thomas J. 1979. *Macroeconomic Theory.* New York: Academic Press.

Shaikh, Anwar. 1989. "Accumulation, Finance, and Effective Demand in Marx, Keynes, and Kalecki." In *Financial Dynamics and Business Cycles: New Perspectives,* ed. Willi Semmler. Armonk, NY: M.E. Sharpe.

———. 1992. "A Dynamic Approach to the Theory of Effective Demand." In *Profits, Deficits, and Instability,* ed. Dimitris Papadimitriou. New York: St. Martin's Press.

Shaked, Avner, and John Sutton. 1984. "Involuntary Unemployment as a Perfect Equilibrium in a Bargaining Model." *Econometrica* 52, no. 6 (November): 1351–64.

Skillman, Gilbert L. 1988. "Bargaining and Replacement in Capitalist Firms." *Review of Radical Political Economics* 20, no. 2–3 (Summer–Fall): 177–83.

———. 1991. "Efficiency vs. Control: Strategic Bargaining Analysis of Capitalist Production." *Review of Radical Political Economics* 23, no. 1–2 (Spring–Summer): 12–21.

Skillman, Gilbert L., and Harl E. Ryder. 1993. "Wage Bargaining and the Choice of Production Technique in Capitalist Firms." In *Markets and Democracy: Participation, Accountability, and Efficiency,* ed. Samuel Bowles, Herb Gintis, and Bjorn Gustafsson. Cambridge: Cambridge University Press.

Stiglitz, Joseph E., and Andrew Weiss. 1981. "Credit Rationing in Markets with Asymmetric Information." *American Economic Review* 71, no. 3 (June): 393–410.

Tobin, James. 1965. "Money and Economic Growth." *Econometrica* 33, no. 4 (October): 671–84.

———. 1969. "A General Equilibrium Approach to Monetary Theory." *Journal of Money, Credit, and Banking* 1, no. 1 (February): 15–29.

———. 1975. "Keynesian Models of Recession and Depression." *American Economic Review* 65, no. 2 (May): 195–202.

———. 1980. *Asset Accumulation and Economic Activity.* Chicago: University of Chicago Press.

———. 1982. "Money and Finance in the Macroeconomic Process." *Journal of Money, Credit and Banking* 14, no. 2 (May): 171–204.

———. 1993. "Price Flexibility and Output Stability: An Old Keynesian View." *Journal of Economic Perspectives* 7, no. 1 (Winter): 45–66.

6

Heather Boushey

MACROECONOMIC PERFORMANCE AND LABOR MARKET DISCRIMINATION

I. Introduction

Discrimination in the labor market is a continually pressing concern in the United States. Even with policies such as Affirmative Action and the Equal Pay Act, disparities in pay and employment rates by gender and race still exist. Human capital factors, such as differences in educational attainment or job tenure, cannot fully explain differences in labor market outcomes by gender or by race. Recent research still finds an unexplained "residual" in wage functions, and African American unemployment continues to be consistently twice the rate of white unemployment. Standard microeconomic models of explaining discrimination, which only look to individual characteristics, cannot explain the persistence of discrimination in the United States.

To understand discrimination and its persistence in the face of rising parity in human capital characteristics, we must look beyond supply-side factors and turn to an exploration of the role of demand-side factors and macroeconomic conditions in perpetuating discrimination in the labor market. Research that focuses on persistent inequality and looks to the role of labor demand and discrimination by employers suggests that employers may be unwilling to hire low-skill African Americans— especially men—because of the perception that these workers do not display appropriate attire or have the necessary soft skills and positive work attitudes (Holzer 1996; Kirschenman and Neckerman 1991; Moss and Tilly 2000). These models, however, look to the actions of individuals and deficiencies in the populations that experience discrimination rather than to systemic market forces. Spriggs and Williams (2000) document that the unemployment rate of African American workers has been consistently much higher than that of white workers since the U.S. gov-

138

ernment began looking at unemployment by race. They argue that changes in macroeconomic conditions affect the level of discrimination. The African American unemployment rate is less sensitive to changes in the general economy, and the portion of the gap in unemployment rates between African American and white workers explained by skill differences is also sensitive to the general economy.

The theory of social structures of accumulation, pioneered by David Gordon, points to a method for understanding the relationship between the macroeconomy and labor market outcomes, which can be extended to an understanding of the relationship between macroeconomic performance and discrimination. The social structures of accumulation (SSA) model addresses the relationship between the functioning of the macroeconomy—the profitability of the economic system—and the structure of the labor market where elements "exogenous" to the strictly defined economic system have profound effects on the profitability of the overall system. Among the most important of these exogenous institutions are those ensuring the availability of money and credit, those relating to state involvement in the economic process, and the nature of the class struggle. The structure of the labor market dictates the extent to which labor or capital garners the dividends from productivity increases, and hence the profitability of the system—what we typically think of as the macroeconomy—is fundamentally related to the form and function of the labor market.

A key factor framing the analysis of labor market dynamics and macroeconomy in the SSA approach is the cost of job loss. The cost of job loss index is an empirical method developed to explore the microdynamics behind the macroeconomics of the unemployment-wage trade-off. It describes the loss in income that individuals will experience if they lose their current job, and helps to capture the effects of unemployment and wages (and to some extent, social policy) on worker productivity (Schor 1987; Schor and Bowles 1987; Weisskopf, Bowles, and Gordon 1983). One simple formula for the cost of job loss is:

$$(1) \qquad CJL = UD(W - UI)$$

where CJL = the cost of job loss; UD = duration of unemployment spells; W = the average weekly earnings; and UI = the value of unemployment insurance and other income-replacing social programs. This index extends the SSA model by establishing a method to understand the costs to individuals of unemployment. It also is a measure of job insecurity that is linked to macroeconomic conditions and social safety nets. High unemployment will raise the cost of job loss and reduce worker bargaining power. If social insurance programs are generous, this may moderate a worker's proclivity to accept their working conditions or pay, because they know that they can rely on the state to help them if they lose their jobs.

Building on the SSA model, this chapter introduces an ancillary model, the social structures of *insulation*, which also focuses on the safety net–labor market–macroeconomy nexus.[1] This model develops the notions implicit in the cost of job loss and presents them as important to the profitability of the entire system. The social structures of insulation model addresses questions that the SSA model does not, such as what is the degree of vulnerability that particular individuals experience with respect to the market? Do individuals have choice with respect to the jobs they take? To what degree are individuals insulated from market forces? Most importantly, the social structures of insulation model can address the relationship between discrimination and macroeconomic performance through an understanding of the role of exogenous elements in maintaining the profitability of the system that are particular to individuals. The social structures of insulation model enriches our understanding of the social institutions and practices behind the cost of job loss. Importantly, this model extends the concepts of SSA and the cost of job loss by bringing gender and race to the forefront of the analysis and seeing discrimination as an allocative mechanism that assigns individuals to places within a particular labor market structure. This assignment determines the degree of vulnerability an individual has with respect to unemployment and low pay and is a crucial component to understanding the social structures of insulation.

There are three key elements in the social structures of insulation model:

1. The manner in which unemployment regulates pay—that is, the relationship between unemployment and the wage level.
2. The manner in which this process of regulation differs for groups of workers—that is, the relationship between unemployment and wage differentials. The process of regulation will differ among workers depending on the extent of labor market discrimination and the ways in which social policy does or does not insulate workers from unemployment.

3. The manner in which the degree of insulation is determined by family structure. The structure of the family, the number of family members working in the paid labor market, and the interaction between social policy and family structure all affect a worker's degree of dependence on the market.

The approach is based on an understanding of the labor market, and its relationship to the macroeconomy, that sees unemployment as the regulator of wages—a starting point common in the heterodox economics literature, and based on the observation that unemployment is a permanent feature of the capitalist economy. Individuals, due to their race-ethnicity, gender, marital status, age, disability, education, or other characteristics, do not all have the same relationship to unemployment and paid labor. The theory of the social structures of insulation seeks to explain how social structures and safety nets insulate workers to varying degrees from unemployment and its effects on wages.

Both the SSA model and the social structures of insulation model accept that the economic system is embedded in power relations. However, the subjects of analysis of the two approaches differ. The SSA model focuses on the relationship between *profitability* and a given social system—that is, exogenous elements that affect accumulation. The social structures of insulation model focuses on the relationship between *individuals* and the economic system—that is, the exogenous elements that affect an individual's insulation from unemployment, low wages, and poverty. Where one approach focuses on profits the other focuses on poverty. Exogenous elements in the social structures of insulation model include the strength of social safety nets and community and labor organizations, which help to protect workers' rights, the provision of services to help families manage both parenthood and employment, and the extent to which any (or all) of these factors protect all individuals equally. The social structures of insulation approach is a structural model that explains differences in labor market outcomes for individuals at the micro level, while not denying that there are differences in human capital across individuals.

The remainder of this chapter is organized as follows. The theoretical analysis in Section II develops the social structures of insulation model, beginning with the abstract relationship between unemployment and the wage level and moving on to the more concrete relationships between unemployment, wages, and inequality. The empirical discussion in Section III provides a case study of how the social structures of insulation play out in the labor market by testing the hypothesis that unemployment does not affect the wages of all workers equally.

II. Theoretical Perspectives: The Social Structures of Insulation

Under capitalism, individuals experience varying degrees of economic vulnerability. This vulnerability is manifest in three basic ways. First, an individual may be unable to find employment, which leaves her without income. Second, an individual may be able to find employment, but not at a living wage. Thus, he may be working, but still very poor. Third, an individual may have limited familial resources or be less able to qualify for income maintenance from government safety-net programs, which may increase her economic vulnerability when she is either unemployed or earning poverty-level wages.

Social policy plays an integral role in the social structures of insulation. The extent to which social policy provides a buffer between individuals and economic distress affects individuals' insulation from unemployment. Social policy, however, often mirrors trends that appear in the labor market. Workers who experience labor market discrimination are often ineligible for the more generous social programs. Programs that serve people who are not in the labor market, often referred to as the "undeserving poor" and disproportionately likely to be women and people of color, are less generous than programs that serve those workers who are referred to as "deserving poor" and are disproportionately white and male (Boushey 1997; Katz 1989; Quadagno 1994). Prior to understanding the role of social policy in perpetuating or alleviating discrimination, however, we must address the relationship between the macroeconomy and the labor market.

The first two manifestations of economic vulnerability—unemployment and low wages—are, in theory and practice, linked phenomena. Unemployment acts to discipline labor. Concretely, unemployment keeps wages in check by putting downward pressure on wages at the bottom end of the income spectrum. Insulation from unemployment is, in effect, insulation from the negative effects of unemployment on pay. The negative effects of unemployment on pay differ among workers; this difference depends on a worker's relative degree of insulation from unemployment. The present model contends that workers are not equally threatened by rising unemployment rates: workers have differing degrees of insulation from the market and from unemployment or underemployment. A list of factors, including gender and race, determine the placement of workers within the wage structure, and thus the degree of insulation a worker enjoys from unemployment and its deleterious effects on wages. This set of factors together constitutes the social structures of insulation.

This approach provides a method for understanding the links between the mechanisms that create and maintain the dynamics between unemployment and wages and the concrete ways that this process occurs in any historical epoch. The model begins with an analysis of the general process of accumulation, whereby changes in the rate of accumulation bring on changes in labor demand, which in turn change the level of unemployment in the economy and, given the relative bargaining strength of capital and labor, wages. Social processes —the elements of the social structures of insulation—mediate the links in the dynamics of the process of accumulation. The theory of social structures of insulation takes this analysis of abstract, theoretical processes, and elucidates how the labor market will look in any particular historical configuration. Through exploring the links between unemployment and wages, this analysis sheds light on the interaction between the macroeconomy and the microeconomic processes. Thus, the model begins at a highly abstract level and proceeds to a concrete analysis of the social structures of insulation.

Relationships Between the Macroeconomy and the Labor Market

The first step in understanding the social structures of insulation is to understand the general relationship between unemployment and pay. At the most abstract level, high unemployment is associated with lower pay. This relationship is at the core of Marx's analysis of the accumulation of capital (Marx 1986) and the basic logic behind the theory of the reserve army of labor. During the process of accumulation, capitalists will employ new technologies to cheapen the value of labor power and employ fewer workers. Competition between labor and capital over wages, and among laboring populations over employment, will push down wages. Unemployment disciplines wages by exerting a downward pull on wages. Heterodox models share the view that unemployment may be a permanent feature of the labor market and that it serves to discipline labor. There is empirical support for this view: for example, movements in the unemployment rate have been found to affect nominal wages (Rebitzer 1988).

Within the neoclassical tradition, the efficiency wage model also builds on the notion that there is a negative relationship between unemployment and pay. Shapiro and Stiglitz (1984) argue that to induce workers not to shirk, firms will pay more than the prevailing wage. If it pays one firm to raise wages, however, it pays all firms to do so. Therefore, where firms pay efficiency wages there will be unemployment in equilibrium.[2] These findings are consistent with Blanchflower and Oswald (1994), who document the existence of a stable, negative relationship between unemployment and the level of pay, which they term the "wage curve." Through random samples of nearly four million people from sixteen countries, they find that the local unemployment rate affects pay levels such that "a worker who is employed in an area of high unemployment earns less than an identical individual who works in a region with low joblessness" (p. 5).

Unemployment, Pay, and Income Inequality

The social structures of insulation model takes as its starting point the notion that unemployment (and the threat of unemployment) regulates wages and labor discipline. However, unemployment occurs to actual individuals and thus unemployment does not affect everyone identically. Some individuals experience *actual* unemployment and some only experience the *threat* of unemployment. Not all workers have similar probabilities of being unemployed. African Americans have consistently experienced an unemployment rate twice the white unemployment rate, and workers with less education are more likely to be unemployed than workers with higher levels of education (Mishel, Bernstein, and Schmitt 1999). Social institutions and practices also mediate the negative relationship between unemployment and pay. Particular social institutions and practices may moderate or amplify the relationship between unemployment and pay, depending on the particular historical configuration. In taking the abstract notion of a relationship between unemployment and pay and exploring it concretely, the social structures of insulation model does not assume that the disciplinary effect of unemployment is uniform across individuals.

Empirical analysis demonstrates support for the hypothesis that workers are insulated to varying degrees from the effects of unemployment on pay. Workers with greater levels of social protection—those in unions and in firms which have a high level of industry and product-market concentration—are also less susceptible to the negative effects of unemployment on pay than workers who are not in such firms (Nickell and Kong 1988). These differences are not uniform across countries, indicating that different social configurations affect the degree of insulation workers have from the negative effects of unemployment on pay (Weisskopf 1987). Low unemployment also increases wages for African Americans (Freeman 1991; Spriggs and Williams 2000).

The variance in the relative degrees of insulation from actual or threatened unemployment leads to differences in wages for groups of workers. Here, the model builds particularly on the work of Patrick Mason and Rhonda Williams, who explore exclusion and discrimination in the labor market. Mason (1993) extends Botwinick's (1993) analysis of wage differentials to include the possibility of racial exclusion within competitive capitalism. Access to high-wage jobs is the concrete expression of the abstract notion that discrimination is a labor allocation device for "determining service in the reserve army" (p. 6). Williams explores how the constructs of gender and race provide the framework for competition among workers over access to good jobs. She argues that "workers seeking to shelter themselves from bourgeois society's most fragile and despised existence—life among the low-waged and unemployed—have ample reason to create and wield weapons to shelter themselves from other members of the working class" (1991, 77). Their analysis suggests that discrimination becomes endemic to the capitalist labor market through the process of accumulation, which entails systemic wage differentials.

Variance in the degree of insulation is also foundational for the social structures of accumulation model, but there the focus is on the relationship between profitability and the overall economic system. In *Segmented Work, Divided Workers* (1982), David Gordon, Richard Edwards, and Michael Reich develop an analysis of the labor market that is intimately tied to the cycles of capitalist accumulation and their relationship to the form of production, building on the work of Doeringer and Piore (1971) and Edwards (1979). They argue that segmentation characterizes the U.S. labor market and that there is little mobility among labor market segments. Productivity conditions determine the segmentation of firms, which then determines the types of jobs they offer. In the United States in the post-war period, large corporations became the core firms of the economy and workers in these industries soon made up the primary labor market. This labor market is characterized by stable, well-paid employment, wage increases that are tied to productivity, workers who possess a relatively high degree of bargaining power, and internal job ladders. Peripheral firms, which constitute the secondary labor market, service the core firms. A relatively low degree of bargaining power, relatively low-wage employment, and little job stability characterize the secondary labor market.

The SSA view of dual labor markets emphasizes the class relations in labor markets and the ways in which both productivity and profitability derive from labor market structure. The analysis focuses on the characteristics of jobs, not job occupants. However, as pointed out by Albelda and Tilly (1994), "the segments have a striking racial and gender complexion to them" (p. 214). The capacity of employers to maintain a division of labor with segmented labor markets and limited mobility between segments is conditioned on social structures that allow systemic discrimination. Just as the profitability of the entire system is interconnected to institutions that enable stable accumulation, the structure of the labor market is interconnected with the social processes that shape social life beyond the purely economic sphere. Social status and power dynamics that reside in non-economic spheres play a crucial role. Considering the impact of social structures of insulation extends the model by bringing gender and race to the forefront of the analysis and examining the relationship between individuals and the economic system, rather than looking to the relationship between profitability and the economic system.

Gender and race are allocative mechanisms by which individuals are assigned places along the employment–unemployment spectrum. Figure 6.1 traces out the dynamics of the social structures of insulation. First, on the macroeconomic side, there is a relationship between unemployment and wages whereby unemployment disciplines the wage level. On the microeconomic side, discrimination leads to wage differentials between women and men and whites and non-whites. There is a link between these two processes: unemployment occurs to actual workers and discrimination plays a role in access to employment. As discrimination lessens the job opportunities for discriminated-against workers, wage differentials increase, and this may have an effect on the wage level.

Figure 6.1 **The Dynamics of the Social Structures of Insulation**

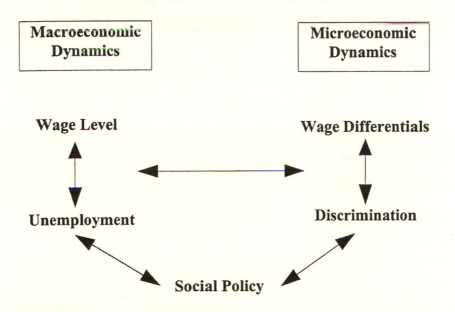

The relationship between the macro and the micro is mediated by social policy. Social policy has a role both in reinforcing or eradicating discrimination and in providing insulation from unemployment. In this manner, social policy also protects employed workers from downward wage pressure from the unemployed because, with generous social benefits, the unemployed are less likely to rapidly underbid the wages of the employed.

III. Empirical Evidence

This section presents some empirical evidence for these theoretical propositions. This model uses the method employed by Blanchflower and Oswald (1994) to test whether there are different wage curves for different groups of workers and how these differences affect the average level of pay and the differences in pay between these groups of workers.[3] Theories of labor market discrimination and labor market segmentation suggest that there is extensive labor market segmentation, and that African Americans and women are discriminated against in terms of wages and employment. If this is true, then the wage curve should take a different shape when disaggregated by gender and by race. Further, differences in disaggregated wage curves should affect the aggregate wage curve in specific ways. Prior research lends support to the hypotheses that there are specific wage curves for different groups of workers, depending on their relative degrees of insulation from the negative effects of unemployment on pay, and that institutions matter in determining the shape of the wage curve (Bratsberg and Turunen 1996; Winter-Ebmer 1996).

Empirical Method

Blanchflower and Oswald document the wage curve as:

(2) $\ln w = -0.10 \ln U +$ other terms

where $\ln w$ is the natural log of the wage, $\ln U$ is the natural log of unemployment in the worker's local region, and other terms are control variables for worker and sectoral characteristics. The log of wages is a monotonically decreasing and convex function of local unemployment rates. The unemployment elasticity of pay is estimated to be -0.10 so that, all else equal, a region with an unemployment rate twice as high as another region will have wages that are 10 percent lower.

To test the hypothesis that individuals are insulated to varying degrees from the effects of unemployment on wages, the wage curve is disaggregated by gender and race:

(3) $w_{ij} = f(U, X_{ij})$

where w_{ij} is the wage of person i in the jth group; X_{ij} is a set of measured characteristics of individual i (such as gender, age, and education) in the jth group; and U is the local unemployment rate. For this equation, the expectation is that the wage curve will be more elastic for subgroups of workers who are more vulnerable to being unemployed and less insulated from the negative effects of unemployment on their pay. The social structures of insulation model argues that women and people of color experience discrimination within the labor market in the United States and so we expect that they experience an amplified wage curve.

Data

Following Blanchflower and Oswald (1994),[4] Katz and Krueger (1991), and Freeman (1991), this study uses data from the CPS Annual Merged File for selected years from 1986 to 1996 for the individual-level employment, earnings, and background data.[5] The CPS Annual Merged File consists of extracts from the Monthly Current Population Survey (CPS).[6] The Annual Merged File is a good dataset for weekly and hourly earnings equations. Unlike the March CPS files, the CPS Annual Merged File includes variables for earnings per week and earnings per hour. In the March CPS, analysts must use three retrospective variables—annual earnings, weeks worked, and usual weekly hours worked—to calculate hourly wages. Although both of these CPS datasets have the advantage of being large enough to generate reliable estimates for different subgroups within the population, there are several well-known problems, including the fact that various components of income are underreported. Income at the high end (for confidentiality reasons) is top-coded. There is evidence that these caps are not consistent over time: a larger share of incomes are capped over time and the omission of capital gains created a larger bias over the 1980s.

The sample of the dataset used for this analysis includes only individuals who (1) are between 18 and 64 years old; (2) are employed in either the private or public sector excluding those who are self-employed; and (3) live in one of the fifty largest metropolitan statistical areas (MSA).[7] The CPS Annual Merged File identifies both an individual's MSA and his state of residence.[8]

Tables 6.1 and 6.2 summarize key characteristics of the sample used. For the sample, the mean earnings for men are greater than for women, and mean earnings for whites are greater than for all other racial categories. Whites have a higher degree of educational attainment than other racial groups, and whites are twice as likely as African Americans to possess an advanced degree.

Table 6.3 reports the mean unemployment rate for the aggregate population and for disaggregated groups from 1986 to 1997. This table clearly indicates that the unemployment rate of African American workers is double that of white workers for the entire period. This table also indicates that the business cycle has a greater effect on African American unemployment; it is more volatile over time than white unemployment and is more volatile than female unemployment.

Table 6.1

Mean Earnings per Week by Sample by Race and Gender, 1986–1996

	Earning per week
Mean earnings per week for all workers	$601.46
By race	
White	$622.45
African American	$484.73
American Indian	$547.82
Asian and Pacific Islander	$616.08
Other (including Hispanic)	$429.42
By gender	
Male	$707.52
Female	$481.98

Source: Author's calculation from the CPS Outgoing Rotation Groups, 1986–1996.
*All values are in 1996 dollars.

The Effects of Discrimination on Wages

To examine whether unemployment has a different effect on workers' wages based on their gender or race, the following specification of the wage curve is tested:

$$(4) \qquad \ln w_{ij} = f_0 + f_1 \ln U + f_2 X_{ij} + f_3 D_{ij} + e_{ij}$$

where ln w is the log of earnings per week or the log of the hourly wage (earnings per week over usual hours) for individual i, where the labor market is defined by the MSA an individual lives in; ln U is the natural log of the unemployment rate defined at the level of the MSA; X is a vector of characteristics particular to individual i; and D_{reg}, D_{indy}, and D_{occ} are state, industry, and occupational dummies. The variables in X are dummies for gender, race, marital status, union membership, private sector employee, part-time (less than 30 hours/week), and paid hourly; variables for educational attainment (less than high school, high school graduates, some college, four years of college, and beyond four years of college), and age and its square (to measure for experience). Each specification also includes thirteen dummies for industry classification, fourteen dummies for occupational grouping, and state dummies.

There are two differences between this specification and the one used by Blanchflower and Oswald. First, this model separates the labor mar-

Table 6.2

Educational Attainment by Sample by Race and Gender, 1986–1997

	African American	White
Some high school	13	11
High school degree	38	32
Some college	31	27
College degree	13	19
Advanced degree	6	12
	Female	Male
Some high school	9	13
High school degree	34	31
Some college	29	26
College degree	18	19
Advanced degree	10	12

Source: Author's calculation from the CPS Outgoing Rotation Groups, 1986–1996.

ket into groups defined by gender and race and estimates the wage curve for each group using the MSA unemployment rate. The expectation is that groups which are less insulated from unemployment—those that experience a higher degree of discrimination in the labor market—will have a more elastic wage curve. The negative effect of unemployment on their pay should be larger than for the aggregate population.

Second, the regressions are corrected for the fact that the standard errors in Blanchflower and Oswald's regressions are most likely too small (Card 1995). Although their model runs regressions using pooled cross-sections of micro data and it appears that they have many degrees of freedom, the actual number of degrees of freedom involved in the estimation of the wage curve elasticity is far less than the number of individual wage observations. In actuality, the model only has as many degrees of freedom as there are grouped variables, which here is the unemployment rate (Kloek 1981; Moulton 1990; Riddell 1981). To fix this problem, the present specification uses the Hoover–White Sandwich estimators to recalculate the standard errors. This estimator weights the standard variance by one plus an additional term, based on the variance of the number of observations in each group.

Table 6.4 shows the results of the estimates for various years. For each demographic group, the table shows only the estimated coefficient on the MSA unemployment rate, although each regression includes all

Table 6.3

Unemployment in the Fifty Largest Metropolitan Areas in the United States, 1986–1997

Unemployment rate	1986	1987	1988	1989	1990	1991	1992	1993	1994	1995	1996	1997
Aggregate	6.28	5.77	5.19	4.94	5.34	6.61	7.39	6.81	6.27	5.53	5.14	4.68
African American	13.70	12.71	11.30	10.93	11.35	12.57	14.64	12.92	11.83	10.23	10.01	9.67
White	5.20	4.74	4.28	4.04	4.43	5.73	6.30	5.82	5.80	4.69	4.32	3.89
Female	6.43	5.65	5.28	5.06	5.23	6.35	6.87	6.42	5.96	5.47	5.19	4.75
Male	6.15	5.88	5.12	4.84	5.42	6.83	7.85	7.13	6.19	5.61	5.09	4.61
African American female	12.84	12.43	11.08	10.08	11.05	12.08	13.38	11.80				
African American male	13.65	11.61	11.78	11.06	11.77	13.17	15.02	13.37				
White female	5.33	4.51	4.26	4.14	4.29	5.37	5.77	5.50				
White male	5.10	4.91	4.35	3.97	4.55	6.03	6.77	6.09				

Source: Bureau of Labor Statistics, *Geographic Profile*, 1986–1996. The BLS stopped tabulating separate unemployment rates for African American women and men and white women and men as of 1994.

Table 6.4

Wage Curves: Selected Years

	1987	1989	1991	1993	1996
Aggregate population	−0.15	−0.15	−0.17	−0.10	−0.13
	(.03)***	(.03)***	(.05)***	(.04)**	(.03)***
African American	−0.18	−0.16	−0.33	−0.29	−0.10
	(.07)***	(.04)***	(.10)***	(.09)***	(.04)**
White	−0.14	−0.14	−0.16	−0.07	−0.15
	(.03)***	(.04)***	(.06)***	(.05)***	(.03)***
Female	−0.14	−0.14	−0.18	−0.09	−0.09
	(.03)***	(.05)***	(.06)***	(.05)*	(.03)***
Male	−0.17	−0.17	−0.16	−0.10	−0.16
	(.03)***	(.03)***	(.06)***	(.04)**	(.03)***
African American female	−0.19	−0.14	−0.30	−0.23	−0.03
	(.08)***	(.05)***	(.10)***	(.11)**	(.05)
African American male	−0.18	−0.21	−0.35	−0.34	−0.18
	(.06)***	(.03)***	(.12)***	(.08)***	(.05)***
White female	−0.12	−0.13	−0.17	−0.07	−0.11
	(.04)***	(.06)***	(.07)***	(.07)	(.04)***
White male	−0.17	−0.15	−0.15	−0.07	−0.18
	(.03)***	(.04)***	(.07)**	(.05)	(.04)***

Standard errors in parentheses under each coefficient.

*Significant at the 10 percent level, **significant at the 5 percent level, ***significant at the 1 percent level.

the other variables listed above. This table suggests that the elasticity of unemployment for the fifty largest U.S. cities is generally higher than the −.10 that Blanchflower and Oswald found for the nation as a whole, indicating that the wage curve is more elastic in urban areas than in the country as a whole. The estimates also show that in the fifty largest cities in the United States, the wage curve varies over the business cycle. The largest elasticities are in the recession year of 1991 and the smallest elasticities are in the boom year of 1996.

African American wages are more sensitive to changes in the unemployment rate in the MSA in which they live than are white workers, and they are more sensitive to business cycle fluctuations. In 1991, the elasticity of earnings for African American workers with respect to the MSA unemployment rate is −0.33, while it is only −0.16 for white workers. In other years, the elasticity of African American earnings is closer to that of whites, but in every year except 1996, African Americans have a higher elasticity. African American males have higher elasticities than

African American females and white males generally have higher elasticities than white females, except for the recession year of 1991.

IV. Conclusions

The empirical section of this chapter demonstrates that not only are African American workers more likely to experience unemployment, but the elasticity of their pay with respect to the aggregate unemployment rate in the fifty largest cities in the United States is larger than the elasticity of pay for other groups of workers. This is consistent with the theoretical premise of this chapter: that workers who are less insulated from unemployment are also less insulated from the negative effects of unemployment on their pay.[9]

These disturbing empirical results push us to rethink our employment and wage policies. Unfortunately, these results substantiate the point made by Massey and Denton (1993), who argue that "racial segregation—and its characteristic institutional form, the black ghetto— are the key structural factors responsible for the perpetuation of black poverty in the United States" (p. 9). The results in this chapter point to the conclusion that the separation of the labor markets for African American and white workers has a strong negative effect on African American wages. The physical separation of the two labor markets may explain the wage gap (the gap left over after accounting for observable human capital characteristics) between African American and white workers.

In his last published work, *Fat and Mean* (1996), David Gordon argues that the United States has taken the "low road in managing the relationships between productivity, profitability and distribution. This 'low road' emphasizes discipline and supervision in the workplace, and inequality and poverty in the community" (p. 144). Evidence from the preceding wage curves suggests that we may indeed be on such a path. Part of the reason employers have been able to suppress wage growth despite low overall rates of unemployment has been because the labor market is bifurcated and workers have varying degrees of insulation from unemployment, low wages, and poverty. Limiting the insulation workers have from unemployment is merely one method of enacting the foundations for the current social structure of accumulation —a structure built on taking the "low road," on increasing wage inequality, and on the elimination of social safety nets.

The social structures of insulation model extends the SSA model originally pioneered by Gordon. The model presented here explores the elements that determine an individual's degree of economic vulnerability, developing an approach to analyze discrimination, social policy, and the relationship between unemployment and pay across space. This model provides a link between the macroeconomy and the continued re-creation of a labor market that is strongly segmented along gender and race lines. In addition, this model also reflects Gordon's work with respect to the spatial dimension of capital accumulation (Gordon 1978).

Finally, this chapter also poses a challenge to the work of David Gordon. It argues that gender and race play important roles in the determination of wages and employment. The allocation of workers by their gender and race to jobs in the wage/employment hierarchy is as important as are the reasons for that hierarchy—reasons that Gordon studied so astutely. This is not to say that gender and race did not figure prominently in his work, but that the determinants of profitability were primary to the analysis, and gender and race were only secondary, albeit important, aspects. This analysis posits that discrimination is actually part of the accumulation process and that differentiation among workers is key to enabling firms to segment their labor markets. Access to employment and to fair wages delineates an individual's degree of economic vulnerability. Women and minorities still struggle for the right to have "good" jobs and the right to fair pay. The heightened sensitivity of African Americans to unemployment's negative effects on pay is indicative of this vulnerability.

Notes

I am grateful to Ellen Houston and Jim Stanford for their careful editing of this chapter. The errors, of course, are my own.

1. This model had its genesis in a paper I wrote for David Gordon's Labor Seminar in 1995 and I am greatly indebted to him. See Boushey (1997).
2. The efficiency wage model, while predicting that unemployment may exist, is limited because it leads to the conclusion that involuntary unemployment cannot persist. Although unemployment may exist in equilibrium in the short run, it may not exist in the long run as the imperfections—the need to pay workers efficiency wages—may not exist if this market imperfection can be eradicated (Darity 1991).
3. Another way of empirically evaluating the social structures of insulation could be through the cost of job loss. For example, Bowles (1985) develops a model where the cost of job loss varies positively with employment but negatively with social programs, using a labor extraction function based on the cost of job loss and supervision. He argues that this model provides a way to explain Marx's reserve army of

labor that is consistent with neoclassical competitive assumptions. He argues that labor markets do not clear in equilibrium and, thus, excess labor supply does not lead to a competitive decrease in the wage. Given a positive cost of surveillance and a conflict of interest between employer and worker over work-effort, the wage rate offered by the competitive profit-maximizing employer will exceed the worker's next best alternative, as in the case of the efficiency wage model.

4. Blanchflower and Oswald use the CPS March Files for most of their analysis. They use the CPS Annual Merged Files for their analysis using MSA level unemployment for 1987.

5. This analysis uses separate years, rather than pooling the data as Blanchflower and Oswald do, because there are problems with some years' data. For example, in 1995, MSA fips codes are not available for a full quarter and the Bureau of Labor Statistics further cautions that all MSA fips codes are suspect for that year. There also appear to be problems with the 1992 data. Further, separating out the regressions by year allows us to explore differences in the wage curve over the business cycle.

6. Each household entering the CPS is administered four monthly interviews, then ignored for eight months, then interviewed again for four more months. Since 1979, only households in months four and eight reported their usual weekly earnings and usual weekly hours of work. These are the outgoing rotation groups and each year the Bureau of Labor Statistics gathers all these interviews together into a single *Annual Merged File*. The National Bureau of Economic Research prepares *CPS Labor Extracts*, 3d ed., *NBER 50 Variable Uniform Extract* with information appropriate for analysis of labor market issues from the monthly outgoing rotation group files.

7. The Census Bureau defines an MSA as "an urban area that meets specified size criteria—either it has a city of at least 50,000 inhabitants . . . or it contains an urbanized area of at least 50,000 inhabitants and has a total population of at least 100,000." Primary and consolidated MSAs are larger urban metropolitan areas (Bureau of Labor Statistics 1995).

8. There is some degree of sample selection bias that occurs when choosing individuals who are working, excluding those who may have higher reservation wages and therefore be unemployed.

9. It is also true that workers who are more likely to be unemployed are also less likely to benefit from wage-replacing social policies when they are unemployed.

References

Albelda, Randy, and Chris Tilly. 1994. "Towards a Broader Vision: Race, Gender, and Labor Market Segmentation in the Social Structure of Accumulation Framework." In *Social Structures of Accumulation: The Political Economy of Growth and Crisis*, ed. David M. Kotz, Terrence McDonough, and Michael Reich. New York: Cambridge University Press.

Blanchflower, David G., and Andrew J. Oswald. 1994. *The Wage Curve*. Cambridge: MIT Press.

Botwinick, Howard. 1993. *Persistent Inequalities: Wage Disparity Under Capitalist Competition*. Princeton: Princeton University Press.

Boushey, Heather. 1997. "Embracing Discrimination? The Relationship between Low-Wage Labor Markets and Policies in Aid of the Poor." In *Gender and Political Economy: Incorporating Diversity into Theory and Policy*, ed. Ellen Mutari, Heather Boushey, and William Fraher. Armonk, NY: M.E. Sharpe.

Bowles, Samuel. 1985. "The Production Process in a Competitive Economy: Walrasian, Neo-Hobbesian, and Marxian Models." *American Economic Review* 75, no. 1 (March): 16–36.

Bratsberg, Bernt, and Jarkko Turunen. 1996. "Wage Curve Evidence from Panel Data." *Economic Letters* 51, no. 3 (June): 345–53.

Bureau of Labor Statistics. 1995. *Geographic Profile of Employment and Unemployment*. Washington, DC: Department of Labor.

Card, David. 1995. "The Wage Curve: A Review." *Journal of Economic Literature* 33, no. 2 (June): 785–99.

Darity, William. 1991. "Efficiency Wage Theory: Critical Reflections on the Neo-Keynesian Theory of Unemployment and Discrimination." In *New Approaches to Economic and Social Analyses of Discrimination*, ed. Richard Cornwall and Phanindra Wunnava. New York: Praeger.

Doeringer, Peter, and Michael Piore. 1971. *Internal Labor Markets and Manpower Analysis*. Lexington, MA: Lexington Books.

Edwards, Richard. 1979. *Contested Terrain: The Transformation of the Workplace in the Twentieth Century*. New York: Basic Books.

Freeman, Richard. 1991. "Employment and Earnings of Disadvantaged Young Men in a Labor Shortage Economy." In *The Urban Underclass*, ed. Christopher Jencks and Paul E. Peterson. Washington, DC: Brookings Institution.

Gordon, David M. 1978. "Capitalist Development and the History of American Cities." In *Marxism and the Metropolis*, ed. William Tabb and L. Sawers. New York: Oxford University Press.

———. 1996. *Fat and Mean: The Corporate Squeeze of Working Americans and the Myth of Managerial "Downsizing."* New York: Free Press.

Gordon, David M., Richard Edwards, and Michael Reich. 1982. *Segmented Work, Divided Workers: The Historical Transformation of Labor in the United States*. New York: Cambridge University Press.

Holzer, Harry. 1996. *What Do Employers Want?* New York: Russell Sage Foundation.

Katz, Lawrence, and Alan B. Krueger. 1991. "Changes in the Structure of Wages in the Public and Private Sectors." In *Research in Labor Economics*, ed. Ronald Ehrenberg. Greenwich, CT: JAI Press.

Katz, Michael B. 1989. *The Undeserving Poor*. New York: Pantheon Books.

Kirschenman, Joleen, and Kathryn M. Neckerman. 1991. " 'We'd Love to Hire Them, But. . . .' The Meaning of Race for Employers." In *The Urban Underclass*, ed. Christopher Jencks and Paul Peterson. Washington, DC: Brookings Institution.

Kloek, T. 1981. "OLS Estimation in a Model Where a Microvariable Is Explained by Aggregates and Contemporaneous Disturbances Are Equicorrelated." *Econometrics* 49, no. 1 (January): 205–7.

Marx, Karl. 1986. *Capital: A Critique of Political Economy, Volume I*. Moscow: Progress Publishers.

Mason, Patrick L. 1993. "Accumulation, Segmentation and the Discriminatory Process in the Market for Labor Power." *Review of Radical Political Economics* 25, no. 2 (June): 1–25.

Massey, Douglas S., and Nancy A. Denton. 1993. *American Apartheid: Segregation and the Making of the Underclass*. Cambridge: Harvard University Press.

Mishel, Lawrence, Jared Bernstein, and John Schmitt. 1999. *The State of Working America 1998–99*. Ithaca, NY: Cornell University Press.

Moss, Philip, and Chris Tilly. 2000. "How Labor Market Tightness Affects Employer Attitudes and Actions toward Black Job Applicants." In *Prosperity for All? The Economic Boom and African Americans*, ed. Robert Cherry and William Rodgers. New York: Russell Sage Foundation.

Moulton, Brent R. 1990. "An Illustration of a Pitfall in Estimating the Effects of Aggregate Variables on Micro Units." *Review of Economics and Statistics* 72, no. 2 (May): 334–38.

Nickell, Stephen J., and Paul Kong. 1988. "An Investigation into the Power of Insiders in Wage Determination." Oxford, UK: Oxford Applied Economics Discussion Paper #49, June.

Quadagno, Jill. 1994. *The Color of Welfare: How Racism Undermined the War on Poverty*. New York: Oxford University Press.

Rebitzer, James. 1988. "Unemployment, Labor Relations, and Unit Labor Costs." *American Economic Review* 78, no. 2 (May): 389–94.

Riddell, W. Craig. 1981. "Contemporaneous Correlation in Wage Contract Studies." *Econometrica* 49, no. 2 (March): 515–16.

Schor, Juliet. 1987. "Does Work Intensity Respond to Macroeconomic Variables? Evidence from British Manufacturing, 1970–86." Cambridge: Department of Economics, Harvard University. Mimeo.

Schor, Juliet, and Samuel Bowles. 1987. "Employment Rents and the Incidence of Strikes." *Review of Economics and Statistics* 69, no. 4 (November): 584–92.

Shapiro, Carl, and Joseph Stiglitz. 1984. "Equilibrium Unemployment as a Labor Discipline Device." *American Economic Review* 74, no. 3 (June): 433–44.

Spriggs, William E., and Rhonda Williams. 2000. "What Do We Need to Explain about African American Unemployment?" In *Prosperity for All? The Economic Boom and African Americans*, ed. Robert Cherry and William Rogers. New York: Russell Sage Foundation.

Weisskopf, Thomas. 1987. "The Effect of Unemployment on Labor Productivity: An International Comparison." *International Review of Applied Economics* 1, no. 2 (July): 129–51.

Weisskopf, Thomas, Samuel Bowles, and David Gordon. 1983. "Hearts and Minds: A Social Model of Aggregate Productivity Growth in the United States, 1948–79." *Brookings Papers on Economic Activity* 2: 381–441.

Williams, Rhonda. 1991. "Competition, Discrimination, and Differential Wage Rates: On the Continued Relevance of Marxian Theory to the Analysis of Earnings and Employment Inequality." In *New Approaches to Economic and Social Analyses of Discrimination*, ed. Richard Cornwall and Phanindra Wunnava. New York: Praeger.

Winter-Ebmer, Rudolf. 1996. "Wage Curve, Unemployment Duration and Compensating Differentials." *Labor Economics* 3, no. 4 (December): 425–34.

Part III

Power and the Global Economy

7

Jim Stanford

SOCIAL STRUCTURES AND ECONOMIC MOBILITY

WHAT'S REALLY AT STAKE?

I. Introduction

This chapter investigates David Gordon's long-standing skepticism regarding the alleged importance of "globalization" in explaining recent regressive trends in the economic development of the United States and other industrialized economies. This skepticism was perhaps expressed most succinctly in a 1988 *New Left Review* article, entitled "The Global Economy: New Edifice or Crumbling Foundations?" Ask a dozen of Gordon's colleagues to list his five most important writings, and this article is unlikely to appear on many of these lists; it was written for a popular audience, is relatively non-technical, and concretely policy-oriented. Yet it has proven to be enduringly influential (and controversial) in left discussions regarding the importance or non-importance of international commodity trade and capital mobility in the restructuring of the post-war social accord, and whether or not the prospects for rebuilding that accord (or, more likely, a different one) have been fundamentally undermined by globalization.

The argument contained in "The Global Economy" is classic David Gordon: sweeping in its historical and spatial perspective, richly abstract in its theorizing about the contrasting roles of private markets and institutional structures, yet concrete and detailed in the wealth of empirical evidence brought forward to support his case. His main concern—restated in smaller ways in subsequent writings—was that both progressive economists and political activists have vastly overstated the importance of globalization (measured especially by the increasing im-

portance of trade flows and foreign investment) in determining the recent course of economic and social change in the developed capitalist
economies. He challenged the notion that globalization is either "new"
or even has become more "important," once current international trade
and investment patterns have been placed in longer-term perspective.
He rejected the idea that globalization has somehow undermined the
power or importance of governments and state policies—if anything, he
argued, institutions and policies have become *more* important in determining where capitalism is vibrant and successful, and where it is not.
Progressives should not implicitly accept the neoclassical assumption
that a "perfect market" is identical to an absence of regulation; it takes
far more than the dismantling of rules constraining international commodity trade and capital mobility to ensure that a viable and dynamic
regime of accumulation is established.[1]

Most importantly, Gordon rejected the political conclusions implied
by what he termed the "New International Division of Labor/Globaliza-
tion of Production" (NIDL/GOP) analysis. If capital can indeed so readily
use its access to foreign markets and foreign production platforms to
escape domestic efforts to regulate it and improve working and social
conditions, then the "spreading political fatalism" (Gordon 1988, 64)
that he bemoaned in the advanced countries would seem to be quite
justified. In contrast, Gordon saw little in the "new" global economy to
indicate that capitalism has indeed reestablished a more dominant and
regressive regime:

> The breakdown in the postwar system has reflected an erosion of socially
> determined institutional relationships. TNC responses since the early 1970s
> reflect their own political and institutional efforts to erect some shelters
> against the winds of spreading economic instability. The TNCs are nei-
> ther all-powerful nor fully equipped to shape a new world economy by
> themselves. They require workers and they require consumers. Workers
> and consumers helped shape the structure of the postwar system, and we
> are once again in a position to bargain over institutional transformation.
> The global economy is up for grabs, not locked into some new and im-
> mutable order. (1988, 64)

The issues raised in the 1988 article seem all the more relevant in the
wake of the immense policy controversies that have erupted in both
North America and Europe regarding the continuing course of international economic integration (such as the political struggles surrounding

the negotiation of the NAFTA, the establishment of the WTO, and monetary union in Europe). Indeed, Gordon continued to engage in these debates, suggesting that the general decline in U.S. labor and social standards that has characterized the last two decades has had far more to do with domestic institutional and political factors than with the alleged impact of globalization—and arguing strategically that at least as much emphasis should be placed on reversing those domestic setbacks (through measures such as increasing the minimum wage or improving the institutional structures governing union organizing and collective bargaining) as on opposing new trade and investment treaties. Whether it is accepted or not, Gordon's critique of the simple-minded anti-globalization mentality has at least forced progressive economics to develop a more sophisticated and complex analysis of globalization and its consequences; this chapter represents one effort to respond to this challenge.

The chapter is structured as follows. Section II situates the argument in the context of a critique of both orthodox and radical visions of the consequences of international economic integration. Section III describes a hybrid general equilibrium system that preserves the budget constraints and microeconomic foundations of traditional Walrasian models, while relaxing some of the Walrasian assumptions (in particular the assumption of self-clearing factor markets) which heterodox critics have found to be particularly odious. Section IV reports on a series of simulation experiments that test the properties of this hybrid model under several different open-economy scenarios. These simulation results contradict both the blissful optimism of Walrasian models and the simple-minded pessimism of some of their radical critics regarding the impact of globalization on labor market outcomes.

II. Straw Men on Either Side

David Gordon's stated intention was clearly not to trivialize the importance of international trade and investment patterns in structuring recent global capitalist development. Rather, he was reacting against the more unbalanced and shallow conclusions of NIDL/GOP proponents—namely that globalization is all-powerful and destructive in its impact on progressive social and economic policies. Yes, globalization is probably important; but that importance is subtly and variably constrained by countervailing economic and institutional forces that need to be considered by the model. Yet at the same time, perhaps the more extreme statements of the NIDL/GOP perspective have themselves represented a re-action against the stereotypical view—held so dear by mainstream economics—that international economic liberalization is a mutually beneficial, efficiency-enhancing policy change that could only be opposed by narrow vested interests. Since the traditional neoclassical faith in the virtues of globalization rests on the analytical assumptions that underpin the entire Walrasian model (and in particular on the assumed power and efficiency of self-adjusting factor markets), it will hardly inspire confidence among those who have already rejected these analytical starting points.

What is needed is a more careful, balanced model that abandons the happy Walrasian assumptions, but that still pays attention to those factors —ranging from the complex institutional determinants of competitive-ness and profitability, to the simple accounting and adding-up require-ments that must be respected by any complete, internally consistent economic model—which will shape and constrain the process of glo-balization. Then we can gain a better understanding of precisely what *forms* of globalization may be harmful to progressive policy (commod-ity trade? capital mobility? labor mobility?), and what factors may serve to *limit* the damage.

Table 7.1 summarizes the key features of these two contrasting ste-reotypical perspectives of globalization and its effects, in opposition to which the model described later in this article will define itself. These features are stated deliberately in a blunt, simplistic fashion, so as to highlight and contrast their key conclusions; Table 7.1 obviously does not do justice to the depth of analysis reflected in more complete origi-nal statements of either of the summarized perspectives.

The tenets of the Walrasian analysis of international economic liber-alization are well known. Specialization in an open economy will be guided by *relative* costs only. Absolute costs, or the overall *competitive-ness* of economies, are not relevant: the self-adjusting behavior of fac-tor markets, which ensures that all resources are *fully employed* both before and after liberalization, dictates that each economy continues to operate on its production possibilities frontier. These efficient factor markets, by determining competitive factor price outcomes on the basis of supply and demand only, also guide the direction of specialization.[2] An open global economy offers various "routes" by which the efficiency and welfare gains accruing from this specialization can be accessed. For example, a relatively high-wage economy could export capital-inten-sive products, invest its capital abroad, or import migrant labor: these

Table 7.1

Contrasting Stereotypes of Globalization

Walrasian "Bliss"	Radical "Angst"
Every national or regional economy is inherently and automatically competitive. *"Competitiveness" is not an issue.*	*Cost competitiveness is absolute and variable,* and is a crucial determinant of the aggregate performance of national or regional economies.
Relative factor prices determine only the *direction of specialization* in an open economy (not its overall performance).	Wage levels are the crucial measure of the competitiveness of an open economy, and hence affect its *overall performance.*
Market-clearing processes ensure that all resources are *fully employed* under globalization.	International commodity trade and capital mobility *undermine aggregate employment* and investment in high-wage economies (and ultimately undermine pro-labor social and economic policies).
Under global liberalization, a high-wage economy will export capital-intensive commodities, and/or invest its capital abroad, and/or attract inward migration. These are *substitutes* that attain the same specialization and welfare gains.	In a liberalized global economy, a high-wage economy will experience *trade deficits, a loss of domestic investment, and the decline of employment.*
Commodity trade and/or factor mobility will reduce or eliminate the factor price differentials that give rise to international specialization. The *specialization* process is stopped by global *"equality."*	Employment and investment will shift from high-wage to low-wage areas until all countries establish equally attractive conditions for investors. The *restructuring* process (the "race to the bottom") is stopped by maximum global "*inequality.*"
International economic liberalization *"perfects"* the market system (enhancing the efficiency of production and exchange).	International economic liberalization *"cements"* the market system (enhancing the power of private investors).

actions are *substitutes* that all achieve the same result (overcoming the relative domestic scarcity of labor). The specialization process is stopped once the motive for that specialization—differences in relative factor prices—is eliminated by the demand and/or supply adjustments that accompany international commodity trade and/or factor mobility. In other words, the globalization process generates, and is ultimately limited by, international *equality* in distributional outcomes.[3]

This blissful view of the motives for and consequences of international economic liberalization is reversed completely in the pessimistic understanding of the NIDL/GOP theorists. Rejecting (quite rightly) the supply-side focus of neoclassical models, radical critics stress the important effects of international economic conditions on the *demand constraint* that normally limits domestic output and employment. When the demand constraint can change, then the demand-side effects of shifts in international competition and investment could quite conceivably overwhelm any beneficial supply-side reallocations resulting from Walrasian mechanisms. Competitiveness, on *absolute cost* grounds, becomes relevant—and much writing in the NIDL/GOP tradition has identified (quite wrongly) that cost competitiveness first and foremost with *wage levels*.[4] In an open economy setting, then, a high-wage economy is likely to suffer both from a trade deficit (driven by the import of lower-cost foreign-made goods) and a loss of domestic investment expenditure (as investors shift their capital to more profitable foreign locations).[5] Jurisdictions will be forced to compete with one another in a social and economic "race to the bottom"—continually weakening labor and social standards in an effort to reduce domestic production costs, enhance profitability, and hence win a greater share of world investment and production. What ultimately stops this profit-seeking restructuring process? In a sense, it is the achievement of some maximum level of *inequality* in the global economy: only the creation of equally appealing, high-profit socio-institutional regimes in all jurisdictions will stop the flight of capital and the downward bidding of social standards.[6]

In one sense, however, both the Walrasians and their radical critics agree that international economic liberalization represents an important and powerful step forward for world capitalism. The former model sees the dismantling of barriers to commodity trade and factor mobility as the *perfecting* of the market system, allowing the natural forces of supply and demand to operate more efficiently in seeking and finding a welfare-maximizing outcome. The latter critics see globalization in political-economy terms as representing the *cementing* of the market system, in the sense that geographic mobility greatly enhances the ability of capital to impose social and institutional regimes much more to its liking. The two perspectives seem to agree, however, that globalization is both *important* and *beneficial* for the global free-market or capitalist economy (although the radicals would not assume, of course, that what is good for the system is also good for its citizens).

Clearly, neither of these stereotypical views is going to provide an accurate, balanced analysis of the effects of international economic integration. Heterodox economists immediately abandon, as their starting point, many of the assumptions that underpin the Walrasian model: the faith in factor market clearing and full-employment; the notion that factor prices reflect only supply and demand (not institutions or power); the view that labor and capital relate to each other as "equals" in a fair and mutually beneficial process of exchange. But when we carefully and consistently expand these fundamental critiques of the Walrasian approach into a full-fledged alternative model, we also find that the extreme pessimism of the NIDL/GOP approach needs to be modified and nuanced.

III. The Model

To attempt to illustrate the properties of a more careful heterodox analysis of globalization, we construct a formal general equilibrium system that abandons critical Walrasian assumptions regarding factor market clearing, but still carefully portrays budget constraints, income identities, and the institutional determinants of labor market outcomes and investment. What follows below is a prototypical structuralist analog to the 2x2x2 general equilibrium systems that have long been used to illustrate the properties of the Walrasian model of international economic liberalization.[7]

The basic structure of the model is illustrated in the Social Accounting Matrix presented in Table 7.2. There are two countries, two factors (labor and capital), and two sectors (the first of which is relatively capital-intensive and hence relatively high-wage). All labor is provided by worker households, which also generate a (small) share of total savings; most capital is owned by capitalist households.[8] There are quasi-"banks" that act as pure financial intermediaries: collecting savings from households, allocating them to the sectors for new investment, and distributing profits from the sectors back to the households. There is also a quasi-"retail" sector that translates aggregate expenditure on consumption or investment into demands for specific commodities (namely domestic and foreign national varieties of the output of the two sectors). Domestic absorption (consumption plus investment) is thus translated into domestic demand for domestic output plus imports. Total demand for each sector's output equals domestic demand plus exports. A "government" performs

Table 7.2

A Simple Structuralist General Equilibrium Model, Social Accounting Matrix

Receivers	Payers								Total
	Sector 1	Sector 2	"Banks"	"Retail"	Worker households	Capitalist households	"Gov't."	World	
Sector 1			I_1	$P_1(Q_1 - X_1)$				$P_1 X_1$	$P_1 Q_1 + I_1$
Sector 2			I_2	$P_2(Q_2 - X_2)$				$P_2 X_2$	$P_2 Q_2 + I_2$
"Banks"	rK_1	rK_2			S^w	S^c		$r^* K_l$	$r(K - K_l) + r'K_l + S$
"Retail"	I_1	I_2			C^w	C^c	C^G		$C + I$
Worker households	$w_1 E_1$	$w_2 E_2$	iK^w						Y^w
Capitalist households			$r^* K_l + r(K^c - K_l)$ $+ (r - i)K^w$						Y^c
"Gov't."				$t_1 P^*_1 M_1 + t_2 P^*_2 M_2$					$t_1 P^*_1 M_1 + t_2 P^*_2 M_2$
World			I_l	$P^*_1 M_1 + P^*_2 M_2$					$M + I_l$
Total	$P_1 Q_1 + I_1$	$P_2 Q_2 + I_2$	$r(K - K_l) +$ $r'K_l + I$	$C + I$	$S^w + C^w$	$S^c + C^c$	C^G	$X + r^* K_l$	

only one function: it collects tariffs (at sector-specific rates) on imports, and then consumes that revenue (in the provision of some public good, also purchased from the "retail" sector). The two countries interact through commodity trade (following the standard Armington model of national product differentiation, purchasers in both countries tend to purchase both home and imported varieties of the output of both sectors, hence generating a two-way trade in both commodities) and through foreign investment (with profits on foreign investment repatriated to the home economy's "banks"). The national income account requires that any current account surplus (exports plus net foreign investment income, less imports) be offset by a flow of new foreign investment abroad. The model also allows (if desired) for international labor migration; migrant workers are assumed to move permanently to the host country (so that no flow of migrant remittances is considered).

The bulk of the model's 60-odd equations consist of identities that describe the income-accounting and budget-constraint relationships summarized in Table 7.2. But the model also contains numerous behavioral relationships describing the actions of the specified agents. Many of these behavioral functions are inherited harmlessly from standard neoclassical general equilibrium models of this type: CES-type demand allocation functions (which allocate an aggregate expenditure into product-specific and national-variety-specific commodity demands, based on relative prices and the preferences of purchasers); CES-type household consumption functions (in which household savings increase non-linearly with income, based on the relative "price" of present versus future consumption, namely the interest rate, and on consumer preferences); and CES-type factor demand functions according to which firms will hire a cost-minimizing combination of expended labor services[9] and capital (on the basis of total output, relative factor prices, and technology).

What is it, then, that makes this "structuralist" model structuralist? The following features, which differ fundamentally from Walrasian practice, are sufficient to impart the model with demand-constrained, institutionally influenced properties:

1. Wages are determined not by market-clearing but by a process of conflictual bargaining. They depend positively on average productivity, negatively on the unemployment rate, and negatively on a measure of *employers'* socio-institutional power (assumed to reflect variables such

as unionization, wage regulation, and the extent of wage-replacing social benefits). There is no reason to expect this bargaining process to be
equal across sectors, so inter-sectoral wage differentials are a normal
feature of the system.

2. Consistent with the structuralist literature on the labor extraction
problem facing employers,[10] a distinction is made between actual labor
services *expended* during production (an optimal amount of which is
desired by cost-minimizing firms) and the labor that must be *hired* by
firms to achieve that expended effort (in light of the variability of work
effort). Labor intensity is thus modeled as varying positively with wages
(via an efficiency wage effect), the capital intensity of production (reflecting the role of technology in standardizing and monitoring work
effort), and the measure of employers' power.

3. Aggregate investment is determined not by the passive clearing of
an autonomously endowed capital market, but rather by an independent
profit-driven investment function. Investment varies positively with the
rate of profit (measured relative to the interest rate), and with a measure
of *investors'* socio-institutional power (assumed to reflect the stability
of property relationships and the general "investment climate"). The
interest rate, in turn, varies negatively with investors' power (thus
reflecting an assumed political-economic conflict between the financial
sector and "real" investors). The allocation of aggregate investment
between sectors is then modeled in standard cost-minimizing fashion
(so that the marginal value productivity of capital is equalized between
sectors).[11]

4. Consumption expenditure is modeled *separately* across the two
types of households (rather than as a single "national" decision). Combined with the assumption that capitalist households have higher average incomes, and the assumption of increasing marginal propensity to
save, this produces (via explicit microeconomic mechanisms) the standard "Cambridge" macroeconomic result that total consumer spending
will increase as income is redistributed from profits to wages.[12]

All other variables in the model are treated no differently than would
be the case in a standard neoclassical general equilibrium setting. Yet
the structuralist model behaves very differently—illustrating the extent
to which it is the Walrasian treatment of factor markets (as efficient,
self-clearing, and automatically fully employed) that is the defining feature of neoclassical analysis (including the neoclassical analysis of globalization). The alternative structuralist model, in essence, is a Kaleckian

investment-driven multiplier system, greatly complicated by the portrayal of numerous microeconomic decisions (including the factor-hiring decisions of firms, and the expenditure decisions of households). But the key features of the Kaleckian approach are preserved: an initial volume of aggregate investment is injected into the system (based on expected profit). This investment generates a multiplied volume of total output and employment, depending on numerous factors (including propensities to save, the labor-intensity of production, and the determination of wages). The surplus generated by the system at the end of that process (once wage costs have been deducted) must generate a rate of profit consistent (via the investment function) with the initial injection of investment; the volume of investment actually forthcoming must thus vary until that consistency is attained.

As predicted by Kalecki (1971),[13] the system exhibits an equilibrium level of unemployment—in essence, a kind of structuralist "natural rate" that must be sufficient to moderate wage demands and enforce labor intensity to a degree consistent with the profitability needed to justify the initial investment that gets the whole process rolling. Changes in the intensity of aggregate demand (such as changes in the vibrancy of investment, the propensity to consume, or in other sources of demand—such as government spending or exports) will affect that equilibrium level of unemployment, with important and lasting demand-side consequences for output and employment. Changes in the institutional relationships governing the distribution of income in society (between workers and employers, or between financial capital and "real" capital) also affect equilibrium output and employment.

The Kaleckian, investment-driven roots of this structuralist general equilibrium can be portrayed in a reduced form as the interaction between the independent investment function and a complex function summarizing the relationship between aggregate demand and profitability (see Figures 7.1 and 7.2). This latter function, termed here a "labor cost constraint," exhibits a non-linear pattern in the present model.[14] It first rises, as growing investment and hence aggregate demand increases the output–capital ratio sufficiently to keep the rate of profit growing; but it then ultimately falls at high levels of aggregate demand and employment, as the balance of bargaining power (crucial to the determination of wages and productivity) shifts in favor of workers, and a declining profit share drags down the rate of profit.

Two broad cases are possible. If the intersection of the two functions

Figure 7.1 **A "Profit-Squeeze" Equilibrium**

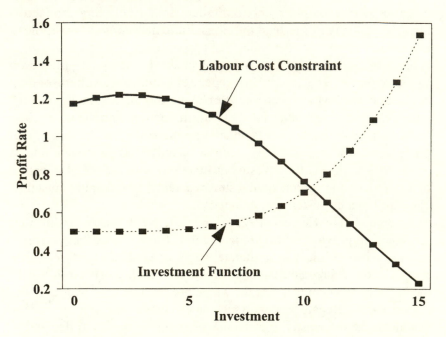

occurs on the declining portion of the labor cost constraint, then the system produces a "profit-squeeze" equilibrium (Figure 7.1). Increasing aggregate demand is accompanied by declining profitability, and this squeeze on profit limits further growth in the absence of some alternative (non-profit-driven) injection of demand. The profit-squeeze case implies a conflictual distributional relation between workers and capitalists (one must receive less for the other to receive more). If the intersection occurs sooner, however, in the rising portion of the labor cost constraint (due to weak investment or a lower, flatter labor cost constraint), then the system produces a "profit-push" equilibrium (Figure 7.2). Investment is held back by demand, not by pressure on profit; increasing aggregate demand then actually *increases* profitability. This implies the potential for a mutually beneficial expansion of demand, employment, wages, and profits—or what Glyn (1995, 35) calls the Keynesian "free lunch."[15] Whether the model produces a profit-squeeze or profit-push equilibrium depends on numerous of the parameters specified within it—including the sensitivity of investment to changes in profitability, the propensity to consume (and the differential between the

Figure 7.2 **A "Profit-Push" Equilibrium**

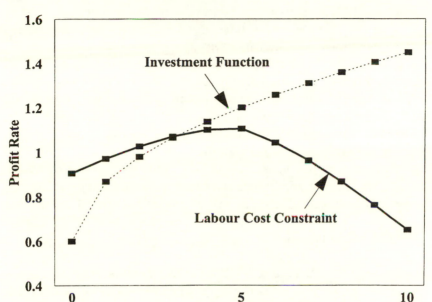

savings propensities of the different classes of household), and the sensitivity of wages and labor intensity to the unemployment rate.

Our prototypical structuralist model considers international economic interactions in the following manner. As mentioned, international commodity trade is modeled in the Armington fashion: purchasers choose between domestic and imported varieties of a product based on their preferences and on relative prices. When allowed, investment migrates from one country to another based on differentials in profitability and in the institutional structure governing investment. We assume that this flow of foreign investment stops once the investment rate (investment as a share of the existing capital stock) is equalized between the two countries.[16] Finally, when allowed, labor migrates from one country to another based on relative wages and employment prospects; we assume that this process equalizes the "average expected wage" between the two countries (that is, the average wage adjusted for the proportionate chance that the migrant is unemployed).[17]

Note that there is little difference between the model's treatment of these international economic linkages and the linkages that would be portrayed in a typical Walrasian model. The treatment of commodity trade is exactly the same, and the portrayal of factor mobility only slightly different (requiring the equalization of investor spirits and expected wages, respectively, rather than the rate of profits and wages in the Walrasian case). This illustrates once again the extent to which it is not their portrayal of the immediate processes of globalization per se that explains the difference between Walrasian and heterodox expectations regarding the effects of those processes. Rather, it is differences in the models of factor markets that *underlie* the respective general equilibrium systems (efficient market-clearing in the Walrasian case, conflictual and institutionally mediated interactions in the structuralist case) that explain why the two approaches can come to such different conclusions regarding the effects of international economic integration.

IV. Model Simulations

Even though the structuralist model described above is relatively simple, in general equilibrium terms,[18] it rapidly becomes extremely difficult to attempt to discover its properties through pure functional analysis. So we adopt the common practice of exploring the properties of a general equilibrium model through illustrative numerical simulations. Indicative values are chosen for the various functional parameters and exogenous variables of the system, and the system is solved numerically.[19] Comparative-static results are then obtained by adjusting one or more of the parameters, resolving the model, and contrasting the two sets of final results.

Since the behavior of the structuralist model depends importantly on whether its equilibrium is "profit-squeeze" or "profit-push," numerical prototypes of each case (corresponding to the two examples illustrated in Figure 7.1) are constructed. To understand the implications of international economic interactions within a structuralist general equilibrium framework, the following experiments are conducted:

- the bilateral reduction of tariffs between two economies (from an assumed 10 percent on both sectors to 5 percent);
- the unilateral reduction of tariffs by the home economy (from 10 percent to 5 percent);
- an increase (of 10 percent) in the total factor productivity of output in both sectors of the foreign economy;

- an increase in the autonomous preference of home purchasers for imported varieties of both products, and a corresponding decrease in their preference for domestically produced varieties;[20]
- an increase in the foreign country's measure of investors' power (from 1 to 2); and
- an increase in the foreign country's measure of employers' power (from 1 to 2).

In each of these six cases, the comparative static simulation is conducted assuming that capital and labor are both internationally immobile (i.e., that the two countries interact only through commodity trade), that only capital is internationally mobile, and that both capital and labor are internationally mobile. This will provide some indication as to how the *form* of international economic integration affects the final consequences of any policy shock.

With six different broad experiments, three different stages of international economic integration, and two types of general equilibrium (profit-squeeze and profit-push), a total of thirty-six comparative static simulations are performed. The results are presented in Tables 7.3 through 7.8, each of which corresponds to one of the six broad experiments. Proportionate changes resulting from the parameter change specified are reported for seven variables: total home employment (E); home GDP (Y); real output of the two home sectors (Q_1 and Q_2); the ratio of real outputs (Q_1/Q_2, a rise in which indicates a relative specialization toward the capital-intensive, high-wage industry); and the ratio of home-to-foreign average wages and unit labor costs (ULC).[21] The left side of each table illustrates the results for a profit-squeeze equilibrium, and the right side for a profit-push equilibrium.[22]

Consider first some general findings that seem to apply across most or all of the six broad experiments. In the majority of cases, the estimated size of effects is larger in the profit-push simulations. The overall strength of demand-side pressures tends to be felt more strongly in a profit-push equilibrium: any initial demand change (positive or negative) is multiplied more forcefully when the labor cost constraint slopes upward. The intuition behind this point can be understood geometrically: in a profit-push equilibrium, both the investment function and the labor cost constraint slope upward, and hence a relatively small shift in one of the curves can produce a larger estimated movement in the point of their intersection than is the case (in a profit-squeeze equilibrium), when the labor cost constraint slopes downward.

In almost every experiment, the estimated size of the comparative static effects is by far the smallest in the case in which factors are immobile (i.e., only final commodities are internationally mobile). Comparative static effects are larger when capital mobility is allowed. And in almost every experiment the estimated size of effects is largest in the case of *full* integration (that is, when commodities and *both* factors are internationally mobile). The greater impact of globalization when capital is mobile is quite consistent with the emphasis placed by NIDL/GOP theorists on the importance of international capital mobility—while being quite inconsistent with the Walrasian conclusion that factor mobility and commodity trade are *substitutes* which have the same ultimate effects.[23] It is interesting to note, however, that even in a structuralist model, when goods and capital are internationally mobile (the scenario that is most commonly assumed within NIDL/GOP writings), the impact of policy changes is still limited in an important way by the lack of labor mobility. This immediately suggests that free trade in goods and international capital mobility alone have not made national borders meaningless.

In most of the full-integration simulations, labor and capital flow in the same direction: toward the more competitive or pro-capitalist economy. In other words, in a demand-constrained structuralist setting, labor migration and foreign investment are likely to be *complements*, not *substitutes*. It is the demand-side expansion arising from the injection of investment expenditure that creates employment opportunities for workers. This is quite different from the Walrasian system, in which labor is automatically fully employed and the only factor determining wages is the relative abundance of capital; thus international factor mobility in the structuralist case is largely driven by demand, as opposed to the factor price effects resulting from the shifts in relative factor supplies that are stressed in the Walrasian tradition. For this reason, the foreign investment of capital tends, when it is able, to "pull along" additional supplies of labor at the same time.

This result reflects a fundamental conceptual difference between the Walrasian and structuralist approaches. In the Walrasian case, the two factors meet in production as equals, in a process of balanced, mutually beneficial exchange. Outward foreign investment and inward labor migration are thus mirror images that attain the same result—namely, an evening out of factor endowment ratios between countries, with consequent and mutual welfare benefits. In the structuralist setting, however, labor and capital are not "equals": labor is fundamentally *dependent* on capital to start the employment-generating production process through an initial injection of investment. Thus if capital leaves, labor (if allowed) is obliged to follow in order to maximize its chances of remaining employed.

Another interesting result when labor is mobile is that the flow of migration typically runs from the *higher-wage* to the *lower-wage* economy—completely contrary to the direction predicted in a Walrasian model. For Tables 7.4 through 7.8 (all experiments other than the bilateral reduction of tariffs), a competitiveness-enhancing policy change is applied to the foreign economy, and the relative demand for foreign-made products increases as a result. Domestic unemployment increases, and in the absence of labor mobility, wages fall. But under labor mobility, labor exits the home economy, drawn by better employment prospects abroad. According to the condition of equalized expected wages, however, this migration can only stop if wages in the home (higher unemployment) economy are left *higher* than in the faster-growing foreign economy—in order to compensate those home workers who remain behind for their greater likelihood of unemployment.[24]

This result is perhaps not quite so surprising in the case of a wage-*reducing* policy change in the foreign country (such as the case of stronger employers' power): here migration will flow toward that country (even though it has lower wages) until the labor cost constraint begins to bind there—pushing up wages and partly eliminating the home wage premium. In this case, factor mobility (albeit in a direction *opposite* to that predicted in a Walrasian model) still helps to narrow a factor price differential. The result is especially surprising, however, in the case of wage-*enhancing* foreign policy changes (such as higher productivity or investors' power). In this case, migration flows toward the foreign economy, drawn both by higher wages and lower unemployment. But that flow of migration is so great that the wage differential between the two economies is actually *reversed*—leaving the home economy (the source of the migration) with higher wages. In these cases the amount of migration required to reestablish conditions of equal expected wages is much larger, and hence the loss of domestic employment and output much greater. In other words, the ultimate potential threat posed to the home economy is all the greater when the ultra-competitive rivalry facing it comes from an economy with *higher* wages. This stands in contrast to the predisposition of NIDL/GOP models to place particular emphasis on the threat posed by low-wage competition.

Finally, note that in most cases, when home output declines as a result of the foreign policy shift, that decline is experienced in both of the domestic sectors: capital-intensive and labor-intensive. This is true regardless of whether the competition for markets and investment comes from a low-wage or a high-wage foreign trading partner. For example, in the case of stronger foreign employers' power (and hence lower foreign wages), the proportionate decline in home production of the capital-intensive commodity actually exceeds the decline in production of the labor-intensive commodity (causing a perverse relative specialization of the *high-wage* economy in the *labor-intensive* commodity). This stands in sharp contrast to the standard Walrasian expectation that a high-wage economy will only experience a reallocation of resources from its labor-intensive to its capital-intensive sectors, following liberalization with a low-wage trading partner. In the demand-constrained structuralist world, on the other hand, relative cost advantages offer no such protection: economic contraction will be experienced *throughout* an uncompetitive economy when exposed to international competition, and there is no guarantee that this contraction will be avoided (or even experienced less forcefully) in those sectors that correspond to the economy's relative (or comparative) cost advantage.

Let us now briefly summarize the more specific results of each broad experiment. Table 7.3 illustrates the case of bilateral trade liberalization. The effects of a two-way reduction in tariffs are very small, and generally benign or even positive. A small specialization toward the capital-intensive sector is experienced in both the profit-squeeze and the profit-push regimes; this is driven by the relative shift in final demand from consumption to investment that results from the decline of government tariff revenue (all of which, recall, was consumed). In the case of unilateral tariff reduction (Table 7.4), however, small declines in output and employment are experienced when factors are immobile. The negative effects are larger when factors are mobile (especially when both capital and labor are mobile, in which case the profit-push system loses 10 percent of its employment and real output). In a demand-led structuralist system, unilateral tariff reduction (long advocated on efficiency grounds by Walrasian trade theorists, but seldom implemented by governments who are apparently unconvinced by the economists' models!) undermines demand for domestic output, and consequently

Table 7.3

Simulation Results: Bilateral Tariff Reduction (percentage change by variable)

	Profit-squeeze system							Profit-push system						
	Emp.	GDP	Q1	Q2	Q1/Q2	Wage	ULC	Emp.	GDP	Q1	Q2	Q1/Q2	Wage	ULC
Goods trade only	0.00	0.03	0.28	−0.19	0.47	0.00	0.00	0.05	0.00	0.14	−0.01	0.14	0.00	0.00
Goods trade and capital mobility	−0.00	0.02	0.26	−0.21	0.46	0.00	0.00	−0.04	−0.05	0.05	−0.09	0.14	0.00	0.00
Goods trade, capital mobility, and migration	0.03	0.04	0.29	−0.17	0.47	0.00	0.00	−0.04	−0.04	0.05	−0.09	0.14	0.00	0.00

Table 7.4

Simulation Results: Unilateral Tariff Reduction (percentage change by variable)

	Profit-squeeze system							Profit-push system						
	Emp.	GDP	Q1	Q2	Q1/Q2	Wage	ULC	Emp.	GDP	Q1	Q2	Q1/Q2	Wage	ULC
Goods trade only	0.15	−1.03	0.50	0.27	0.23	−0.80	1.60	−1.49	−1.80	−1.10	−1.12	0.02	−0.40	0.30
Goods trade and capital mobility	−0.07	−1.37	−0.21	−0.44	0.23	−3.20	−0.70	−5.94	−4.23	−5.54	−5.43	−0.11	−1.00	−4.20
Goods trade, capital mobility, and migration	−3.93	−3.09	−3.56	−3.76	0.22	0.30	−1.30	−10.46	−6.65	−10.08	−10.04	−0.05	0.70	−6.81

undermines both employment and investment in the home economy. Wages decline as a result of the stagnant macroeconomic conditions at home.

Table 7.5 illustrates the case of a unilateral increase in foreign productivity. When only goods are mobile, this change is benign—if anything, the faster foreign growth that is likely to result (especially in a profit-push equilibrium) stimulates domestic output and employment through spin-off income effects on the home country's exports. As one would expect, relative home wages fall (thanks to rising foreign wages), but relative home unit labor costs rise (similarly due to higher foreign productivity). When capital is mobile, however, foreign investment by the home economy expands to take advantage of higher foreign productivity, with consequent negative effects on employment and output. The outward flow of capital is ultimately limited by the tightening of labor market conditions in the foreign economy (a process that takes longer in a profit-push equilibrium, thus explaining the relatively larger shift that occurs in this case). With labor mobility, however, the flow of labor from home to the foreign economy serves to relax this labor cost constraint, facilitating the flow of greater quantities of capital. Once again, international capital flows and labor migration are complements—unlike the Walrasian prediction that they should be substitutes. Moreover, the divergence in wages and unit labor costs is even greater in the case of capital mobility than with commodity trade alone—again contrary to the Walrasian expectation that international factor mobility will serve to eliminate or at least reduce factor price differentials. The contrast to the traditional mainstream comparative advantage conclusion—namely that rising foreign productivity can pose no threat to domestic output and employment[25]—is striking.

Similarly, in Table 7.6, domestic output and employment are undermined by an autonomous shift in the preferences of purchasers toward (presumably higher-quality) products. Whether foreign competitiveness is rooted in cost or non-cost factors, therefore, the results are exactly similar: declining home demand, employment, and wages (when labor is immobile). This can be true even in the case of commodity trade alone—but the negative effects are largest when factors are mobile (especially when both capital and labor are mobile).

Tables 7.7 and 7.8 indicate the effects of pro-capitalist shifts in the socio-institutional structures of the foreign economies. Once again, the consequences when only commodities are internationally mobile are

Table 7.5

Simulation Results: Higher Foreign Productivity (percentage change by variable)

	Profit-squeeze system							Profit-push system						
	Emp.	GDP	Q1	Q2	Q1/Q2	Wage	ULC	Emp.	GDP	Q1	Q2	Q1/Q2	Wage	ULC
Goods trade only	−0.22	1.32	−0.41	−0.58	0.17	−0.90	4.01	7.78	9.38	6.00	5.54	0.43	−1.10	0.20
Goods trade and capital mobility	−0.77	0.46	−2.10	−2.27	0.17	−6.60	−1.30	0.32	4.94	−1.21	−1.33	0.12	−2.50	−6.41
Goods trade, capital mobility, and migration	−9.09	−3.43	−9.29	−9.40	0.13	0.70	−3.20	−9.94	−0.64	−11.40	−11.65	0.29	1.10	−11.61

Table 7.6

Simulation Results: Greater Propensity to Import (percentage change by variable)

	Profit-squeeze system							Profit-push system						
	Emp.	GDP	Q1	Q2	Q1/Q2	Wage	ULC	Emp.	GDP	Q1	Q2	Q1/Q2	Wage	ULC
Goods trade only	0.08	−0.49	−0.07	0.38	−0.45	−0.40	0.80	−0.26	−0.35	−0.31	−0.11	−0.20	−1.10	0.10
Goods trade and capital mobility	−0.03	−0.66	−0.41	0.05	−0.45	−1.60	−0.30	−1.09	−0.78	−1.14	−0.92	−0.22	−0.30	−0.80
Goods trade, capital mobility, and migration	−1.87	−1.48	−2.00	−1.55	−0.46	0.10	−0.60	−2.00	−1.26	−2.05	−1.85	−0.21	1.10	−1.40

Table 7.7

Simulation Results: Stronger Foreign Investors (percentage change by variable)

	Profit-squeeze system							Profit-push system						
	Emp.	GDP	Q1	Q2	Q1/Q2	Wage	ULC	Emp.	GDP	Q1	Q2	Q1/Q2	Wage	ULC
Goods trade only	-0.10	0.61	-0.22	-0.25	0.03	-5.61	-4.71	6.55	7.88	4.97	4.75	0.21	-1.70	-7.62
Goods trade and capital mobility	-0.38	0.05	-1.68	-0.72	-0.97	-8.40	-7.20	-4.48	0.89	-6.01	-4.99	-1.07	-3.60	-15.62
Goods trade, capital mobility, and migration	-12.13	-5.65	-13.54	-9.46	-4.51	1.90	-9.21	-21.53	-8.72	-23.23	-21.67	-1.99	2.20	-23.82

Table 7.8

Simulation Results: Stronger Foreign Employers (percentage change by variable)

	Profit-squeeze system							Profit-push system						
	Emp.	GDP	Q1	Q2	Q1/Q2	Wage	ULC	Emp.	GDP	Q1	Q2	Q1/Q2	Wage	ULC
Goods trade only	-0.09	0.57	-0.17	-0.25	0.07	4.71	1.50	5.64	6.63	3.65	4.61	-0.92	26.73	0.20
Goods trade and capital mobility	-0.29	0.23	-0.81	-0.88	0.07	2.30	-0.60	0.12	2.73	-1.55	-0.26	-1.29	25.20	-4.00
Goods trade, capital mobility, and migration	-3.63	-1.30	-3.70	-3.75	0.05	5.50	-1.20	-7.99	-0.39	-9.95	-8.96	-1.08	29.60	-9.81

quite benign—even positive, in the profit-push case, because the stronger demand-side spin-offs resulting from faster foreign growth stimulate domestic exports. When capital is mobile, however, the negative consequences for the home economy can be quite severe, as investors shift their expenditure toward the more amenable foreign institutional regime. Tightening foreign labor markets limit the outward shift in investment; but labor migration eases this constraint, allowing for a much larger total shift in investment and employment. Once again, equilibrium wages are higher in the home economy, even after the outward flow of capital and labor. Workers are attracted to the foreign economy by the better employment prospects there; even in the wage-suppressing case of higher foreign employers' power, labor flows toward the more pro-capitalist jurisdiction.[26]

Perhaps an interesting real-world application of this sometimes counter-intuitive analysis of the impact of differing social structures on patterns of trade, investment, and migration can be found in the case of north-south economic migration within the United States. Clear regional differences exist in the institutions governing employment relations between the "right-to-work" states of the south, and the "free association" states of the north.[27] Where possible, capital is migrating to take advantage of the more favorable institutional regimes of the south.[28] Labor faces no legal barriers to its inter-state migration (only cultural and economic ones, such as the costs of relocation)—yet labor continues to migrate from the higher-wage north to the lower-wage south (in contrast to the predictions of traditional Walrasian models). Why? Average *expected* incomes may be higher in the south, thanks to more vibrant (though unevenly distributed) economic growth and hence lower unemployment.

Finally, note that some critics of recent international economic liberalization initiatives—noting the emphasis in trade and investment treaties on facilitating and guaranteeing the international movement of goods and capital, but not of labor—have argued that labor's interests could be protected in this process by simultaneously enhancing international *labor* mobility in a parallel fashion.[29] Then workers could migrate toward socio-institutional regimes that are more appealing to labor, in the same manner that (and presumably in the opposite direction as) capital migrates across borders in search of more pro-capitalist institutional regimes. These simulations, however, suggest that the opening of labor migration actually *worsens* the consequences of globalization for less competitive or pro-capitalist economies—by eliminating one of the constraints (namely a supply-side labor market constraint in the more competitive foreign economy) that eventually limits the ability of capital to take advantage of international differentials in social and institutional regimes.

V. Conclusion

On the basis of the simulations reported above, we can reach conclusions that differ from both of the stereotypical portrayals of globalization that were summarized in Table 7.1. To the Walrasian optimists, we would show that by abandoning only a couple of their key initial assumptions—those relating to the ability of competitive factor markets to autonomously create (and re-create) full-employment—many of their conclusions regarding the impacts of globalization are turned upside down. More particularly, the structuralist simulations suggest that:

- *Overall* output and employment will be undermined, in an open-economy setting, by a lack of *absolute* competitiveness.
- Policy shifts that could create or add to such a lack of competitiveness include the unilateral reduction of tariffs, faster growth in foreign productivity, a growing preference for imports by domestic purchasers (or a declining preference for exports by foreign purchasers), and/or the creation of more pro-capitalist institutional regimes in foreign countries governing the processes of employment, distribution, and accumulation.
- The effects of international competition are not limited to a reallocation of factor supplies away from relatively expensive sectors. Output and employment in all sectors can fall in an uncompetitive economy; and the *relative* specialization that may occur in the course of that general decline may be perverse (that is, the high-wage economy may specialize relatively in the labor-intensive sector).
- Factor mobility may exacerbate international factor price differentials. The exit of capital from the home economy toward a more competitive trading partner will widen a wage gap created by an initial loss of domestic competitiveness.
- When labor is mobile, both labor and capital will tend to flow in the same direction (toward the more competitive or pro-capitalist jurisdiction). Moreover, labor may tend to flow toward the *lower-wage* economy.

In short, within a quite plausible and internally consistent general equilibrium system—one that fully respects budget constraints and income identities, and differs only in a couple of key equations from a traditional Walrasian system—globalization can indeed be seen to have negative, unbalanced, and demand-side consequences. When considering the impact of international economic integration, therefore, the sanguine mainstream conclusions that have been handed down through nearly two centuries of "comparative advantage" thinking do not provide a convincing refutation of current fears regarding unemployment and rising inequality in a globalized economy.

At the same time, however, the preceding simulations also raise important questions regarding the extreme pessimism reflected in the NIDL/GOP portrayal of the impacts of globalization. The following specific findings seem particularly at odds with much of the NIDL/GOP accepted wisdom:

- Bilateral trade liberalization has little if any effect on domestic output and employment, even when the trading partner involved is characterized by differing or more pro-capitalist institutional regimes, and even when factors are mobile. In a context where only commodities are internationally mobile, international shifts in relative competitiveness similarly have at most modest impacts on home output and employment. This suggests that the preoccupation of many critics of globalization with bilateral or multilateral commodity trade liberalization initiatives has been misplaced—or at least that it needs to be clarified that the focus of concern with more multi-faceted agreements (such as the NAFTA, which promotes a range of investment liberalizations in addition to the reduction of tariffs and non-tariff barriers to commodity trade) does not lie with their trade-liberalizing components. It needs to be made far clearer, from a heterodox perspective, that the problem with "globalization" is not a problem with "free trade." This result also suggests that visioning and developing mechanisms to limit the profit-seeking international mobility of capital (perhaps through restrictive means such as capital controls, or pro-active measures such as the development of democratically controlled pools of social capital) might be a particularly productive policy direction to pursue.
- A domestic economy can indeed be undermined by a lack of competitiveness (especially when factors are mobile). But competitive-

ness cannot be identified with *low wages*. A country can be characterized by high or low wage levels, and be competitive or uncompetitive. Indeed, it is when an international pressure for markets and investments comes from a competitive economy characterized by relatively higher wages that the damage to an uncompetitive economy tends to be worse (especially when factors are mobile).

- Even when commodities and capital are internationally mobile, important factors still limit the loss of output and employment experienced by a relatively uncompetitive home economy.[30] In particular, we cannot forget that firms even in a more competitive foreign jurisdiction still face the fundamentally difficult task of extracting labor effort from their workforce at profitable wages; this constraint becomes all the more difficult as output grows and unemployment declines in a booming, competitive economy. Similarly, a stable and accumulation-enhancing set of institutions governing the investment process is also required to maintain the appeal of foreign economies in the eyes of investors. As David Gordon stressed in his 1988 article, the task of building and maintaining these institutional regimes is far more complex and difficult than is often supposed (and than is suggested by our simple increase of the "investors' rights vector" from 1 to 2 in the preceding numerical simulations). We can hardly assume that a foreign jurisdiction has succeeded in this task simply because its government is repressive, pro-business, and lays out a welcome mat to foreign corporations.

In one sense, the simulations here are quite consistent with a basic point made in the NIDL/GOP literature: when commodities and especially capital are internationally mobile, it can become more difficult for an economy to maintain or implement relatively pro-labor employment and social policies without experiencing a loss of investment and employment. It is clear that David Gordon would not have disagreed with this point in principle. The issue then becomes one of how relatively important this economic mobility has been, or is likely to become, in explaining changes in competitiveness and employment—and subsequently explaining the political-economic pressures for socioinstitutional change that are likely to arise in the wake of changes in competitiveness and employment. For this reason, the pressures created by globalization need to be placed in perspective against the other pressures that have emerged since the breakdown of the post-war golden age. In contrast to the abstract modeling exercise that has been reported here,[31] we will need further concrete, case-specific, and empirical studies of the relative importance of the contrasting factors affecting employment, distribution, and accumulation in an open-economy setting, in order to attain a proper balance in our analysis. This is exactly the type of research that David Gordon was famous for—and hence exactly why we will so badly miss his creative and exacting analysis.

Notes

The research presented here was initially conceived and carried out while the author was completing his Ph.D. dissertation under the supervision of David Gordon, to whom the author remains greatly thankful. The author also thanks Andrew Glyn and Lance Taylor for comments on an earlier draft.

1. In this, the argument is appropriately reminiscent of the structuralist development literature.

2. In the strict Heckscher-Ohlin model, in which technology and preferences are identical across countries, it is therefore only relative factor supplies that determine relative factor prices. But even in a more general Walrasian model (in which technology and preferences may vary), the guidance provided by autarky relative factor prices is efficient.

3. This, of course, was one of the great benefits of free world trade in the eyes of the early neoclassical liberals. See the chapter by William Milberg in this volume for a critical summary of these traditional assumptions.

4. Given his life-long interest in productivity issues, it is not surprising that David Gordon should have been particularly dismayed by this reduction of competitiveness to a simple question of wage levels.

5. That a simultaneous trade deficit and capital export is impossible, on national income accounting grounds, for more than just a very short period of time only reemphasizes the need to consider issues of open-economy competitiveness and growth within a more careful and complete analytical framework.

6. The global equality predicted in the Walrasian model is defined with respect to equality of factor price outcomes across countries. The global inequality predicted by the "race to the bottom" hypothesis is defined with respect to the division of income between labor and capital; of course, this also implies a perverse type of international wage equality, with wages being pushed down to some uniform minimum.

7. For reasons of space a full listing of the equations in the model is not provided here, but is available from the author. For a more complete description of the model and its theoretical pedigree, see Stanford (1995), Chapters 3–5.

8. It is assumed that worker households are paid the going rate of interest on their savings. Capitalist households, on the other hand, by assuming the entrepreneurial "risk" associated with investing, are paid the full value of profits on their savings, plus the difference between the interest rate and the profit rate on workers'

savings. This specification seems most consistent with the real-world division of income, but is not essential to the properties exhibited by the model.

9. This is distinguished from actual employment, as shown below.

10. See Bowles (1985), and the empirical operationalization of that model in Weisskopf, Bowles and Gordon (1983).

11. The crucial difference between the present model and the Walrasian approach on this point is that in the latter case the rate of profit will equal this marginal value product of capital, while in the structuralist model the independence of the aggregate investment function breaks the link between the two (leaving the rate of profit to be determined, in "surplus approach" fashion, as the national output remaining after wages have been paid, divided by the capital stock).

12. Some Walrasian general equilibrium models include the disaggregated modeling of household consumption decisions; see, for example, models described in Dervis et al. (1982). But when the overall model is still based on a Walrasian, full-employment foundation, then this disaggregated treatment of households loses the demand-side significance that it carries in structuralist models.

13. This is explored subsequently by other writers in the structuralist tradition, such as Skott (1989) or Glyn (1995).

14. David Gordon identified this non-linear function (in profitability-investment space or profitability-utilization space) as a defining characteristic of what he called the "left-structuralist" approach; see Gordon (1994). The labor cost constraint in Figure 2.1 was constructed through numerical simulation—by replacing the investment function with varying exogenous injections of investment expenditure, and then noting the resulting rates of profit generated as a "surplus" by the macroeconomic system.

15. The exploration of these contrasting possibilities, of course, has been a central focus of the modern structuralist economic literature. Note that the categorization defined here in profitability–investment space differs from the "stagnationist" (or wage-led) versus "exhilarationist" (or profit-led) categorization developed by Bhaduri and Marglin (1990), among others, in wage–employment space. Similarities and differences between these approaches are beyond the scope of the present discussion, but are certainly worthy of further study.

16. An alternative approach would have been to simply require that the rate of profit be equalized between the two countries, as is typically assumed in neoclassical models of factor mobility; this would ignore, however, the non-profit determinants of investment (including the interest rate and the institutional regime) that are included in the present model. If interest rates and investment regimes are constant across countries, then the equalization of the investment rate reduces to the equalization of profitability.

17. Neoclassical migration models typically only assume the equalization of wages, on the implicit assumption that labor is fully employed. Of course, even the more elaborate treatment here ignores many factors affecting migration (including migration costs, cultural and communication factors, the variability of immigration enforcement, etc.).

18. The model contains no portrayal of behavioral relations in the financial sector, no government, no non-traded sector, and an extremely simplistic depiction of the institutional influences on wages, productivity, and investment.

19. The simulations reported here were solved using the GAMS modeling sys-

tem. The use of numerical simulations to explore the properties of general equilibrium systems is quite common in the international economics literature; see, for example, Brown (1992). If "real-world" numbers were chosen for the exogenous parameters, such that the output of the model replicated the corresponding data for a real-world economy (and this can be easily accomplished by adjusting the scale parameters that appear in all of the behavioral functions), then the exercise becomes equivalent to the computable general equilibrium (CGE) analyses that are now common in the fields of trade and development policy, tax policy, and environmental policy.

20. Technically this is accomplished by increasing the import "share" parameter in the CES consumer demand allocation functions, and by decreasing the domestic share parameter. This is assumed to reflect some growing preference for imports on non-price (or quality) grounds.

21. A rise in these ratios indicates that home wages (or unit labor costs) rise relative to those in the foreign country. The unit labor cost is defined as average wages divided by average labor productivity; it is also equal to labor's share of output.

22. Note that a more elaborate set of experiments could be conducted if we combined a profit-squeeze home-economy equilibrium with a profit-push foreign-economy equilibrium, and vice versa; these permutations would double the number of results presented here. These experiments were conducted, but their results were not found to significantly affect the broad conclusions stated here, and so they are not reported.

23. Some caution must be exercised in making this latter point: the difference between a 5 percent tariff and a 10 percent tariff is not entirely comparable to the difference between capital mobility and no capital mobility (since the former is a matter of degree, while the existence or non-existence of the latter will cause structural changes). So even in a Walrasian understanding one might expect the effect of policy changes to be larger when capital is mobile.

24. Bowles (1988) explores—also in a structuralist, demand-constrained context—the interesting and surprising results obtained when labor (not just goods and capital) is mobile between regions.

25. See Krugman (1994) for an especially forceful recent statement of this view. In fact, if anything foreign productivity growth should benefit the home economy in a full-employment Walrasian model by virtue of terms-of-trade effects (that is, the relative cheapening of the foreign export). The structuralist case described here is reminiscent of the result in a Ricardian trade model when one or more factors are mobile—namely, all mobile factors migrate toward the higher-productivity economy; see Brewer (1985).

26. In the profit-push equilibrium, the decline in foreign wages is doubly severe following the increase in employers' power there (totaling 30 percent in these simulations): the wage-suppressing institutional change is supplemented, in this case, by the contractionary demand-side consequences for the foreign economy of reducing wages in a profit-push equilibrium (a contractionary pressure that is only partly offset by the expansion of foreign exports). Nevertheless, labor migrates toward this ultra-low-wage economy—in hot pursuit of the capital which moves to take advantage of repressive labor institutions.

27. Right-to-work laws are the most visible, but not the only manifestations of

the differing institutional regimes; also evident in the south are lower (or non-existent) state minimum wages, much less generous state unemployment and welfare programs, and weaker health and safety or employment standards.

28. One important factor limiting this migration, but not reflected within the present structuralist model, is the importance of non-traded production.

29. See, for example, Edwards and Garonna (1991).

30. The prototypical model described above does not include other features that might also serve to limit the potentially negative effects of globalization; two that are particularly worth mentioning are exchange rate fluctuations and the role of non-tradable sectors.

31. See Stanford (1999) for a more empirically grounded examination of the relative importance of global versus domestic determinants of employment and distribution in the Canadian case.

References

Bhaduri, Amit, and Stephen Marglin. 1990. "Unemployment and the Real Wage: The Economic Basis for Contesting Political Ideologies." *Cambridge Journal of Economics* 14, no. 4 (December): 375–393.

Bowles, Samuel. 1985. "The Production Process in a Competitive Economy: Walrasian, Neo-Hobbesian and Marxian Models." *American Economic Review* 75, no. 1 (March): 16–36.

———. 1988. "Profits and Wages in an Open Economy." In *The Three Worlds of Labor Economics*, ed. Garth Mangum and Peter Phillips. Armonk, NY: M.E. Sharpe.

Brewer, Anthony. 1985. "Trade with Fixed Real Wages and Mobile Capital." *Journal of International Economics* 18, no. 1–2 (February): 177–186.

Brown, Drusilla. 1992. "Properties of Computable General Equilibrium Trade Models with Monopolistic Competition and Foreign Direct Investment." In *Economy-Wide Modeling of the Economic Implications of a FTA with Mexico and a NAFTA with Canada and Mexico*. Washington: United States International Trade Commission.

Dervis, Kemal, Jaime de Melo, and Sherman Robinson. 1982. *General Equilibrium Models for Development Policy.* Cambridge, UK: Cambridge University Press.

Edwards, Richard, and Paolo Garonna. 1991. *The Forgotten Link: Labor's Stake in International Economic Cooperation.* Savage, MD: Rowman and Littlefield.

Glyn, Andrew. 1995. "Social Democracy and Full Employment." *New Left Review* 211 (May–June): 33–55.

Gordon, David M. 1988. "The Global Economy: New Edifice or Crumbling Foundations?" *New Left Review* 168 (March–April): 24–64.

———. 1994. "Growth, Distribution and the Rules of the Game: Left Structuralist Macro Foundations for a Democratic Economic Policy." In *Investment, Saving, and Finance: A Progressive Strategy for Renewed Economic Growth*, ed. Gerald Epstein and Herb Gintis. Cambridge, UK: Cambridge University Press.

Kalecki, Michal. 1971. *Selected Essays on the Dynamics of the Capitalist Economy.* Cambridge, UK: Cambridge University Press.

Krugman, Paul. 1994. "Competitiveness: A Dangerous Obsession." *Foreign Affairs* 73, no. 2 (March–April): 28–44.

Skott, Peter. 1989. *Conflict and Effective Demand in Economic Growth.* Cambridge, UK: Cambridge University Press.

Stanford, Jim. 1995. "Social Structures, Labor Costs, and North American Economic Integration: A Comparative Modeling Analysis." New York: New School for Social Research. Unpublished dissertation.

———. 1999. "Openness and Equity: Managing Labor Market Outcomes in a Globalized Economy." In *Globalization and Progressive Economic Policy*, ed. Gerald Epstein et al. Cambridge, UK: Cambridge University Press.

Thirlwall, Anthony P. 1979. "The Balance of Payments Constraint as an Explanation of International Growth Rate Differences." *Banca Nazionale del Lavoro Quarterly Review* 128, no. 791 (March): 45–53.

Weisskopf, Thomas J., Samuel Bowles, and David M. Gordon. 1983. "Hearts and Minds: A Social Model of U.S. Productivity Growth." *Brookings Papers on Economic Activity* 2: 381–441.

8

William Milberg

INSTITUTIONS AND THE PERSISTENCE OF GLOBAL INEQUALITIES

I. Introduction

Recent theories of economic growth and international trade have indicated that increased capital mobility and liberalized trade will reduce global income inequality. Trade theories predict that trade liberalization will equalize wages among countries and reduce the wage differential within developing countries. Meanwhile, the new growth theories posit that under certain conditions the level of per capita income across countries will converge. There is ample evidence, however, that despite considerable financial deregulation and trade liberalization over the past twenty years, wages have not converged across countries and wage differentials between high- and low-skill workers within developing countries have grown. While risk-adjusted rates of return on capital across countries have largely equalized, and wages of skilled workers have also converged across countries, the earnings of low-skill workers in developing countries have stagnated, creating an increase in wage (and income) differentials in developing countries even more severe than that in developed countries.

New theories of economic growth, which predict convergence in income levels across countries conditional on rapid investment in R&D and human capital, fail to consider the role of weak and volatile aggregate demand and the segmentation of labor markets in explaining the persistence of both cross-country and within-country income inequality. In retrospect, the early tests of these theories of trade and growth suffered from sample selection bias, whereby the theory appears valid for a small sample of countries, but is rejected when a larger group of countries is considered. Invariably, this larger sample includes developing countries.

This chapter will critically review the recent growth and trade theories and assess their empirical support, referring both to the literature and to a survey of wages in specific occupations in major developing country urban centers. I show that the theoretical predictions are generally not borne out by the empirical evidence. The main point, however, is not the esoteric methodological issue of sample selection bias, but the more fundamental problem of model choice. Traditional trade theory views trade outcomes as reflecting factor endowments and competitive market processes. New growth theory amends the traditional model to incorporate the endogenous effects of fixed and human capital investments (rather than assuming a static stock of capital). Both are theories based on the efficiency and naturalness of market systems, which are driven largely by supply-side factors. Considerations of both aggregate demand and institutions are largely absent. I argue that observed labor market outcomes, especially of rising wage inequality in developing countries and international income divergence, can be traced to slow demand growth and labor market segmentation—two factors that have gone largely ignored in the recent revival of trade and growth theories.

The implication is of considerable importance for policy—both in terms of domestic macro policies and international policies regarding trade liberalization and the system of international payments. Widespread adoption of the Washington consensus array of market liberalization and restrictive macroeconomic policies has not generated the foreign investment demand in developing countries necessary to produce rates of economic growth sufficient for reduced inequality. And trade liberalization alone has not brought sufficient growth in demand for low-wage workers in developing countries. Thinking through a more institutional lens gives a very different set of policy options, for individual countries and for the international regulation of the globalization of production and finance. In the concluding section I focus on some policy alternatives to neoliberalism. But first, I begin with a review of the revival of mainstream free-market theories of international trade and economic growth.

II. Static Neoclassical Trade Theory

David Ricardo's theory of comparative advantage forms the basis for the modern theory of international trade and for the analysis of the implications of trade liberalization for income distribution. According to the principle of comparative advantage, free trade will be mutually beneficial if countries specialize in the production and export of those goods for which they have a relative cost advantage. The development of Ricardo's theory by Heckscher, Ohlin, Samuelson, and others in the 1930s and 1940s was to locate each country's relative cost advantage in its factor endowments, typically understood as its stocks of labor and capital. Accordingly, free trade should lead to a (mutually beneficial) pattern of specialization whereby capital-abundant countries produce and export capital-intensive goods and labor-abundant countries produce and export labor-intensive goods.

Protection and Real Wages

The implications of the factor endowments model for the distribution of income were laid out in two basic theorems developed by Paul Samuelson. The first relates directly to the question of trade liberalization and income distribution. According to the Stolper-Samuelson theorem, the imposition by one country of a tariff on its imports will result in an increase in the remuneration of the country's scarce factor relative to that of its abundant factor. Conversely, trade liberalization will raise the remuneration of a nation's relatively abundant factor of production and reduce that of its scarce factor.

With the publication of Adrian Wood's (1994) book, the Stolper-Samuelson theorem from 1941 re-emerged in the debate over the role of international trade in the growing gap between the wages of skilled and unskilled workers in industrialized countries. Wood reinterpreted the basic model in terms of two types of labor: low-skill and high-skill. In this case, the Stolper-Samuelson theorem predicts that trade liberalization will lead to a larger gap between wages of skilled and unskilled labor in those countries that are abundant in skilled labor, and reduce this gap in countries that are abundant in unskilled labor.

There has been a flurry of recent studies of the validity of the Stolper-Samuelson theorem for developed countries, especially the United States. Wage differentials in the United States have risen steadily over the past twenty years. The ratio of the wage of college graduates to that of high school graduates increased substantially between 1979 and 1997, from 1.56 to 2.24.[1] At the same time, import penetration has also grown. Despite the apparent positive correlation between the wage differential and import propensity in the United

States, studies vary widely in the estimated importance of changing trade patterns on the rising wage differential. Trade flows are variously reported to explain from 5 percent to 50 percent of the growth in the wage differential, with most studies placing the importance at 15–20 percent.[2]

The implications of the Stolper-Samuelson theorem for developing countries have received much less attention, although the theorem itself is logically symmetrical: trade liberalization should raise the wage differential in skilled-labor-abundant countries and at the same time lower the wage differential in countries abundant in unskilled labor. This optimistic prediction for developing countries has served to support the policy of trade liberalization in developing countries.

Until recently there was little available evidence on the impact of trade liberalization on the relative wages of workers by skill level in developing countries. But recent studies provide evidence that wage differentials are rising in many developing countries, too—contrary to the prediction of Stolper-Samuelson. Mexico has received more attention than most developing countries, no doubt because of its participation in NAFTA. Between 1984 and 1990, the ratio of average hourly compensation between skilled and unskilled rose over 25 percent (Hanson and Harrison 1995). Many other countries have also experienced a rise in the relative wage of skilled workers. A detailed study of nine countries— Argentina, Chile, Colombia, Costa Rica, Malaysia, Mexico, Philippines, Taiwan, and Uruguay—found that, after netting out labor supply changes, trade liberalization was associated with a rising wage differential in all cases except for the second liberalization episode in Argentina (1989–1993), when relative wages were stable (Robbins 1996). That is, "instead of trade liberalization compressing relative wages in LDCs, liberalization may sometimes widen wage dispersion" (Robbins 1996, 57). It should be noted that the second Argentine liberalization was also the only case in which trade liberalization was associated with *reduced* trade openness (as measured by exports plus imports as a share of GDP), largely due to an overvalued exchange rate that dampened exports. Moreover, even this result is overturned when we consider a longer time period: between 1986 and 1994 there was an increase in the return on investment in college education in Argentina and a decline in the return on investment in less-than-college education.[3]

Evidence from the Union Bank of Switzerland's survey of earnings by occupation in different cities reveals that the increase in the wage

Figure 8.1 **Ratio of Bank Clerk to Bus Driver Wages, Selected Cities**

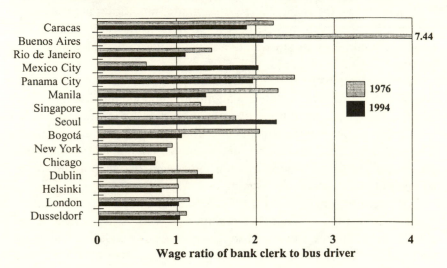

Source: Prices and Earnings Around the World, Union Bank of Switzerland, various issues. Bank clerk defined as "completed bank training and has about 10 years of experience." Bus driver defined as "unskilled or semi-skilled worker."

gap in developing countries from the late 1970s to 1994 was in many cases more pronounced than in developed countries. Some examples are shown in Figures 8.1 through 8.3, which take the occupation of bank teller as the benchmark "skilled" occupation and look at relative wages of bus drivers, construction workers, and textile workers—all described as "unskilled occupations."[4] In the developed countries, the ratio of the bus driver or construction worker wage to the bank clerk wage remained constant or rose slightly, indicating little change in the ratio of the wage of skilled to unskilled workers. In the developing countries, the ratios rise dramatically in most cases, and fall only for bus drivers in Singapore and Mexico City. For construction workers the ratio rose in every city surveyed, but the increases are by far the greatest in the Latin American cities, especially Bogotá, Panama City, Mexico City, Rio de Janeiro, and Buenos Aires. The case of textile workers is more mixed. In all developed countries sampled, the textile worker wage actually rose relative to that of the bank clerk. This was also true in some developing countries, most dramatically in Singapore and Mexico City. In Seoul, Rio de Janeiro, and Buenos Aires the relative skilled worker wage rose.

Figure 8.2 **Ratio of Bank Clerk to Construction Worker Wages, Selected Cities**

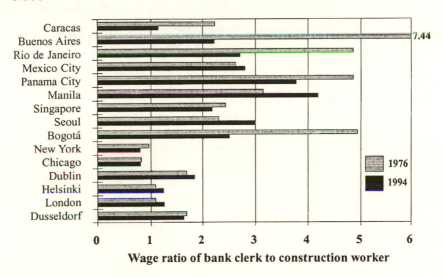

Source: Prices and Earnings Around the World, Union Bank of Switzerland, various years. Bank clerk defined as "completed bank training and has about 10 years of experience." Construction worker defined as "unskilled or semi-skilled worker."

The Paradox of Rising Wage Differentials

The Stolper-Samuelson theorem seems to fit the experience of many developed countries, especially the United States, where rising imports from low-wage countries are seen as contributing to the skill-biased technical change that is driving the growing wage gap. But when developing countries are considered, the theory fares less well.[5] Two explanations have been offered for the rising wage differential in many developing countries. One is that the theory functions at the regional level more than it does globally. Thus, while from a global perspective some countries are low-skill abundant, within their own region (sometimes referred to as "cones of diversification") they are in fact high-skill abundant (Davis 1996).

A second explanation is that trade liberalization accelerates the shift in labor demand toward the high-skilled through an increase in the degree of mechanization (and thus skill requirement) of production resulting from highly capital-intensive imports. Lowering tariffs raises the

Figure 8.3 **Ratio of Bank Clerk to Textile Worker Wages, Selected Cities**

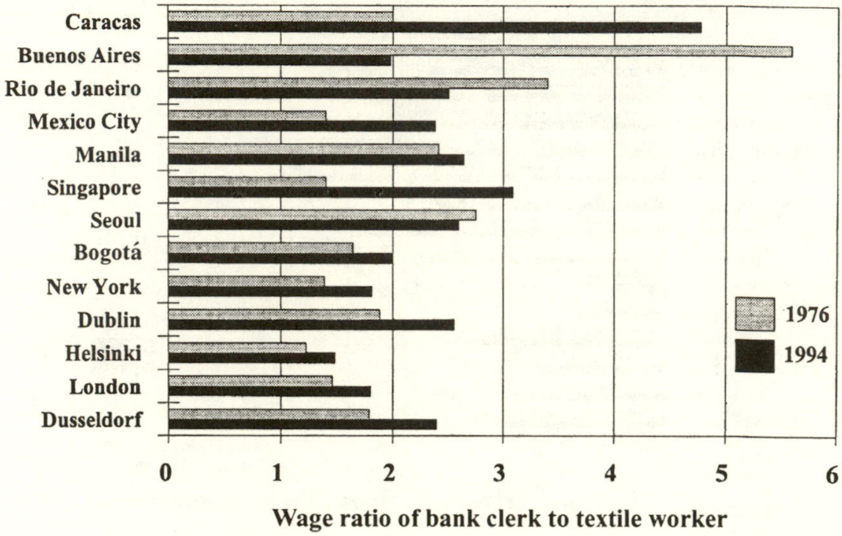

Wage ratio of bank clerk to textile worker

Source: Prices and Earnings Around the World, Union Bank of Switzerland, various years. Bank clerk defined as "completed bank training and has about 10 years of experience." Textile worker defined as "unskilled or semi-skilled worker."

ratio of imported capital to GDP and, in turn, the overall ratio of capital to output. This capital deepening brings a transfer of skill-biased technical change from developed countries. The same labor demand shift can result even without the import effect. If capital is mobile, then trade liberalization can shift the production of low-skill-intensive sectors in developed countries to developing countries where they are relatively skill intensive. Robbins (1996) refers to this phenomenon as "skill-enhancing trade." Markusen and Venables (1995) and Markusen (1996a, 1996b) associate the phenomenon with the activity of transnational corporations, but Feenstra et al. (1998) identify it more generally with outsourcing, which may be associated with arm's-length or non-arm's-length international trade. They write, "if skilled and unskilled labor are used in different intensities along the value chain of a product, outsourcing from a host to recipient country reduces the relative demand for unskilled labor *in both locations*" (p. 1, emphasis added). Using regional data from Mexico, Feenstra and Hanson (1997) find that in regions where foreign direct investment is concentrated, over half of the rise in the skilled labor wage share that occurred in the 1980s is associated with foreign outsourcing. I argue below that labor market segmentation under conditions of weak and volatile aggregate demand may also be important for the persistent (and in some cases growing) wage inequality in developing countries.

Equalization of Wage Levels

The second theorem on income distribution implied by the factor endowments model of trade is that of "factor price equalization," according to which free trade in goods and services creates a tendency for factor prices to equalize across countries, both relatively and absolutely. That is, both the ratio of factor prices—for example the ratio of the wage rate to the profit rate—and the absolute wage rates and profit rates in different countries should converge across countries when trade is liberalized. The logic of factor price equalization is close to that of the Stolper-Samuelson theorem. Under conditions of full employment, perfect competition and globally identical and constant returns to scale technology, free trade raises the remuneration to each country's relatively abundant factor. Since countries are, by definition, relatively abundant in different factors, the adjustment continues until factor prices are equalized across all countries. The astonishing insight from this theorem is that factor prices should equalize even in the absence of any international movement of the factors themselves.[6]

While there is some support for the view that trade liberalization has led to the equalization of rates of return on similar capital assets, there is much less evidence that globalization has brought an equalization of wages around the world.[7] In the absence of complete wage equalization, we should at least see some *tendency* for wage equalization when trade is liberalized—that is, factor price convergence. When we consider a sub-sample of countries that are similar in level of development, there is some evidence that wages across countries have converged. The evidence gets weaker as the number of countries included is increased. Focusing on the European Union, a number of studies find limited support for the hypothesis of cross-country convergence (as opposed to complete equalization) of wages and prices as a result of trade liberalization (van Mourik 1987). When the OECD as a whole is considered, the evidence is more mixed. From 1961 to 1984, rising international trade openness of OECD countries was associated with a convergence of wages across countries (Mokhtari 1992). After 1984, no clear convergence pattern is observed, and a number of industrialized countries, such as the United States and the United Kingdom, saw average real wages of production workers diverge notably from that of the highest-wage countries such as Germany. Table 8.1 reports an index of real compensation for manufacturing production workers in various countries. Among developed countries, German real wage growth was more rapid than in the United Kingdom or Japan, and the U.S. real wage actually fell. In Table 8.2 the real wages of all countries have been converted into U.S. dollars and then compared to German wages. The large and protracted appreciation of the U.S. dollar in the first half of the 1980s is evident in the rise in U.S. real wages relative to Germany. But after 1985, this exchange rate effect was reversing itself and U.S. real wages fell rapidly in relation to those in Germany, as did all countries in the sample with the exception of South Korea and Singapore. Even in own currency terms, average wages in the United States have fallen relative to other OECD countries, reflecting deindustrialization in high-wage manufacturing industries, declining unionization, a falling real minimum wage, and an increase in part-time employment. Especially notable about rising wage inequality in the United States is the collapse of wages for low-wage workers (see Howell et al. in this volume).

In sum, there appear to be at least four distinct patterns of countries. In addition to the two groups of industrialized countries—one divergent, but with positive wage growth (e.g., Japan and United Kingdom), the other experiencing stagnant or falling average real wages (e.g., United States)—there are also two groups of developing countries: one whose average real wages converge and one whose wages diverge from the level in the high-wage industrialized countries. The Asian NICs have had wages converge toward the level in the highest wage countries. Other developing countries (e.g., Mexico, Pakistan, Sri Lanka) have seen their already low wages diverge from—that is, grow at a slower rate than—that of the developed countries.

Regional data for real earnings in manufacturing confirm this pattern. Of the three developing regions, only East and Southeast Asia saw positive real wage growth since 1970, and at a robust rate of over 5 percent per annum. Real manufacturing wages in Latin America and the Caribbean declined by over 2.5 percent in the same period. And sub-Saharan Africa shifted from a period of stagnant real wages in the late 1980s to one of declines of over 12 percent from 1980 to 1988 (see

Table 8.1

Index of Real Hourly Compensation in National Currency, 1975–1995 (1975 = 100)

Year	Germany	U.S.	U.K.	Japan	Mexico	Pakistan	Sri Lanka	Korea	Singapore
1975	100	100	100	100	100	100	100	100	100
1976	104	103	100	99	133	102	102	112	108
1977	108	106	96	101	125	117	143	136	110
1978	112	107	104	104	154	139	182	162	113
1979	115	105	106	104	143	132	141	180	124
1980	118	101	109	102	121	111	113	168	133
1981	117	101	109	104	144	105	106	164	146
1982	118	102	110	106	132	111	121	175	156
1983	119	103	113	106	105	111	123	191	171
1984	119	102	114	107	97	100	118	203	187
1985	123	102	115	108	96	116	136	219	193
1986	127	102	120	110	84	131	135	229	175
1987	133	101	122	110	78	136	136	253	175
1988	138	100	125	114	72	127	133	290	190
1989	139	98	126	119	74	134	135	362	212
1990	144	97	127	124	74	N/A	140	411	228
1991	148	97	131	127	75	N/A	147	485	242
1992	148	97	133	131	79	N/A	140	550	254
1993	150	97	133	132	80	N/A	144	584	262
1994	152	96	131	134	84	N/A	147	623	287
1995	156	96	132	138	72	N/A	N/A	663	303

Source: Department of Labor, 1996. Series are deflated by CPI indexes from IMF International Financial Statistics, 1997.

Table 8.2

Real Hourly Compensation: Comparison to Germany, 1975–1995 (Germany = 100)

Year	Germany	U.S.	U.K.	Japan	Mexico	Pakistan	Sri Lanka	Korea	Singapore
1975	100	154	124	51	48	6	14	13	13
1976	100	156	100	49	51	6	12	15	13
1977	100	143	82	49	29	6	14	16	12
1978	100	121	81	54	30	6	8	15	11
1979	100	106	82	46	24	5	6	15	11
1980	100	98	89	42	20	4	4	11	12
1981	100	122	96	55	27	5	4	12	16
1982	100	132	90	53	12	5	5	13	18
1983	100	139	84	59	5	5	5	14	21
1984	100	153	83	66	3	4	4	16	26
1985	100	154	81	66	2	4	5	16	26
1986	100	110	69	68	1	3	3	12	17
1987	100	85	62	63	0.19	3	3	11	14
1988	100	80	65	69	0.10	2	2	13	15
1989	100	83	63	71	0.10	2	2	19	18
1990	100	68	58	58	0.07	N/A	2	17	17
1991	100	68	59	65	0.07	N/A	2	19	19
1992	100	64	56	66	0.07	N/A	1	19	20
1993	100	67	50	80	0.07	N/A	1	21	22
1994	100	65	49	85	0.06	N/A	1	21	24
1995	100	55	43	83	0.03	N/A	N/A	20	24

Sources: U.S. Department of Labor (1995). IMF (1997).

Note: Real compensation is the level of compensation in national currency divided by the market exchange rate, adjusted for changes in the CPI.

Table 8.3

Growth Rate of Real Earnings in Manufacturing by Region, 1970–1990

Region	Years	Average annual growth rate (%)
Sub-Saharan Africa	1975–80	−0.6
	1980–88	−12.3
Latin America and the	1971–80	−2.13
Caribbean	1971–92	−3.13
East and Southeast Asia[a]	1971–80	5.32
	1981–90	5.12

Source: Singh (1997).
[a] Includes Indonesia, Republic of Korea, Malaysia, Philippines, and Thailand.

Table 8.3). One clear implication from this is the divergence of average wages among developing countries themselves. In one dramatic example, real wages in South Korea have grown almost 700 percent since 1975, while real wages in Mexico fell 28 percent in the same period.

The focus on convergence or divergence of *average* wages veils important differences among workers of different skill levels or in different occupations. Wages of high-skilled workers across countries are converging onto those in high-wage countries, while wages of low-skill workers have diverged. This pattern can be seen in Figure 8.4, which shows wage dispersion (measured by the standard deviation divided by the mean) in different occupations for a sample of cities worldwide. From 1988 to 1994, the dispersion of wages of experienced bank clerks—a relatively skilled occupation—narrowed, while that of bus drivers rose slightly. The dispersion of construction worker wages was down slightly from 1988 to 1994, but remained at a much higher level than for bank clerks.

The lack of wage equalization has been attributed to two main factors: large differences in relative factor abundance and persistent differences in technology. Large differences in factor abundance imply that even with free trade the specialization pattern will not change enough to greatly alter relative factor demand. The other explanation of the failure for factor prices to equalize—the persistence of technological differences across countries—is also the best documented. The factor price equalization theorem is based on the assumption that all countries share the same technology and that the scale of production has no effect on

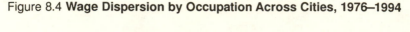

Figure 8.4 **Wage Dispersion by Occupation Across Cities, 1976–1994**

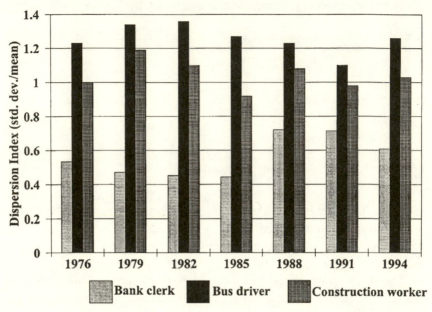

productivity. This will result in identical levels of productivity in each industry across countries. On the surface this might seem like a plausible assumption, given the expansion of international trade in relation to total output, and especially the rise in trade in intermediate products and the surge in foreign direct investment in the 1980s that give firms across countries access to inputs and technology at the same cost. But many studies have shown that technology differs widely across countries, especially at the level of particular industries (see, for example, Elmslie and Milberg 1992; or Trefler 1993, 1995).

More important than the fact that countries have different technology and productivity at the level of specific industries is that such technological differences across countries reveal a particular pattern: countries with high average productivity tend to have a high level of productivity across most sectors. A survey of twenty-eight industries in thirteen OECD countries revealed systematic differences in labor productivity across countries, even when an adjustment is made for differences in sectoral capital–labor ratios. The authors of this survey conclude:

What emerges most clearly is that the industrial countries use different techniques of production at the industry level, suggesting that factor prices are not equalized. In particular, *countries using more capital per worker in the manufacturing sector as a whole, tend to use more capital per worker in every industry, contrary to the prediction of the factor price equalization model.* (Dollar et al. 1988, 42 [emphasis added])

In fact, productivity gaps across sectors within a country are generally smaller than the productivity differences across countries within a given sector. Table 8.4 indicates the high positive and statistically significant correlation coefficient between sectoral productivity and the economy average for the G-7 countries.

One reason for this pattern is that innovation in a given sector may rapidly influence other sectors in the same economy. And these spillovers can have a cumulative effect. Numerous studies have shown that manufacturing productivity growth spurs productivity growth economywide, evidence of the well-known Verdoorn's Law. Moreover, differences in technology and productivity across countries persist despite the surge in international capital flows since 1980. Why do such technology "gaps" exist? While the expanded operations of transnational corporations certainly create more channels for the international diffusion of new technologies, there is considerable evidence that innovation and technological change are particular to each country, its set of institutions and regulations (Lundvall 1992; Nelson 1993). Moreover, the diffusion of technology internationally is not instantaneous or straightforward, and obviously depends not only on the level of international trade and foreign investment, but also on the form that such an operation takes—that is through direct investment or joint venture or licensing or other channels.

III. Mainstream Theories of Economic Growth

Globalization and Convergence

Economic globalization is the internationalization of production and finance. This process has taken place at least since the end of World War II and at an increased pace since the 1970s, when the Bretton Woods agreement collapsed, leading to the privatization of foreign exchange risk. Trade and foreign direct investment have grown more rapidly than output, and gross international financial flows have grown at explosive

Table 8.4

Correlations Between Average and Sectoral Productivity Levels, G-7 Countries, 1993

Industry	Pearson	Spearman
Food, beverages, and tobacco	0.8113*	0.5714
Textiles, apparel, and leather	0.7784*	0.4286
Wood products and furniture	0.8923**	0.8929**
Paper, paper products, and printing	0.9037**	0.7500
Chemicals and drugs	0.9569**	0.7500
Petroleum refineries and products	−0.3257	−0.2857
Rubber and plastic products	0.7981*	0.6071
Non-metallic mineral products	0.9207**	0.8571*
Iron and steel	0.9175**	0.8929**
Non-ferrous metals	0.4879	0.7500
Metal products	0.9479**	0.8929**
Electrical equipment and machinery	0.9833**	0.9286**
Shipbuilding and repairing	0.2657	0.5714
Motor vehicles	0.8500*	0.7857*
Aircraft	0.9575**	0.7857*
Other transport equipment	0.5203	0.8286*
Professional goods	0.8876*	0.2571
Other manufacturing	0.4369	0.4643
Average	0.7217	0.6516

Source: Milberg (1997b).
Notes: Productivity is value added per unit of output in 1985 U.S. dollars converted with actual exchange rates. Asterisks (* and **) indicate significance at the 5 and 1 percent levels, respectively, using two-tailed tests.

rates. The process, spurred to an important extent by a combination of financial deregulation and trade liberalization, was expected to bring a harmonization of different national economies through the unification of capital markets, increased competitive pressures on prices, and more rapid international diffusion of technology. The result would be a unified world economy, characterized by a convergence of prices and productivity and ultimately of standards of living.

The globalization ideal of economic convergence was supported by the dominant theory of economic growth, the Solow-Swan model (Solow 1956; Swan 1956). The model predicts that all economies will converge to a single level of average per capita income, a result known as "absolute convergence." The logic of this strong prediction is that if countries differ only in terms of the size of their capital stock (i.e., assuming technological change, population growth, and saving rates are similar across countries), then because of diminishing returns to capital, countries with a relatively large capital stock will have a low rate of return on capital and less incentive for the accumulation of new capital. Conversely, in countries with a relatively small initial endowment of capital, the presence of diminishing returns means there will be a high rate of return on capital and relatively strong incentives for capital accumulation. This implies that countries with little capital will have a lower income level initially but grow more rapidly than the relatively rich countries with a large initial stock of capital, resulting in convergence.

The recognition of a persistence in the gap in living standards across countries (as well as the availability of new, large data sets making it possible to measure such persistence) led, in part, to a reconsideration of the theory of economic growth. The past ten years have seen a rejection of the traditional model of economic growth and the rise of new models of endogenous growth, with novel implications for the convergence of growth rates and in living standards across regions and countries.[8] In particular, the new growth theories reject the possibility of absolute convergence, and raise the likelihood that convergence will not occur at all or will occur only when a series of other conditions are the same in all countries, including the rate of national saving and population growth as well as the rate of growth of investment in education and R&D. The inverse relation between the initial level of income and the rate of economic growth predicted by the Solow-Swan model depends on the assumption that countries differ only in terms of the size of their capital stock. In reality they differ in many other respects. When other factors affecting growth, such as the propensity to save, the rate of population growth, the level of educational attainment, or the degree of trade openness, are explicitly taken into account, then the same inverse relationships between the initial level of per capita income and the rate of economic growth is called "beta convergence" or "conditional convergence."[9]

The main difference between the new and old theories of growth is that the new models reject the assumption of diminishing marginal returns of factors of production and allow for the possibility that the rate of productivity growth is not given, but can vary across countries depending on the rate of investment in human capital and R&D and from "learning by doing." In the Solow-Swan model, growth can come from growth in the stock of inputs—capital or labor—or from increased efficiency of these inputs. The growth rate is thus given exogenously, that is, it depends on the given rate of investment, population growth, and the rate of technological progress. Adding to the stock of capital or labor will increase economic output, but with diminishing returns to each input. Functional income distribution (the wage and profit rates) is determined by the marginal productivity of each factor, and thus depends on the given technology. Economic growth alters the distribution of income, since it results in a change in the productivity of each of the factors of production. Economic policy plays little role in the growth process according to this theory, since the sources of growth are not determined within the economic process itself, but are assumed given.[10]

In the new theories of economic growth, technology and technological change are endogenous in that they depend on the cost of, and thus relative rate of return on, inventing and adopting new technologies. Moreover, capital is redefined to include human capital and infrastructure. The models do not predict absolute convergence, since countries with an initial advantage in terms of capital stock may enjoy a growing gap between themselves and those countries with a small initial endowment.

Evidence on Growth Rate Convergence

One of the reasons for the rejection of traditional growth theory was that its prediction of absolute convergence was simply not supported for a large sample of countries since 1960 (Sala-i-Martin 1996). When industrialized countries alone are considered, absolute convergence was strong from 1960 to 1973 and then slowed afterwards. But when a larger sample of countries is included, the opposite pattern emerges, especially in the period since 1973.

The difference in the results from these two samples of countries comes from the fact that, on average, poor industrializing countries have grown more slowly than rich industrialized ones since 1973. Verspehagen (1992) divided the larger sample of countries into four groups—developed market economies, NICs, oil exporting countries, and others—and performs a similar test of absolute convergence. His results show that of these four groups there was convergence in every case except "other," which is the non-OPEC, non-NIC, developing countries. Specifically, the developing country group ("other") was the only group that saw the gap in per capita income compared to the United States grow over the period 1960–1986 (Verspehagen 1992, 81–82).

IV. Demand Stagnation and Segmented Labor Markets

The distributional effects of globalization predicted by the mainstream economic models have not been realized. International wage equalization has not occurred. Wage differentials have risen as predicted in the industrialized countries but, contrary to prediction, the wage differential between high- and low-skill jobs has also grown in many developing countries. And the convergence of rates of economic growth and national income levels predicted by the neoclassical growth model has also not taken place in the post–Bretton Woods era. To the contrary, divergence is the more commonly observed pattern, whether it is characterized as such, or as "conditional" or "club" convergence. The factor price equalization and Stolper-Samuelson theorems are based on a static model of factor price determination and are inadequate for tracking the dynamics of productivity and wage growth or stagnation. But more important than the success of any particular theory is to understand why economic integration has not brought the expected beneficial effects on growth and distribution in developing countries and to find policies that encourage the beneficial aspects of globalization without inducing its regressive distributional effects.

An alternative is to look at labor market institutions and macroeconomic forces to explain the global rise in wage inequality and the persistent differences in wages between developed and developing countries. Such factors have been largely absent in the recent revival of trade and growth theories, since these theories typically assume full employment and allow only for human capital differences across workers. But employment and wage growth are closely linked. This is especially true for the wages of low-skilled workers. For example, during the years of rapid growth in the U.S. economy, 1948–1973, low-skill workers saw their wages rise at the same rate as the wages of high-skilled (or highly educated) workers (Mishel and Bernstein 1996). For developing countries, significant growth in employment and wages can only come with structural economic change—that is, industrialization. Successful industrialization has, in most cases, been preceded or accompanied by a significant rise in productivity in agriculture (Syrquin 1996). At the same time, as I argued above, countries that enjoy a high level of average productivity usually demonstrate high productivity across a broad spectrum of industries.

But while average wages typically rise with productivity, increases in productivity require demand and output growth as much as improvements in human capital and R&D expenditure. Thus it is likely that wages of low-skill workers in developing countries have stagnated not only because of insufficient investment in human capital, but because of inadequate demand and investment growth. We have seen that in industrialized countries, high rates of labor productivity growth are positively associated with high rates of growth of output. And of course output growth depends on demand. Thus the problem of rising wage differentials within developing countries and the persistent gap in real wages between developed and developing countries cannot be adequately explained by a skill bias toward high-skill workers on the demand side of the labor market, be it the result of technological change or international trade. A combination of low aggregate demand growth and segmented labor markets—that is, significant portions of the labor force whose labor is undervalued compared to other segments—is sufficient to bring about a failure of both wage convergence between developed and developing countries and a narrowing of the wage gap in developing countries. Moreover, these tendencies may be mutually reinforcing: when aggregate demand is weak or volatile, labor market segmentation is likely to become more rigid. Conversely, lower average wages can dampen both consumption demand and profit expectations on which investment demand hinges.[11]

When labor markets are segmented, such as between unionized and non-unionized sectors or between male and female occupations, then the effect of slow aggregate demand growth on wages will be different for different segments. Well-organized workers, for example, may continue to see their wages rise, while low-skill and poorly organized workers may not be able to achieve wage gains of the same magnitude.[12] In some countries, wages of low-skill workers have even fallen in absolute terms over the past twenty-five years.

V. Policy Alternatives to Neoliberalism

The new growth theories have provided an explanation of absolute growth rate divergence. But by focusing only on the supply side, these theories tend to oversimplify the task facing those countries that are not on a convergence path. To the extent that trade liberalization encourages some countries to specialize in non-dynamic sectors, these countries may get locked into a low-growth path (Dixon and Thirlwall 1975; Elmslie and

Milberg 1996). This is particularly important in light of the discussion above of the high degree of correlation in productivity across sectors within countries. Thus, the basis for questioning the relevance of the factor price equalization theorem—the persistence of technology gaps across countries over time—is also important for an understanding of the divergence of growth rates across countries.

By definition, jumping from one convergence club to another is a difficult task. For one, specialization and trade patterns are relatively fixed over time.[13] But clearly some countries—in particular the Asian NICs—have broken out of the straightjacket of static comparative advantage. In no case have supply-side policies alone been adequate. Intervention to spur demand growth (whether through trade policy or industrial policy), and the increased ability of workers to organize and bargain, has featured prominently in every case.

Globalization and Demand Expansion

What are the potential areas for more rapid growth in aggregate demand? Most studies find, not surprisingly, that investment, and particularly fixed investment, is a key variable (DeLong and Summers 1991).[14] That is, developing countries that experience a significant and sustained increase in investment are most likely to see a rise in economic growth. Rodrik (1999) defines an "investment transition" as a "sustained increase in the investment/GDP ratio of five percentage points or more" and finds that "investment transitions are associated with significant increases in economic growth" (pp. 58–59).

The weakness of this solution is that investment growth is itself mainly a function of the growth of economic activity that raises profit expectations. Higher savings alone will not generate greater investment.[15] One implication of this view is that public investment can "crowd in" private investment. What about foreign direct investment as an engine of demand growth? Relative to the domestic investment needs of most developing countries, the pool of available foreign direct investment is relatively small. Overall, foreign direct investment has rarely been the driving force for growth. In fact, it has often lagged, following in the path of politically stable, growing economies. Moreover, the suppression of labor and environmental standards as a means to attract foreign capital is often ineffective (Milberg 2000).

Export growth is a second key source of demand acceleration. Export-led growth is certainly not a new idea, but it is often ignored in the recent literature on endogenous growth. The new growth theories focus largely on the supply side, and especially the increasing returns to human capital accumulation. Thus trade is assumed in these models to affect growth not because of its impact on demand, but because of supply-side effects from technological diffusion and knowledge spillovers (Grossman and Helpman 1991). The demand-side impact of trade comes from export growth, not from trade openness per se. According to McCombie and Thirlwall (1997, p. 23), "the degree of openness may pick up the static gains from trade and the scope for knowledge spillovers, but not the dynamic benefits brought about by a faster growth of exports allowing other components of demand to grow faster." Trade influences economic growth both directly, by affecting demand for final goods, and indirectly, through its influence on investment. In general, increased export growth means that other components of demand can grow without tightening the balance-of-payments constraint.

Of course not all countries can simultaneously enjoy export-led growth in the sense of running a trade surplus, since total world exports cannot exceed world imports. But certainly the rate of growth of exports can be raised simultaneously for all countries without necessarily worsening the trade balance in *any* country. This will hinge on more rapid growth in developed countries, and especially among countries enjoying a surplus in the balance of payments. Thus a third aggregate demand management policy concerns the organization of the global payments system, which currently has a built-in deflationary bias in its requirement of balance-of-payments adjustment by deficit countries. Davidson (1997) has rekindled Keynes's post-war idea of a payments system in which surplus countries would bear some burden of adjustment, encouraging more trade, foreign direct investment, or foreign aid.

Labor Standards and International Trade

With respect to trade, one policy response is the linking of labor standards to trade liberalization. Labor standards refer to factors affecting the process of labor markets and their outcomes. The five most widely recognized *process* standards are the right of association (ILO Convention 87), the right to organize and bargain collectively (ILO Convention 98), the prohibition of forced labor (ILO convention 105), limitations on child labor (ILO Convention 138), and non-discrimination in employment (ILO Convention 111). Labor market *outcome* standards include a minimum wage, limits on working hours, and workplace health and safety standards. Proposals to link labor (and environmental) standards to trade liberalization take a variety of forms, but generally call for a penalty, such as a temporary tariff, to be imposed on the country that is found to be in violation of those rights or standards.

The economic argument for labor standards is a variant of the standard market failure argument: if even segments of the labor force are undervalued relative to their true economic contribution, then raising the value of that labor will not only benefit those workers affected directly, but also lead to a more efficient use of resources and greater overall output.[16] At the extreme, the labor market is "monopsonistic"; that is, there is a single employer who more or less dictates the wage. But undervaluation also arises if the labor market is segmented, so that pay for groups with similar productivity is not uniform, due to discrimination or inadequate information. According to Sengenberger and Wilkinson:

> The case for labour standards—universally applied equitable terms and conditions of employment—rests on the recognition that labour markets are deeply segmented by power relationships so, in the absence of countervailing regulation, labour is undervalued to varying degrees. Far from determining equal pay for work of equal value . . . the institutions on the supply and demand sides of the labour markets operate so as to discriminate between claimants in the allocation of job opportunities and in doing so generate wage inequalities which bear little or no relationship to the value contribution of individual workers. (1995, 118–119)

The pervasiveness of labor market segmentation in developing countries gives support to the view that labor standards are justified on efficiency grounds.[17] Lee (1996, 385) puts the issue succinctly: "Labor that is cheap because workers are denied the right to join a union is fundamentally different from labor that is cheap because it is plentiful."

VI. Conclusion

The revival of trade and growth theories supporting economic liberalization gives important intellectual support for the recent wave of neoliberalism. To acknowledge that market liberalization in practice has not had its theoretically predicted effects is not to deny the socially de-

sirable aspects of competition, in particular its promotion of technological innovation, organizational efficiency, and even the creation of new
wealth. But to recognize the inequalizing and deflationary effects of
global liberalization as presently constituted is to open up the possibility of removing these from the competitive process and focusing competition on those aspects that are deemed socially desirable.

Notes

I am grateful to Jim Stanford and to Richard Kozul-Wright for suggestions on an
earlier draft, and to Josh Bivens for excellent research assistance. This research was
supported in part by the Global Interdependence Division of UNCTAD.

1. This growing wage gap is the result of a rise in the real wage of those with
college or more advanced education, and a fall in the wage of those with less than a
four-year college education.
2. See Belman and Lee (1996) for a survey of the literature.
3. Pessino (1995), cited in Amadeo (1998).
4. The precise descriptions of the occupations are contained in the notes to the
Figures.
5. Howell et al. (1998) argue that the evidence does not support the theory even
in the case of developed countries.
6. The dramatic prediction of the factor price equalization theorem hinges on
the stringent assumptions listed above. As a result, even some of the original theorists doubted the empirical relevance of the theorem (see Leamer and Levinsohn
1995, 1356). But factor price equalization has also been proven to be logically consistent with conditions of imperfect competition and strategic firm behavior. See
Helpman and Krugman (1985).
7. The focus of this chapter is labor market, not capital market, outcomes. Regarding the latter, empirical studies generally confirm covered but not uncovered
interest rate parity across major industrialized countries. See Piggot (1993/94).
8. Early versions of this approach are Romer (1986) and Lucas (1988).
9. "Sigma convergence" is defined as a reduction in the dispersion of income
levels across the sample of countries. Not all cases of beta convergence also exhibit
sigma convergence. "Club convergence" is the clustering of countries at different
levels of income. For a comparison of these alternative definitions, see Sala-i-Martin (1996). Note also that there is considerable debate about the type of convergence
implied by each of the particular growth models (Galor 1996).
10. For this reason, Syrquin (1996) argues that the Solow-Swan model is of little
relevance for developing countries.
11. On the volatility of aggregate demand, see UNCTAD (1995). On the link
between volatility and labor market segmentation, see Saint-Paul (1997, Chapter 3).
12. See Sengenberger and Wilkinson (1995). For a detailed discussion of the
shift in labor market norms as an alternative explanation of rising wage differentials
in the United States, see Howell (1997).
13. See Wolff (1996) and Gagnon and Rose (1995). Lee (1995) documents the

exceptional performance of South Korea in successfully altering the composition of its exports by moving into higher value added sectors between 1965 and 1992.

14. Blomstrom et al. (1996) provide evidence that the causality is in fact reversed and that investment is "caused" by prior output growth. Rodrik (1999, 65), however, argues that increased profitability will initially spur output and only later investment, thus supporting the view that over time investment drives output.

15. This Keynesian view on the direction of causality between saving and investment has been confirmed empirically in a number of recent studies. See, for example, Gordon (1995).

16. Swinnerton (1998) reviews each of the core labor standards individually to assess the degree to which they raise efficiency. He shows that all of them, except child labor restrictions, are unambiguously efficiency improving.

17. A dynamic complement to this view is that labor productivity may rise in response to higher wages or improved working conditions. In this case, raising standards could raise the international competitiveness of the low-standard countries, increasing world welfare, but with different distributional consequences than those hoped for by any "disguised protectionist." See Piore (1994) for a discussion of the possibility that higher standards promote more efficient and flexible production techniques.

References

Amadeo, Eduardo. 1998. "Wage Inequality in the New and Old Trade Theories." In *Transnational Corporations and the Global Economy*, ed. Richard Kozul-Wright and Robert Rowthorn. London: Macmillan Press.

Belman, Dale, and Thea Lee. 1996. "International Trade and the Performance of U.S. Labor Markets." In *U.S. Trade Policy and Global Growth*, ed. Robert Blecker. Armonk, NY: M.E. Sharpe and The Economic Policy Institute.

Blomstrom, Magnus, Robert E. Lipsey, and Mario Zejan. 1996. "Is Fixed Investment the Key to Economic Growth?" *Quarterly Journal of Economics* 111, no. 1 (February): 269–276.

Davidson, Paul. 1997. "Are Grains of Sand in the Wheels of International Finance Sufficient to Do the Job When Boulders Are Often Required?" *Economic Journal* 107, no. 442 (May): 71–86.

Davis, Donald. 1996. "Technology, Unemployment, and Relative Wages in a Global Economy." Harvard Institute for International Development. Development Discussion Paper no. 549.

DeLong, J. Bradford, and Lawrence H. Summers. 1991. "Equipment Investment and Economic Growth." *Quarterly Journal of Economics* 106, no. 2 (May): 445–502.

Dixon, Robert, and Anthony Thirlwall. 1975. "A Model of Regional Growth Rate Differences on Kaldorian Lines." *Oxford Economic Papers* 27, no. 2 (July): 201–214.

Dollar, David, William Baumol, and Edward Wolff. 1988. "The Factor Price Equalization Model and Industry Labor Productivity: An Empirical Test Across Countries." In *Empirical Methods for International Trade*, ed. R. Feenstra. Cambridge, MA: MIT Press.

Elmslie, Bruce, and William Milberg. 1992. "International Trade and Factor Intensity Uniformity: An Empirical Assessment." *Weltwirtschaftliches Archiv* 128, no. 3: 464–486.

———. 1996. "The Productivity Convergence Debate: A Theoretical and Methodological Reconsideration." *Cambridge Journal of Economics* 20, no. 2 (March): 153–182.

Feenstra, Robert, and Gordon Hanson. 1997. "Foreign Direct Investment and Relative Wages: Evidence from Mexico's Maquiladoras." *Journal of International Economics* 42, no. 3/4 (May): 371–393.

Feenstra, Robert, Gordon Hanson, and Deborah Swenson. 1998. "Offshore Assembly from the United States: Production Characteristics of the 9802 Program." University of California-Davis. Mimeo.

Gagnon, Joseph, and Andrew Rose. 1995. "Dynamic Persistence of Industry Trade Balances: How Persistent Is the Product Cycle?" *Oxford Economic Papers* 47, no. 2 (April): 229–248.

Galor, Oded. 1996. "Convergence? Inferences from Theoretical Models." *Economic Journal* 106, no. 437 (July): 1056–1069.

Gordon, David M. 1995. "Putting the Cart before the Horse: The Investment–Saving Relation Revisited." In *Macroeconomics after the Golden Age*, ed. Gerald Epstein and Juliet Schor. Cambridge, UK: Cambridge University Press.

Grossman, Gene, and Elhanan Helpman. 1991. *Innovation and Growth in the Global Economy*. Cambridge, MA: MIT Press.

Hanson, Gregory, and Anne Harrison. 1995. "Trade, Technology, Wage Inequality." Cambridge: National Bureau of Economic Research. Working Paper no. 5110.

Helpman, Elhanan, and Paul Krugman. 1985. *Market Structure and Foreign Trade*. Cambridge, MA: MIT Press.

Howell, David. 1997. "Institutional Failure and the American Worker: The Collapse of Low-Skill Wages." Annandale on Hudson, NY: The Jerome Levy Economics Institute of Bard College. Public Policy Brief no. 29.

Howell, David, Margaret Duncan, and Ben Harrison. 1998. "Low Wages in the U.S. and High Unemployment in Europe: A Critical Assessment of the Conventional Wisdom." New York: New School for Social Research, Center for Economic Policy Analysis. Working Paper no. 5.

Howell, David, Ellen Houston, and William Milberg. 2000. Chapter in this volume.

International Monetary Fund. 1997. *International Financial Statistics*. CD-ROM.

Leamer, Edward, and James Levinsohn. 1995. "International Trade Theory: The Evidence." In *Handbook in International Economics*, vol. 3, ed. Gene Grossman and Ken Rogoff. Amsterdam: Elsevier.

Lee, Jaimin. 1995. "Comparative Advantage in Manufacturing as a Determinant of Industrialization: The Korean Case." *World Development* 23, no. 7 (July): 1195–1214.

Lee, Thea. 1996. "Trade Policy and Development: Spurring Good Growth." *Current History* 95, no. 604 (November): 382–387.

Lucas, Robert. 1988. "On the Mechanics of Economic Development." *Journal of Monetary Economics* 22, no. 1 (July): 3–42.

Lundvall, Bent, ed. 1992. *National Systems of Innovation*. London: Pinter.

McCombie, John, and Anthony P. Thirlwall. 1997. "The Dynamic Harrod Foreign

Trade Multiplier and the Demand-Oriented Approach to Economic Growth: An Evaluation." *International Review of Applied Economics* 11, no. 1 (January): 5–26.

Markusen, James. 1996a. "Multinational Production Skilled Labor and Real Wages." Cambridge, MA: National Bureau of Economic Research, Working Paper no. 5483.

———. 1996b. "The Theory of Endowment, Intra-Industry, and Multinational Trade." Cambridge, MA: National Bureau of Economic Research, Working Paper no. 5529.

Markusen, James, and Anthony Venables. 1995. "Multinational Firms and the New Trade Theory." Cambridge, MA: National Bureau of Economic Research, Working Paper no. 5036.

Milberg, William. 2000. "Foreign Direct Investment and Development: Balancing Costs and Benefits." *International Monetary and Financial Issues*. Geneva: UNCTAD, forthcoming.

Mishel, Lawrence, and Jared Bernstein. 1996. *The State of Working America*. 1995–96. Armonk, NY: M.E. Sharpe.

Mokhtari, Manocher. 1992. "Do Wages and International Trade Follow an Equilibrium Path?" University of Maryland. Mimeo.

Nelson, Richard, ed. 1993. *National Innovation Systems*. New York: Oxford University Press.

Pessino, Charles. 1995. "The Labour Market during the Transition in Argentina." Buenos Aires: CEMA. Mimeo.

Piggot, Charles. 1993–1994. "International Interest Rate Convergence: A Survey of the Issues and Evidence." *Federal Reserve Bank of New York Quarterly Review* 18, no. 4 (Winter): 24–37.

Piore, Michael. 1994. "International Labor Standards and Business Strategies." In *International Labor Standards and Global Economic Integration: Proceedings of a Symposium*, ed. Gary Schoepfle and Kenneth Swinnerton. Washington, DC: U.S. Department of Labor.

Robbins, Donald. 1996. "Evidence on Trade and Wages in the Developing World." Paris: OECD Development Center, Technical Paper no. 119.

Rodrik, Dani. 1999. *Making Openness Work*. Washington, DC: Overseas Development Council.

Romer, Paul. 1986. "Increasing Returns and Long Run Growth." *Journal of Political Economy* 94, no. 5 (October): 1002–1037.

Saint-Paul, Gilles. 1997. *Dual Labor Markets: A Macroeconomic Perspective*. Cambridge, MA: MIT Press.

Sala-i-Martin, Xavier. 1996. "The Classical Approach to Convergence Analysis." *Economic Journal* 106, no. 3 (July): 1019–1036.

Sengenberger, Werner, and Frank Wilkinson. 1995. "Globalization and Labour Standards." In *Managing the Global Economy*, ed. J. Michie and J. Grieve Smith. Oxford: Oxford University Press.

Solow, Robert. 1956. "A Contribution to the Theory of Economic Growth." *Quarterly Journal of Economics* 70, no. 1 (February): 65–94.

Swan, Trevor. 1956. "Economic Growth and Capital Accumulation." *Economic Record* 32, no. 2 (November): 334–361.

Swinnerton, Kenneth. 1998. "An Essay on Economic Efficiency and Core Labor Standards." *World Economy* 20, no. 1 (January): 73–86.

Syrquin, Moshe. 1996. "Modern Economic (Endogenous) Growth and Development." Mimeo.

Trefler, Daniel. 1993. "International Factor Price Differences: Leontief Was Right." *Journal of Political Economy* 101, no. 6 (December): 961–987.

———. 1995. "The Case of the Missing Trade and Other Mysteries." *American Economic Review* 85, no. 5 (December): 1029–1046.

Union Bank of Switzerland (various issues). "Prices and Earnings Around the World." Geneva.

UNCTAD. 1995. *Trade and Development Report*. Geneva: United Nations.

United States Department of Commerce. Bureau of Labor Statistics. 1996. "International Comparisons of Hourly Compensation Costs for Production Workers in Manufacturing, 1975–1995." Supplementary Tables for BLS Report 909.

van Mourik, A. 1987. "Testing the Factor Price Equalisation Theorem in the EC: A Comment." *Journal of Common Market Studies* 26, no. 1 (September): 79–86.

Verspehagen, Bart. 1992. *Uneven Growth between Interdependent Economies*. Maastricht: University of Limburg.

Wolff, Edward. 1996. "Productivity Growth and Shifting Comparative Advantage on the Industry Level." New York University. Mimeo.

Wood, Adrian. 1994. *North-South Trade, Employment and Inequality: Changing Fortunes in a Skill-Driven World*. Oxford: Clarendon Press.

9

Isabella Bakker

ENGENDERING THE ECONOMICS OF GLOBALIZATION

I. Introduction

The work of David Gordon is marked by a deep concern for challenging injustice and inequality. His writings reflect a dynamic approach imbued with an analysis of power that recognizes the co-existence of exchange and coercion in economic relations. In this sense, his work is the expression of what Sam Bowles and Richard Edwards (1993) have referred to as "three-dimensional economics." Three-dimensional economics goes beyond the one-dimensional view of neoclassical accounts of markets as sites of competition and exchange. Markets, and all of the relationships that go with markets, are in this view also inscribed by aspects of command—that is, economic relationships in which power plays a predominant role—and change—which refers to the way in which the operation of the economic system alters over time. This time dimension captures the historically embedded nature of social systems and of social relations. All three aspects—competition, command, and change—are also a focus of the writings of the heterodox tradition within feminist economics.[1]

Along with insights on the complex working of economies, David Gordon's intellectual contributions are also grounded within a tradition of ethical dialectical reasoning suggesting a constant process of debate. Part of an Aristotelian tradition of putting forth a thesis to an audience, it presumes an interaction with a community involved in deliberation and evaluation. Ultimately, ethical dialectical reasoning involves making a choice or considering what action or policy is best (Waller and Jennings 1990). This normative dimension of engaging in shaping public action also informs feminist economic discourse as does Gordon's recognition of the situatedness and partiality of knowledges.

These dual insights about the nature of knowledge and the multidimensional character of economics are central to the epistemological debates within feminist economics. I would like to further engage in the ethical dialectical dialogue that runs through Gordon's writings by reflecting on some of the scholarship that incorporates gender into the economic paradigm. Recent efforts to "engender economics" offer new entry points to one of the central concerns of David Gordon's work—the critical analysis of social structures and relations in the context of the global political economy.

The scholarship on engendering economic analysis facilitates a deeper understanding of the processes of globalization, restructuring, and economic crises by foregrounding absences in economic accounts of sustainability. Feminist economists see globalization as part of a broader process of restructuring of the state and civil society, of political economy and culture, and of the domestic sector. Gender is seen as important to extending our analysis of globalization and the political and policy responses to that process in a number of sites. This chapter will consider how markets, states, and the domestic sector constitute and re-constitute gender orders in the context of globalization.

The current phase of globalization is marked by an extension and deepening of market relations. More and more aspects of everyday life have become pervaded by market values and symbols, as hyper-mobile capital and scientific and technological innovation compress time and distance. Commodification becomes all-encompassing, yet at the same time, large numbers of people are almost totally marginalized from sharing in its outcomes (Gill 1995). These changes do not necessarily affect men and women in the same way, suggesting that they are positioned differently with respect to market transformations. Although more women are being drawn into market relations as workers, consumers, shareholders, and investors, a large proportion continue to be only indirectly linked to the market. Women continue to be disproportionately concentrated in unpaid production, including subsistence production, informal paid work, domestic production, and volunteer work (Beneria 1999; UNDP 1999).[2]

Moreover, as markets spread, people become increasingly dependent on the workings of markets for survival through the selling of goods or labor. This can create opportunities, but also increases the vulnerability of many people. In particular, markets can play a role in entitlement failures. Entitlement refers to the combined effect of owning resources and being able to use them. Someone may own assets and have labor power (what Dreze and Sen 1989 refer to as endowments) yet they will lack entitlement if they cannot sell their assets or are unable to find paid employment (see Wuyts, Mackintosh, and Hewitt 1992, Chapter 1). Entitlement failures can result from a sudden rise in prices of necessities such as food, a drop in wages, or job loss. Feminist economics has illustrated how entitlement failures occur along gender lines. An example is legislation that limits women's access to land and productive resources and restricts their rights to employment, income, and personal safety (Beneria and Bisnath 1996). While neoclassical economics tends to emphasize women's and men's entitlements and their resulting location in the economy as the outcome of preferences and choices, feminist economics introduces institutional barriers and obstacles to exercising choices as well as the limits set by initial entitlements.

The other issue crucial to a consideration of globalization and its impact on gender orders is that of public provisioning—the ways in which societies provide goods and services through non-market institutions (Wuyts, Mackintosh, and Hewitt 1992). There are many variations in the mix of public provisioning depending on the wealth of a country and its political traditions of public action for the improvement of living standards. Public provisioning includes state, charitable, and voluntary provision of goods, services, and social security benefits. A gender-sensitive notion of provisioning would capture, in addition to the state and voluntary sectors, the provisioning through the domestic sector of both human capacities and the provisioning values that distinguish the domestic sector from the commercial values of the private sector and the regulatory values of the public sector. The circulation of values adds to an analysis of flows of money and real resources. By incorporating provisioning values of the domestic sector, this model introduces the idea that the moral order is something produced in part by activities within the sectors and transmitted between them. Hence, it does not remain as an assumed parameter exogenous to political economy (Elson 1998).

One aspect of globalization related to public provisioning has been the simultaneous redeployment and "hollowing out" of national state powers (Jessop 1997). States have redeployed their energies toward international markets and investments. At the same time, there has been a hollowing out of the state's policy capacity, especially at the level of macroeconomic policy. Declining fiscal capacity and the streamlining of policy toward a more laissez-faire model has shaped both the nature and quantity of state public provisioning. The restructuring of states has involved both downsizing and a change in how remaining public goods and services, such as education, health, and environmental standards, are delivered to citizens. Not only have states withdrawn from the public economy, forcing people to rely on the private sphere of the family, but remaining public-sector activities are also being reshaped according to private-sector rules and criteria. This is often a function of both national political decision making and international trade agreements such as NAFTA and Mercosur (see Bakker 1999, for a more detailed discussion).

This chapter will link a discussion of the economic sites and socially embedded economic processes of globalization to a gender-aware framework. Several contributions of feminist economics to macroeconomic frameworks in particular will be highlighted:

- Gender bias results from both the absence of a gender-aware framework and the ways in which gender *is* incorporated into economic analysis.
- A three-dimensional view of economic processes offers both a power dimension as well as a temporal dimension to neoclassical notions of competition and exchange. Gender relations constitute an important element of each of these three dimensions.
- Three distinct levels of economic analysis characterize feminist heterodox economics (Figure 9.1). Bringing a gender-aware approach to these three levels creates the foundations for a more complete economics based on provisioning, which recognizes that human capacities require both care and material goods to thrive.

II. Conceptual Starting Points

From Gender-Neutral to Gender-Biased

A major question that separates neoclassical and critical approaches within feminist economics is how gender bias is construed: Is the problem one of actual policies and concepts that are gender-biased, or one of pre-existing gender relations? Generally, feminist neoclassical econo-

Figure 9.1 **Engendering Economics**

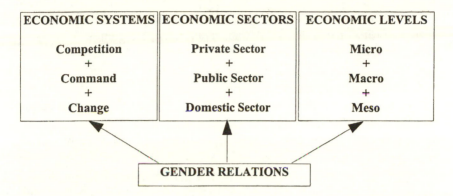

mists would subscribe to the former view, feminist critical economists to the latter. Mukhopadhyay (1994), for example, suggests that it is the social context rather than the economic concepts themselves that are to blame for gender bias in macro outcomes. It is the possibility of bias in the *use* of conceptual frameworks rather than bias in macro policies per se that is the issue, according to this perspective. One key starting point for feminist critical economics is the observation that gender imbalances cannot be rectified primarily through human capital accumulation, that more structural factors may persist which need to be addressed. These structural factors are not simply the problems related to the "incompleteness" of markets (see below), but are also due to the unequal distribution of resources and decision-making power, and the power relations that underpin a fluid and culturally determined gender division of labor reflected in markets and the domestic sector.

Economic Sectors

Feminist economics foregrounds the interaction of productive and reproductive activities, creating the foundations for a more complete economics (Nelson 1996). Fundamentally, economies are a collection of labor processes, some paid and others unpaid, each of which has distinct inputs and outputs. Productive activities refer to the process of creating goods and services that are consumed in society. The reproductive economy consists of people, not merely the process of biological reproduction but also the feeding, caring, replenishing, and daily maintenance of family, household, and community members. Reproductive work and voluntary community work could, in principle, be done by men or women—but provisioning has been socially constituted as mainly the responsibility of women rather than men in most societies. A focus of feminist economics is to make this unpaid work visible and to restructure the provision of care in a more equal fashion between women and men, private and public institutions.

This requires a wider vision of the economy that sees national output as a product of the interaction of the domestic sector alongside the public and the private sectors, producing services including the reproduction of the labor force on a daily and generational basis.

Figure 9.2 (from Elson 1998) depicts a gender-aware circular flow of the national economy, showing the flows of values between sectors as well as flows of money and real resources. The diagram illustrates the production of goods, services, and values by the three sectors. Contrary to conventional economic accounts, the public sector is not simply seen as redistributing income through taxation, benefits, and expenditure; the public sector is also a producer of public services. Similarly, the labor force is treated as a produced means of production rather than as a natural resource like land; the domestic sector produces labor services, including physical, technical, and social capacities.

Captured in Figure 9.2 is also the issue of the depletion and replenishment of human energies and provisioning values in the domestic sector. As Elson notes:

> The production of labor capacities (physical, technical and social) depletes human energies, which need replenishing if the level of labor services is to be maintained. Replenishment requires inputs from the public and private sectors. The domestic sector cannot therefore be seen as a bottomless well upon which the other sectors can draw: unless the inputs from the public and private sector are sufficiently nourishing, human capacities and provisioning values will be destroyed and they will drain away from the circular flow. . . . (1998, 203)

Feminist economists have related these insights to the restructuring of the public and private sectors prompted by policy-induced measures such as Structural Adjustment Policies (SAPs) and broader globalization forces that reinforce tax competitiveness, discourage deficit financing, and enshrine private property rights through trade agreements (Bakker 1994; Brodie 1997; Grunberg 1998; Young 1999).

Figure 9.2 **Business, States, and Households in the Organization of Production**

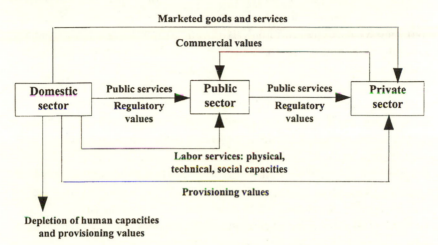

Marketed goods and services

Commercial values

| Domestic sector | Public services / Regulatory values | Public sector | Public services / Regulatory values | Private sector |

Labor services: physical, technical, social capacities

Provisioning values

Depletion of human capacities and provisioning values

Note: Figure 2. "The Circular Flow of Output of Goods and Services" from "The Economic, the Political and the Domestic: Business, States and Households in the Organisation of Production" by Diane Elson, *New Political Economy* 3:2 (1998), 189–208.

Reprinted with permission from the publisher, Taylor & Francis Ltd., P.O. Box 25, Abingdon, U.K., OX14 3UE, www.tandf.co.uk.

Economic Levels

In addition, feminist critical economics recognizes three distinct levels of analysis—the macro, the meso, and the micro—with corresponding gender biases built in at the analytical level which then shape subsequent policy responses. Male bias is the result of an inadequate account of the inequalities between women as a gender and men as a gender (Elson 1994; Bakker 1994). Neoclassical economics treats the micro, meso, and macro levels as fully integrated: the macro level focuses on monetary aggregates like total output and expenditure, which are seen as the coherent result of the activities of millions of individuals (micro), which are integrated by the institutions of the meso level (markets, firms). Feminist critical economics unpacks each level of the economy for male bias and critiques the microfoundations of neoclassical economics.

At the micro level, differences and inequalities between women and men are not simply explained as a matter of differences in preference and resource endowments; power and preferences are analyzed as socially constructed and socially entrenched asymmetries in rules and resources giving certain individuals power over others to shape their options. At the meso level, markets are not intrinsically gendered (that is, biased toward men or women), but do become the "bearers of gender," that is, gender relations shape the relations between women and men as they participate in markets. Labor markets, for example, create separate male and female spheres based on distinct gender hierarchies and social norms about femininity and masculinity. The macro level of monetary aggregates is criticized as male biased because it omits from its analysis a whole area of production—the unpaid production of human resources. While micro level analysis is criticized for the way in which it conceptualizes gender, meso and macro level analyses are criticized for the activities and values that are left out. In particular, the view that the reproductive economy will continue to function no matter what changes in the rest of the economy leads to policies that may not be sustainable (in economic and human terms) in the long run.

How heterodox feminist economics "engenders" the three dimensions of economic analysis—competition, command, and change—will be the focus of the rest of this chapter.

III. Engendering Competition, Command, and Change

Gender, Competition, and Command: The Horizontal and Vertical Dimensions

Markets may represent a positive development for groups previously excluded from economic independence; however, like other institutions guided by social relations, markets are very likely to reflect and reify existing resource allocations and socially constructed gender divisions of labor that influence endowments. While markets entail opportunities (the exchange dimension) they also involve risk such as unemployment and changes in demand for certain goods. So in order to counteract market insecurity, non-market safety nets (kin, community, state provisions) are necessary (Razavi and Miller 1997). This insight highlights one of the limits of a purely production-oriented approach to political and economic globalization. Non-market relations are key to gauging the nature and depth of the globalization process as it plays itself out in the daily lives of real people, of women and men.

Market-based regulation and coordination of disparate economic activities influence what kind of people we become through the shaping of preferences and values; they are, as Bowles suggests, "social settings that foster specific types of personal development and penalize others"

(Bowles 1991, 13). The operation of markets, the formation of prices, and the organization of production intrinsically rely on the operation of social and institutional norms that reflect the incompleteness of contracts. Supplementing the analysis of market relations with insights from institutions operating at the meso level—that is, the structures that mediate between individuals and the economy, such as public-sector agencies—would allow for social norms and networks to be introduced into the analysis of behavior and decision making. For instance, laws in many countries continue to be based on the assumption that women are dependents of men (Equality Now 1999), and their use of public services, their access to land and credit, are therefore mediated through men rather than directly secured by women as independent persons. Similar restrictions apply in advanced industrial economies in terms of welfare state and social security provisions.

The non-market relations that surround and structure all markets also become important in considering the terms on which people come to the market (Mackintosh 1990). This is significant for a gender-aware economic analysis because it introduces space for the notion that market goods and services are allocated through the political structure and social relations of markets, which may promote dominance and subordinacy between parties to an exchange (the command dimension). Sharing similarities with some of the institutional economics literature, these writings introduce the importance of social norms, values, and networks into economic analysis. On the one hand, family and kinship relations are gender ascriptive—the terms of wife, husband, sister, and brother ascribe male and female gender. Conversely, relations between a buyer and a seller, or an employer and employee, taxpayers and citizens, are not intrinsically gendered but become the bearers of gender as the social norms and networks that underpin them are profoundly gendered (Elson 1994).

A gendered dynamic process shaping institutions beyond the household sees gender relations as constituting institutions in such a way that they reproduce gender inequalities to varying degrees. Specifically gendered market failures have been identified, such as markets not investing in and rewarding women's productive and reproductive work, financial intermediaries excluding women (and the poor), and public institutions failing to include women in an equal manner in terms of services and expenditures (Goetz 1997, 5). The research on financial and agricultural sector reform and gender (see below) offers a number of good examples of how the horizontal (exchange) and vertical (command) dimensions of markets shape women's supply responses.

Economists working within the neoclassical tradition, influenced by institutional economics, have conducted studies that recognize the barriers that exist to achieving neoclassical goals of utility maximization and efficient resource allocation. For example, Haddad et al. (1995) cite studies showing that women are less able than men to reallocate their time between different activities. This is related to two factors stemming from the asymmetry in men's and women's obligations, rights, and bargaining positions within the household: the gender-based assignment of household roles restricts the substitution of male and female labor time; and women's labor immobility is also explained by the failure of the household economy to transmit changing price incentives to women. Ingrid Palmer refers to these gender-based distortions as a "reproductive labor tax," which she sees as a kind of tithe levied against women's unpaid work in reproduction, distorting their ability to engage in income-generating activities and acting as a kind of externality to their maximal resource allocation. She argues that, "like all taxes it influences the allocation of resources, in this case in the form of penalizing women's labor time in other activities which are both remunerative and more open to productivity increases" (Palmer 1992, 79).

Sally Baden (1998) has argued that the failure to take gender issues into account when designing and implementing liberalization policies may lead to inefficient outcomes in terms of women's access to markets be it as buyers, sellers, or traders. Financial liberalization addresses the conditions in formal financial markets and macroeconomic aggregates such as saving, investment, and interest rates. Baden uses a gender analysis to reveal gender-based institutional biases in financial and agricultural markets undergoing liberalization. This then is one aspect of the feminist economics literature that can help to engender the competition and command aspects of markets. Table 9.1 (from Baden) highlights key gender issues in financial liberalization based on an evaluation of Latin America and Asia since the 1970s, and more recently, the experience of sub-Saharan Africa.

The work in feminist economics on hierarchies in labor markets, states, and bureaucracy can enhance our understanding of competition and command. This raises the more general issue of gender balance in economic decision making at the macro, meso, and micro levels of the economy. Who decides and who participates in formal and informal decision-making structures? At the macro level, is economic policy a male domain?

Table 9.1

Gender Issues in Finance at the Macro, Meso, and Micro Levels

The Macro Level: Gender variables, such as the degree of feminization of the labor force, may have an association with, or influence on, aggregate investment and savings patterns. The allocation of credit between different sectors (e.g., formal vs. informal; different sectors of activity) may have implications for gender-differentiated access to credit. For example, concentration of credit in manufacturing and cash crops, rather than services or food crops, would create an implicit bias against women's access in many countries.

The Meso Level: Gender may have a significant bearing on transactions costs and issues of imperfect information, which affect the functioning of financial markets. Financial institutions exhibit gender biases, sometimes rationing credit along gender lines, in terms of the proportion of women served, or the loan size granted. Relationships of *market interlinkage* and *trust* built up around financial transactions clearly have gender dimensions, in terms of women's cumulative disadvantage. Women are disadvantaged not just by their limited property rights but also by their relatively low engagement in formalized economic activity and by social barriers to women's mobility and interactions with men, in some societies. This often leads to segmentation of markets along gender lines.

The Micro Level: Gender divisions of responsibility and labor and power within the household lead to gender-differentiated patterns of demand for financial services, and differing patterns of control over financial and other assets. Women's responsibility for day-to-day expenditures combined with their weaker bargaining position will tend to make it harder for them than for men to set aside savings and keep them separate. On the other hand, their responsibility for household budgets may afford opportunities for discreet accumulation.

At the meso level of state and market institutions and organizations, whose voices are heard? Here a gender-aware analysis of government departments, chambers of commerce, women's groups, farmers' cooperatives, and other organizations could be undertaken. Finally, at the micro level, who participates as a worker, trader, or public service consumer and under what conditions? A series of Gender-Aware Country Analyses have been conducted by a team of economists at the University of Manchester under the leadership of Diane Elson, to apply these questions to sector reform strategies.[3]

Gender and Change: The Temporal Dimension

The time dimension of economic systems has been a focus of feminist economists who analyze restructuring of macroeconomies due to globalization pressures or policy-induced measures such as SAPs. This is a vast literature and cannot be surveyed in detail here. Rather, the focus will be on heterodox attempts at modeling macroeconomic change. This is followed by an example of one policy intervention that incorporates the gender-aware insights of three-dimensional economics: efforts to engender government budgets at the national level.

In a way that is similar to the traditionally gender-neutral conceptualization of markets, the analytical foundations of macroeconomics are not linked to a gender relations analysis. Emerging out of the postwar acceptance of Keynesian, demand-oriented economic policies, macroeconomics is preoccupied by aggregate measures of economic change such as output levels, their fluctuations and relationship to rates of growth, unemployment and inflation, the budget surplus/deficit, levels of government expenditure and taxation, the changing balance between different sectors of the economy, and monetary and exchange-rate policy.

Despite the absence of "people" at the level of macroeconomic theory and measurement, there are, nevertheless, built-in assumptions about the individual—he [sic] is, paradoxically, both a commodity and a rational economic person. There are also assumptions about the determinants of the level and pattern of economic activity; about human capacities, how they are allocated to production, and how they are reproduced and maintained. The conceptual starting points for a gender-aware approach to macroeconomics build on the insights of the previous sections. They are effectively summarized in a special issue of *World Development* edited by Cagatay, Elson, and Grown in 1995:

1. Though social institutions may not be intrinsically gendered themselves, they bear and transmit gender biases. Being socially constructed institutions, "free markets" also reflect and reinforce gender inequalities.
2. The cost of reproducing and maintaining the labor force in a given society remains invisible as long as the scope of economic analysis does not include unpaid "reproductive" labor. Thus, unpaid work needs to be made visible and the economic meaning of work redefined to include unpaid reproductive labor.
3. Gender relations play an important role in the division of labor and the distribution of work, income, wealth, and productive inputs, with important macroeconomic implications. This also implies that economic behavior is gendered.

From these insights four different approaches to gender-aware macro modeling have been developed (Cagatay, Elson, and Grown 1995). The first method[4] involves disaggregation by gender and highlights the implications of differences in the behavior of the two genders. An example is Collier et al.'s model of labor reallocations during structural adjustment (1994). A second approach involves the introduction of the gender dimension of certain macroeconomic variables into the model. For instance, how labor markets, credit and goods markets function is shaped by degrees of gender inequality. Also decision making in the domestic, private, and public sectors depend on various aspects of gender relations. The World Bank's Revised Minimum Standard Model (RMSM) is an example illustrating how potential changes, such as including unpaid labor in the incremental capital–output ratio, would alter the value of the ratio as well as its policy prescriptions (Elson 1995). The third approach divides the economy into a productive sector that comprises the traditional macroeconomic variables, and a reproductive sector that entails provisioning goods and services. The goal is to analyze the interaction of the two sectors in terms of flow and stock variables. Taylor's Social Matrix Model (1995), which inserts different hypotheses about the linkages between the sectors, is an example of a potential method. The fourth approach combines a number of the previous approaches. For instance, Erturk and Cagatay (1995) use a growth cycle model to explore how secular and cyclical changes in the degree of feminization of the labor force and the intensity of female household labor influence macroeconomic variables (Cagatay 1998).

The next section will highlight one example of how insights from these models can be used to scrutinize macroeconomic policies for the gender-based effects.

Policy Innovations: Engendering National Budgets

By the early 1980s, a shift in focus in feminist economics was fueled by a change in the macro policy environment away from Keynesian thinking to neo-liberal economics, which stressed stabilization and structural adjustment policies. For gender practitioners, the need to extend their critical insights beyond discrete micro-level projects to macroeconomic policies became quickly apparent as policy increasingly focused on cutting back aggregate public expenditure and the money supply in order to reduce deficits and curb inflation (Razavi 1996). This meant increasing scrutiny by Ministries of Finance and multilateral development and lending agencies such as the World Bank.

In response, some feminist scholars and activists in the North (Canada, Australia, Switzerland, the UK) and the South (Barbados, Mozambique, Namibia, Tanzania, Sri Lanka, South Africa, Uganda) have begun to concentrate on "engendering" the main economic debates of the day by scrutinizing national budgets (Budlender, Sharp, and Allen 1998; Commonwealth Secretariat 1999; Bakker 1999). Gender-sensitive budgets represent a transition from advocacy to accountability: they audit government budgets for their impact on women and girls, men and boys. Some are conducted from within government (Australia, for example) and some are launched by NGOs, activists, and researchers outside of government.

The Women's Budget Initiative (WBI) in South Africa, started in 1995, is unique as it is a joint effort of parliamentarians and non-governmental organizations. Starting as a research project, six sectors of the budget — welfare, education, reconstruction and development, labor, trade union/ industry, and health—were initially examined from a gender-disaggregated perspective. Also included were taxation and public-sector employment as cross-cutting categories. With the assistance of a cross-country gender-based budget initiative launched by the Commonwealth Secretariat, the 1998 Budget Review issued by the Ministry of Finance included a gender impact analysis of the departments of Land Affairs, Public Service and Administration, Public Works, Trade and Industry, Water and Forestry, Labor, and Art and Culture. Several seminars on gender and public expenditure and on South Africa's Medium Expenditure Framework were also initiated in conjunction with Finance. The introduction of a Medium Term Economic Framework in 1997 meant that government and its agencies would plan programs and budgets on a three-year, rolling basis, which allows for longer-term planning at the macroeconomic and sectoral levels. To date, four women's budgets have been completed covering the full complement of sectors falling under the national budget.

The most visible result of the WBI has been that government reviews of sectors now incorporate a gender-sensitive analysis. In terms of policy change, there has been a fine-tuning and improved targeting of the National Public Works Program (Budlender, Sharp, and Allen 1998). Reprioritization of sectoral expenditures has been the major thrust emerging from the South African WBI. Efforts are currently under way to popularize the WBI material in an effort to reach citizens who are illiterate. To this end, *Money Matters: Women and the Government Budget* was produced in 1998 (Hurt and Budlender 1998). The book is written at a level targeted to a second-language English speaker with ten years of education. A similar "translation" is under way of local government analysis.

Gender-sensitive budget analyses are accountability tools that link a gender-disaggregated analysis of expenditures and revenues to potential losses for national economies in at least three ways: (1) *False economies.* Reductions in public expenditure or the introduction of user fees may add to women's unpaid work. This can have feedback effects on the macro economy due to shifts in time use away from GDP-enhancing activities. (2) *Poor targeting.* The targeting of transfers to households may not recognize that women and men have different priorities and powers within households. This can have an impact on the well-being of children and overall poverty-reduction objectives. (3) *Loss of output.* Not taking gender into account in planning education and other expenditures may impact on national economic growth in the long-run (Elson 1994).

The major argument for a gender-sensitive budget analysis rests with the fact that policy makers cannot assume that government expenditures and taxation measures impact equally on men and women as they generally occupy different social and economic positions complicated by relations of race, class, and other social markers. So good policy making requires a gender-sensitive analysis of fiscal policies. Such an analysis goes beyond considering the size of the national deficit/surplus, and delves into the combination of expenditures and revenues that produce it.

At the level of political economy, gender-sensitive budgets, along with other participatory alternative budget initiatives,[5] can challenge the technical discourse of deficits and balanced budgets that increasingly circumscribe the possibilities of political practice in both the North and the South. Technical discourses remove issues from the realm of public debate by limiting discussion to those who master the required technical language of economics. Those labeled as non-technical advocates—like labor, women's groups, and environmental actors—are quickly dismissed as special interests in contrast to tax lawyers, accountants, and financial experts, who are portrayed as representing the general interest of a good business climate (Philipps 1996). Official discourse about economic restructuring tends to emphasize certain macroeconomic indicators of governmental performance, including deficit reduction and interest rate stability. This is presented as advancing a common good and economic progress. Yet this prescription rests on certain assumptions about the actors who comprise the economy. The individual who underwrites this discursive economy is relatively autonomous and able to participate in markets, is mobile between sectors and regions, and can access a limitless supply of social reproductive services in the family when they are withdrawn from the state (Philipps 1996). This "conceptual silence" obscures the social foundations of market relations— their embeddedness—including their gendered and racial underpinnings (Bakker 1994).

IV. Conclusion

This brings me full circle to the discussion at the outset of this chapter. We began with a recognition of David Gordon's complex understanding of economic systems as both knowledge structures and material social relations. Although not explicitly formulated as competition, command, and change, these three dimensions of economic systems capture many of Gordon's ideas and offer an entry point for heterodox economists to engage with feminist economic scholarship. Feminist economists have argued that each of these dimensions is imbued with social relations marked by gender: the social construction of masculinities and femininities. Gender relations create societal networks of hierarchical, regulated social relations which become institutionalized through social norms, rules, and divisions of labor. Feminist economic research on institutions, the economics of production and provisioning, absent and biased markets, and macroeconomic restructuring enhance a three-dimensional consideration of economies.

New policy interventions, briefly discussed in this chapter, such as gender-sensitive national budgets and gender-aware country reports, bring together a broader vision of the economy and economic decision-making. Such innovations can only strengthen Gordon's critical analysis of social structures and relations in a global political economy marked by both cohesion and crisis.

Notes

I would like to extend deep thanks to Diane Elson for her comments on an earlier draft and her intellectual generosity and kindness. I would also like to thank Hande Keklik and Mumtaz Keklik for their comments and support. Thanks also to Jim

Stanford for asking me to write this chapter and to reflect on the contribution of David Gordon. David was my teacher from 1979 to 1982 at the New School. He was a lovely and generous person, a committed "organic intellectual," and an excellent teacher. I am grateful to have learned from him and miss his spirit.

1. I use the terms "feminist heterodox" and "feminist critical" economics interchangeably to refer to scholars who draw on the Keynesian, Kaleckian, structuralist, and Marxist traditions within economics.

2. See the special issue on unpaid labor of *Feminist Economics* 2, no. 3 (Fall 1996).

3. See University of Manchester, Graduate School of Social Sciences, GENECON Unit, for a series of working papers on sectoral program support (health, transport) and gender-aware country economic reports (Bangladesh, Latin America, Nicaragua, Pakistan, Uganda).

4. This discussion draws heavily on Cagatay's more detailed overview. See Nilufer Cagatay (1998). See also Diane Elson (1995).

5. For other examples, see the United Nations Development Program Website at www.undp.org/poverty/events/budgets_wk.html.

References

Baden, Sally. 1998. "Gender and Market Liberalisation." Conference on Integrating Gender Issues in Programme Aid, Sector Investment Programmes, Market Reform and Other Forms of Economic Policy Assistance, Paris, May 6–7. Mimeo.

Bakker, Isabella. 1994. *The Strategic Silence: Gender and Economic Policy*. London and New York: Zed Press and the North-South Institute.

———. 1999. "Neoliberal Governance and the New Gender Order." *Working Papers* 1, no. 1: 49–59.

Bakker, Isabella, and Diane Elson. 1998. "Toward Engendering Budgets in Canada." *Alternative Federal Budget 1998*. Ottawa: Canadian Centre for Policy Alternatives.

Beneria, Lourdes. 1999. "Globalization, Gender and the Davos Man." *Feminist Economics* 5, no. 3 (November): 61–83.

Beneria, Lourdes, and Savitri Bisnath. 1996. *Gender and Poverty: An Analysis for Action*. New York: United Nations Development Program, GIDP Monograph 2.

Bowles, Samuel. 1991. "What Markets Can and Cannot Do." *Challenge* 34, no. 4 (July/August): 11–16.

Bowles, Samuel, and Richard Edwards. 1993. *Understanding Capitalism: Competition, Command and Change in the U.S. Economy*. New York: HarperCollins.

Brodie, Janine. 1997. "Meso-Discourses, State Forms and the Gendering of Liberal-Democratic Citizenship." *Citizenship Studies* 1, no. 2: 223–242.

Budlender, Debbie, ed. 1998. *The Third Women's Budget*. Cape Town: Institute for Democracy in South Africa.

Budlender, Debbie, Rhonda Sharp, and Kerri Allen. 1998. *How to Do a Gender-Sensitive Budget Analysis: Contemporary Research and Practices*. London: Commonwealth Secretariat.

Cagatay, Nilufer. 1998. "Engendering Macroeconomics Policies." New York: United Nations Development Program, BDP/SEPED Working Paper 6.

Cagatay, Nilufer, Diane Elson, and Caren Grown. 1995. "Introduction: Special Issue on Gender, Adjustment and Macroeconomics." *World Development* 23, no. 11 (November): 1827–1836.

Collier, Paul, A.C. Edwards, and J. Roberts Kalpana Bardhan. 1994. "Gender Aspects of Labor Allocation during Structural Adjustment." In *Labor Markets in an Era of Adjustment, Volume I*, ed. Susan Horton, Ravi Kanbur, and Dipak Mazumdar. Washington, DC: World Bank.

Commonwealth Secretariat. 1999. *Gender Sensitive Budget Initiatives Kit*. London: Commonwealth Secretariat.

Dreze, Jean, and Amartya Sen. 1989. *Hunger and Public Action*. Oxford: Clarendon Press.

Elson, Diane. 1994. "Macro, Meso and Micro: Gender and Economic Analysis in the Context of Policy Reform." In *The Strategic Silence: Gender and Economic Policy*, ed. Isabella Bakker. London: Zed Press/North South Institute.

———. 1995. "Gender Awareness in Modeling Structural Adjustment." *World Development* 23, no. 11 (November): 1851–1868.

———. 1998. "The Economic, the Political and the Domestic: Businesses, States and Households in the Organisation of Production." *New Political Economy* 3, no. 2 (July): 189–208.

Equality Now. 1999. *Words and Deeds: Holding Governments Accountable in the Beijing+5 Review Process*. New York: Equality Now.

Erturk, Korkut, and Nilufer Cagatay. 1995. "Macroeconomic Consequences of Cyclical and Secular Changes in Feminization: An Experiment at Gendered Modeling." *World Development* 23, no. 11 (November): 1969–1977.

Gill, Stephen. 1995. "Globalization, Market Civilisation, and Disciplinary Neoliberalism." *Millennium* 24, no. 3: 399–423.

———. 1998. "New Constitutionalism, Democratisation and Global Political Economy." *Pacifica Review* 10, no. 1 (February): 23–38.

Goetz, Anne Marie, ed. 1997. *Getting Institutions Right for Women in Development*. London and New York: Zed Books.

Grunberg, Isabelle. 1998. "Double Jeopardy: Globalization, Liberalization and the Fiscal Squeeze." *World Development* 26, no. 4, June: 591–605.

Haddad, Lawrence, Lynn Brown, Andrea Richter, and Lisa Smith. 1995. "The Gender Dimensions of Economic Adjustment Policies: Potential Interactions and Evidence to Date." *World Development* 23, no. 6 (June): 881–896.

Hurt, Karen, and Debbie Budlender, eds. 1998. *Money Matters: Women and the Government*. Cape Town: Institute for Democracy in South Africa.

Jessop, Bob. 1997. "Capitalism and Its Future: Remarks on Regulation, Government and Governance." *Review of International Political Economy* 4, no. 3 (Autumn): 561–581.

Kabeer, Naila, and John Humphrey. 1990. "Neo-liberalism, Gender, and the Limits of the Market." In *States or Markets? Neo-liberalism and the Development Policy Debate*, ed. Christopher Coclough and James Manor. Oxford: Clarendon Press.

Mackintosh, Maureen. 1990. "Abstract Markets and Real Needs." In *The Food Question: Profits vs. People?* ed. Henry Bernstein. New York: Monthly Review Press.

Mukhopadhyay, Swapna. 1994. "The Impact of Structural Adjustment on Women: Some General Observations Relating to Concpetual Bias." In *The Strategic Si-*

lence: Gender and Economic Policy, ed. Isabella Bakker. London: Zed Press/ North South Institute.

Nelson, Julie. 1996. "Feminism, Objectivity and Economics." In *Economics as Social Theory*, ed. Julie Nelson. London and New York: Routledge.

Palmer, Ingrid. 1992. "Gender Equity and Economic Efficiency in Adjustment Programmes." In *Women and Adjustment in the Third World*, ed. Haleh Afshar and Caroline Dennis. Basingstoke, UK: Macmillan.

Philipps, Lisa. 1996. "The Rise of Balanced Budget Laws in Canada: Fiscal (Ir)Responsibility." *Osgoode Hall Law Journal* 34, no. 4 (Winter): 682–740.

Razavi, Shahra. 1996. *Working towards a More Gender Equitable Macro-Economic Agenda*. Geneva: UNRISD.

Razavi, Shahra, and Carol Miller. 1997. *Gender Analysis: Alternative Paradigms*. New York: UNDP/BDP/GIDP, Monograph no. 6.

Taylor, Lance. 1995. "Environment and Gender Feedbacks in Macroeconomics." *World Development* 23, no. 11 (November): 1953–1961.

United Nations Development Program. 1999. 1998. 1997. 1995. *Human Development Report*. Oxford: Oxford University Press.

Waller, William, and Ann Jennings. 1990. "On the Possibility of a Feminist Economics: The Convergence of Institutional and Feminist Methodology." *Journal of Economic Issues* 24, no. 2 (June): 613–622.

Wuyts, Marc, Maureen Mackintosh, and Tom Hewitt, eds. 1992. *Development Policy and Public Action*. Oxford: Oxford University Press/The Open University.

Young, Brigitte. 1999. "Globalization and Gender: A European Perspective." In *Globalization and Democratization*, ed. Rita Mae Kelly, Jane Bayes, Mary Hawkesworth, and Brigitte Young. Oxford: Oxford University Press.

10

Lance Taylor

CAPITAL MARKET CRISES

LIBERALIZATION, FIXED EXCHANGE RATES, AND MARKET-DRIVEN DESTABILIZATION

I. Tolstoy Was Wrong (About International Capital Markets, at Least)

Everyone knows the epigraph to *Anna Karenina*, "Happy families are all alike; every unhappy family is unhappy in its own way." Tolstoy may well have been right about families, but the extension of his judgment to economies hit by capital market crises distinctly fails. Their causes and unhappy consequences in Latin America, Asia, and Eastern Europe over the past twenty years have many elements in common.

These boom and bust episodes were *not* caused by excessive fiscal expansion or the creation of wholesale moral hazards by market-distorting state interventions. Rather, they pivoted around the government's withdrawal from regulating the real side of the economy, the financial sector, and especially the international capital market. This premeditated laxity created strong incentives for destabilizing private sector financial behavior, on the part of both domestic and external players. Feedbacks of their actions to the macroeconomic level upset the system.

To think about how markets can be rebuilt in a more stable fashion, we have to understand why the crises happened in the first place. That is not an easy task. A plausible place to begin is with the models economists have designed to explain events such as Latin America's "Southern Cone" crisis around 1980, European problems with the ERM in 1992, Mexico and the "tequila" crisis in 1994, events in East Asia in 1997–98, and the Russian crisis of summer 1998. We start out in Section II with a review of mainstream work—accounting conventions, crisis models, "moral hazards," and other abstract niceties. Then we go on to a narrative proposed by people who operate close to macro policy choices and micro financial decisions. Experience shows that the overlap between mainstream models and the reality they are supposed to describe is slight; the practitioners' framework fits history far better. In Section III, it is used as a basis for suggestions about reasonable policy lines to follow in wake of the recent disasters.

II. Existing Theory

This section comprises a review of existing crisis theories. It begins with relatively innocuous but important accounting conventions, and goes on to present mainstream models and a more plausible alternative.

Accounting Preliminaries

A proper macroeconomic accounting framework is essential for disentangling the causes of financial crises: this subsection is devoted to laying one out. Table 10.1 presents a simplified but realistic set of accounts for an economy with five institutional sectors—households, business, government, a financial sector, and the rest of the world.

How each sector's saving originates from its incomes and outlays is illustrated in the top panel. Households in the first line receive labor income W, transfers from business J_b (that is, dividends, rents, etc.) and from government J_g, and interest payments X_h on their assets held with the financial system. They use income for consumption C_h, to pay taxes T_h, and to pay interest Z_h to the financial system. What's left over is their saving S_h. To keep the number of symbols in Table 10.1 within reason, households are assumed to hold liabilities of the financial system only. That is, their holdings of business equity are "small" and/or do not change, and they neither borrow nor hold assets abroad. The last two assumptions reflect a major problem with the data—it is far easier to register funds flowing into a country via the capital market than to observe money going out as capital flight by numerous less than fully legal channels. Repatriation of such household assets is implicitly treated as foreign lending to business or government in the discussion that follows.

Similar accounting statements apply to the other sectors. Business

Table 10.1

Macroeconomic Accounting Relationships

Generation of Savings

Household:	$S_h = W + J_b + J_g + X_h - C_h - T_h - Z_h$
Business:	$S_b = P - J_b - T_b - Z_b - eZ^*{}_b$
Government:	$S_g = T_h + T_b - C_g - J_g - Z_g - eZ^*{}_g$
Financial system:	$0 = Z_h + Z_b + Z_g - X_h$
Foreign:	$S_f = e[M + Z^*{}_b + Z^*{}_g - E]$
Resource Balance:	$S_h + S_b + S_g + S_f = W + P - (C_h + C_g) + e(M - E)$

Investment–Saving Balance $(I_h - S_h) + (I_b - S_b) + (I_g - S_g) = S_f$

Accumulation

Household:	$(I_h - S_h) = \Delta D_h - \Delta H_h$
Business:	$(I_b - S_b) = \Delta D_b + e\Delta D^*{}_b$
Government:	$(I_g - S_g) = \Delta D_g + e\Delta D^*{}_g$
Financial system:	$0 = \Delta H_h - (\Delta D_h + \Delta D_b + \Delta D_g) - e\Delta R^*$
Foreign:	$0 = S_f - e(\Delta D^*{}_b + \Delta D^*{}_g) + e\Delta R^*$

Spreads

Interest rate:	$\Sigma_i = i - [i^* + (\Delta e/e)^E] = i - (i^* + \hat{e}^E)$
Capital gains:	$\Sigma_G = (\Delta Q/Q)^E - [i^* + (\Delta e/e)^E] = \hat{Q}^E (i^* + \hat{e}^E)$

gets gross profit income P, and has outlays for transfers to households, taxes T_b, and interest payments to the local financial system (Z_b) and the rest of the world. The latter payment, $eZ^*{}_b$, amounts to $Z^*{}_b$ in foreign currency terms converted to local currency at the exchange rate e. Business saving S_b is profits net of these expenditures. It will be lower insofar as interest payments Z_b and $eZ^*{}_b$ are high. As discussed later, firms in Asia are said to suffer from constricted saving possibilities because their debt/equity ratios are high. Standard stabilization programs which drive up interest rates and currency values and thereby Z_b and $eZ^*{}_b$ can easily lead to heavy business losses (negative values of S_b), culminating in waves of bankruptcy.

Government saving S_g is total tax revenue net of public consumption C_g, transfers to households, and interest payments at home (Z_g) and abroad (eZ^*_g). For simplicity, the financial system is assumed to have zero saving, so that its interest income flows from households, business, and government just cover its payments to households. Finally, "foreign saving" S_f in local currency terms is the exchange rate times the foreign currency values of imports (M) and interest payments less exports (E). The implication is that the rest of the world applies part of its overall saving to cover "our" excess of spending over income.

This interpretation shows up clearly in the "resource balance" equation or the sum of all the savings definitions. Total saving results from the excesses of income from production ($P + W$) over private and public consumption ($C_h + C_g$), and of imports over exports. In other words, S_f equals total income minus total outlays and the sum of domestic saving supplies.

Likewise, the "investment–saving balance" shows that the sum over sectors of investment less saving must equal zero. Much of the macroeconomic drama in recent crises results from large shifts in these "financial deficits." They show up in each sector's accumulation of assets and liabilities in the penultimate panel of the table.

Households, for example, are assumed to finance their deficit ($I_h–S_h$) by running up new debt ΔD_h with the financial system, partially offset by their greater holdings of the system's liabilities or the increase ΔH_h in the "money" supply.[1] Business and government both cover their deficits by new domestic (the ΔD_b and ΔD_g terms) and foreign (the ΔD^*_b and ΔD^*_g terms) borrowing.

The accounts for the financial system and the rest of the world are slightly less transparent, but essential to the following discussion. The former's flow balances show that new money creation ΔH_h is backed by increases in domestic debt owed by households, business, and government, as well as by increases in the system's foreign reserves $e\Delta R^*$. In the foreign balance, reserve increments and foreign saving are "financed" by increases in the foreign debts of business and government $e(\Delta D^*_b + \Delta D^*_g)$.

How the "spreads" in Table 10.1's last panel enter the analysis is taken up below. What we can do now is say something about how the public sector was supposed to be the prime culprit for "old" financial upheavals, such as the debt crisis of the 1980s. As will be seen shortly, this assertion is far from the truth, but it is so widely accepted that we must discuss it on its own terms.

Mainstream Crisis Models

The first post–World War II wave of developing economy crises in which external financial flows played a significant role took place around 1980. The countries affected included Turkey in the late 1970s, the Southern Cone in 1980–81, Mexico and many others in 1982, and South Africa in 1985. The Southern Cone collapses attracted great attention. They teach significant lessons about how market deregulation by the public sector and private responses to it can be extremely destabilizing.

The academic models underlying the belief that the public sector "caused" the early crises are built around a regime shift (or "transcritical bifurcation" in the jargon of elementary catastrophe theory). They emphasize how gradually evolving "fundamentals" can alter financial returns in such a way as to provoke an abrupt change of conditions or crisis—a ball rolls smoothly over the surface of a table until it falls off.

The regime change is triggered when the profit from liquidating a "distortion" created by the state intervention becomes large enough—investors choose their moment to punish the government for interfering in the market. Such sentiments underlie balance of payments crisis models of the sort proposed by Krugman (1979) and pursued by many others. They assert that expansionary policy when the economy is subject to a foreign exchange constraint can provoke a flight from the local currency.[2]

In a typical scenario, the nominal exchange rate is implicitly assumed to be fixed or have a predetermined percentage rate of devaluation $\hat{e} = \Delta e \ / \ e$. Moreover, the local interest rate i exceeds the foreign rate i^*. Under a "credible" fixed rate regime, the expected rate of devaluation $\hat{e}^E = (\Delta e \ / \ e)^E$ will equal zero. From the last panel of Table 10.1, the interest rate "spread" $\Sigma_i > 0$ will favor investing in the home country.

Now suppose that the government pursues expansionary fiscal policy, increasing the fiscal deficit $I_g - S_g$. If the household and business sectors do not alter their behavior, the investment–saving balance in Table 10.1 shows that foreign saving S_f or the external current account deficit has to rise. A perceived "twin deficit" problem of this sort lies at the heart of traditional IMF stabilization packages that have thrown many countries (now including those in East Asia) into recession.[3] The external imbalance can lead to crisis via several channels. We describe two.

The first is based on the recognition that the government has to issue more debt—that is, in the "Accumulation" panel of Table 10.1, ΔD_g or ΔD^*_g must rise when $I_g - S_g$ is increased. Assume that the government is credit-constrained in external markets so that ΔD_g expands. To maintain its own balances, the financial system can "monetize" this new debt so that ΔH_h goes up as well. If the domestic price level is driven up by money creation (which does not always happen), then the real value of the currency will appreciate (or decline in absolute value). Imports are likely to rise and exports to fall, leading to greater external imbalance. With more borrowing ruled out by assumption, foreign reserves will begin to erode.

Falling reserves suggest that the trade deficit cannot be maintained indefinitely. When they are exhausted, presumably there will have to be a discrete "maxi"-devaluation, a regime shift which will inflict a capital loss on external investors holding liabilities of the home country denominated in local currency. At some point, it becomes rational to expect the devaluation to occur, making $\hat{e}^E$ strongly positive and reversing the spread. A currency attack follows. As with Hotelling's commodity stocks, the economically untenable fiscal expansion is instantly erased.

A second version of this tale is based on the assumption that the local monetary authorities raise "deposit" interest rates to induce households to hold financial system liabilities created in response to greater public borrowing. In the financial system balance in the first panel of Table 10.1, X_h will increase so that interest rates on outstanding domestic debts have to go up as well. The spread Σ_i immediately widens. Foreign players begin to shift portfolios toward home assets, so that from the foreign accumulation balance in Table 10.1, reserves begin to grow. If the monetary authorities allow the reserve increase to feed into faster growth of the money supply, we are back to the previous story. If they "sterilize" a higher ΔR_h by cutting the growth of household (ΔD_h) or business (ΔD_b) debt, then interest rates will go up even further, drawing more foreign investment into the system. From the foreign accumulation balance, pressures will mount for the current account deficit S_f to increase, say via exchange appreciation induced by inflation or else a downward drift of the nominal rate as the authorities allow the currency to gain strength. A foreign crisis looms again.

Moral Hazards

The notion of moral hazard comes from the economic theory of insurance. The basic idea is that insurance reduces incentives for prudence—the more fire insurance I hold on my house, the more arson becomes an intriguing thought. Insurance companies frustrate such temptation by allowing homeowners to insure their properties for no more than 75 percent or so of their market valuations.

In the finance literature, moral hazard has been picked up in diverse lines of argument. Writing in an American context, the unconventional macroeconomist Hyman Minsky (1986) saw it as arising after the 1930s as a consequence of counter-cyclical policy aimed at moderating real/financial business cycles. As is always the case, such economic engineering had unexpected consequences.

One was a move of corporations toward more financially "fragile" positions, leading them to seek higher short-term profitability. With no fears of price and sales downswings, high risk/high return projects became more attractive. This shift was exemplified by increased "short-termism" of investment activities, and the push toward merger and acquisition (M&A) activity in the 1970s and 1980s.

Second, the intermediaries financing such initiatives gained more explicit protection against risky actions by their borrowers through "lender of last resort" (or LLR) interventions on the part of the central bank. The resulting moral hazard induced both banks and firms to seek more risky placements of resources. Banks, in particular, pursued financial innovations. Among them were the elimination of interest rate ceilings on deposits and the consequent creation of money market funds which effectively jacked up interest rates in the 1970s, the Savings and Loan (S&L) crisis of the 1980s, the appearance of investment funds and "asset securitization" at about the same time, and the later emergence of widespread derivatives markets and hedge funds.

To an extent all these changes were driven by gradual relaxation of restrictions on external capital movements (D'Arista 1998). When Eurocurrency markets began to boom in the 1970s, the higher deposit rates they paid put pressure on U.S. regulators to lift interest rate ceilings. Meanwhile, without reserve requirements off-shore banks (and off-shore branches of American banks) could lend more cheaply in the domestic market, leading to further deregulation. The United States took the lead in pushing for new regulatory mechanisms (e.g., the "Basle" standards for capital adequacy adopted in 1988).

Unfortunately, these changes introduced a strong pro-cyclical bias into regulation, just the opposite of the sort of system that should be in place. In an upswing, banks typically have no problem in building up equity to satisfy adequacy requirements. In a downswing, however, unless they already have the capital they can easily be wiped out. As will be seen, such regulatory structures helped exacerbate developing country financial crises.

So far, the moral hazard theory looks sensible; it can be used to underpin plausible historical narratives. Extensions out of context, however, begin to stretch verisimilitude. Deposit insurance, for example, certainly played a role in the S&L crisis in the United States. In the Garn–St. Germain Act of 1982, depositors were allowed to have any number of fully insured $100,000 accounts with an S&L. With their prudential responsibilities removed by the Act, S&L managers were free to engage in any high risk, high return projects they saw fit—which they immediately proceeded to do.

However, a frequently stated extension of this observation to developing country markets makes less sense. For example, deposit guarantees have been accused of worsening the Southern Cone crises, but in Chile they had been abolished precisely to avoid moral hazard! Similarly, for South Korea Krugman's (1998) assertion that the government provided implicit guarantees for banks and industrial corporations holds no water. He argues that Korean conglomerates or chaebol engaged in reckless investment and had low efficiency as proven by their low profitability. But as Chang, Park, and Yoo (1998) point out, profitability was low only after interest payments, not before. Moreover, over the 1980s and 1990s the government did not bail out any chaebol; in the period 1990–97 three of the thirty biggest ones went bankrupt. The government did have a history of stepping in to restructure enterprises in trouble, but that left little room for moral hazard—managers knew they would lose control over their companies if they failed to perform.

Despite such shaky empirical antecedents, moral hazard is given a central role in mainstream crisis models. In a typical example, Dooley (1997) argues that developing country governments self-insure by accumulating international reserves to back up poorly regulated financial markets. National players feel justified in offering high returns to foreign investors, setting up a spread. Domestic liabilities are acquired by outsiders (or perhaps nationals resident in more pleasant climes or just engaging in off-shore manipulations) until such point as the stock of insured claims exceeds the government's reserves. A speculative attack follows.

The *leitmotif* of an alert private sector chastising an inept government recurs again. This time it encourages reckless investment behavior. All a sensible private sector can be expected to do is to make money out of such misguided public action.

A More Plausible Theory

A more realistic perspective is that the public and private sectors generate positive financial feedbacks between themselves—first at the micro and then at the macro level, ultimately destabilizing the system. This line of analysis is pursued by Salih Neftci (1998), a market practitioner, and Roberto Frenkel (1983), a macroeconomist. Both focus on an initial situation in which the nominal exchange rate is "credibly" fixed (setting the $\hat{e}^E$ terms equal to zero in Table 10.1's equations for spreads), and show how an unstable dynamic process can arise. A Frenkel-Neftci (or FN) cycle begins in financial markets, which generate capital inflows. They spill over to the macroeconomy via the financial system and the balance of payments as the upswing gains momentum. At the peak, before a (more or less rapid) downswing, the economy-wide consequences can be overwhelming.

To trace through an example, suppose that a spread Σ_i (e.g., on Mexican government peso-denominated bonds with a high interest rate but carrying an implicit exchange risk) or Σ_G (e.g., capital gains from booming Bangkok real estate) opens. A few local players take positions in the relevant assets, borrowing abroad to do so. Their exposure is risky but *small*. It may well go unnoticed by regulators; indeed for the system as a whole the risk is negligible.

Destabilizing market competition enters in a second stage. The pioneering institutions are exploiting a spread of (say) 10 percent, while others are earning (say) 5 percent on traditional placements. Even if the risks are recognized, it is difficult for other players not to jump in. A trader or loan officer holding 5 percent paper will reason that the probability of losing his or her job is close to 100 percent *now* if he or she does not take the high risk/high return position. Such potentially explosive behavior is standard market practice, as interview studies by Rude (1998) and Sharma (1998) make clear. In the former's words, "the speculative excesses of the international investors in the Asian financial crisis were not an exception, . . . but instead the result of normal business practices and thus to a certain degree inevitable."

After some months or years of this process, the balance sheet of the local financial system will be risky overall, short on foreign currency and long on local assets.[4] Potential losses from the long position are finite—they at most amount to what the assets cost in the first place. Losses from short-selling foreign exchange are in principle unbounded—who knows how high the local currency-to-dollar exchange rate may finally have to rise?

In a typical macroeconomic paradox, individual players' risks have now been shifted to the aggregate. Any policy move that threatens the overall position—for example cutting interest rates or pricking the real estate bubble—could cause a collapse of the currency and local asset prices. The authorities will use reserves and/or regulations to prevent a crash, consciously ratifying the private sector's market decisions. Unfortunately, macroeconomic factors will ultimately force their hand.

In a familiar scenario, suppose that the initial capital inflows have boosted domestic output growth. The current account deficit S_f will widen, leading at some point to a fall in reserves as capital inflows level off and total interest payments on outstanding obligations rise. Higher interest rates will be needed to equilibrate portfolios and attract foreign capital. In turn, S_b will fall or turn negative as illiquidity and insolvency spread à la Minsky, threatening a systemic crisis. Bankruptcies of banks and firms may further contribute to reducing the credibility of the exchange rate.

A downturn becomes inevitable, since finally no local interest rate will be high enough to induce more external lending in support of what is recognized as a short foreign exchange position at the economy-wide level. Shrewd players will unwind their positions before the downswing begins (as Mexican nationals were said to have done before the December 1994 devaluation); they can even retain positive earnings over the cycle by getting out while the currency weakens visibly. But others—typically including the macroeconomic policy team—are likely to go under.

The dynamic behavior of this narrative differs from that of standard crisis models—it does not involve a regime shift when a spread Σ_i or Σ_G switches sign from positive to negative. Rather, movements in the spread itself feed back into cyclical changes within the economy concerned that finally lead to massive instability. Reverting to catastrophe theory jargon, the standard models invoke a "static" instability such as a buckling beam. More relevant to history are "dynamic" or cyclical instabilities that appear when effective damping of the dynamic system vanishes. A classic engineering example is the Tacoma Narrows suspension bridge. Opened in July 1940, it soon became known as "Galloping Gertie" because of its antics in the wind. Its canter became strong enough to make it disintegrate in a 41-mile-per-hour windstorm in November of that year. Despite their best efforts, economists have yet to design a system that fails so fast.

Finally, a *soupçon* of moral hazard enters an FN crisis, but more by way of pro-cyclical regulation than through "promised" LLR interventions or government provision of "insurance" in the form of international reserves. After a downswing, some players will be bailed out and others will not, but such eventualities will be subject to high discount rates while the cycle is on the way up. In that phase, traders and treasurers of finance houses are far more interested in their spreads and regulatory acquiescence in exploiting them than in what sort of safety net they may or may not fall into, sometime down the road.

III. Policy Alternatives

A companion paper (Taylor 1998) reviews in detail experiences in the Southern Cone around 1980, Mexico in 1994–95, and Asia in 1997–98. Its principal conclusion is that financial crises are not made by an alert private sector pouncing upon the public sector's fiscal or moral hazard foolishness. They are better described as private sectors (both domestic and foreign) acting to make high short-term profits when policy and history provide the preconditions and the public sector acquiesces. Mutual feedbacks between the financial sector and the real side of the economy then lead to a crisis. By global standards, the financial flows involved in a Frenkel-Neftci conflagration are not large—$10–20 billion of capital flows annually (around 10 percent of the inflow the United States routinely absorbs) for a few years are more than enough to destabilize a middle income economy. The outcomes are now visible worldwide.

A number of policy issues are posed by the experiences reviewed herein. It is convenient to discuss them under three headings: steps which can be taken at the country level to reduce the likelihood of future conflagrations; actions both an afflicted country and the international community can take to cope with a future crisis, when and if it happens; and how the international regulatory system might be modified to enhance global economic comity and stability.

Avoiding Frenkel-Neftci Cycles

Rather than a formal model, Neftci and Frenkel provide a framework which can be used to analyze crisis dynamics. There are five essential elements:

1. The nominal exchange rate is fixed or close to being pre-determined;
2. There are few barriers to external capital inflows and outflows;
3. Historical factors and the conjuncture act together to create wide spreads of the form Σ_i and Σ_q in Table 10.1—these in turn generate capital movements which push the domestic financial system in the direction of being long on domestic assets and short on foreign holdings;
4. Regulation of the system is lax and probably pro-cyclical;
5. Macroeconomic repercussions via the balance of payments and the financial system's flows of funds and balance sheets set off a dynamic process which is unstable.

To a greater or lesser extent, national policy-makers can prevent these components from coming together explosively.

The Exchange Rate

There are often very good reasons to have a pegged nominal rate (or one that is limited to fluctuations within a narrow band). It is anti-inflationary, which has been crucially important to Latin American stabilization packages beginning with Mexico's in the late 1980s. It can also enhance export competitiveness, as happened when countries in Southeast Asia pegged to the falling dollar after the Plaza Accord. Problems with a pegged rate arise when it contributes to wide spreads and (especially) when it is over-valued. In the formulas of Table 10.1, for example, a positive value of $\hat{e}^E$ can reduce Σ_i and Σ_G; this is a good argument for a thoughtfully designed crawling nominal depreciation. An even better argument is that such an exchange rate regime can help avoid real appreciation, which in turn can widen the trade deficit, bring in capital inflows or induce reserve losses, and kick off an unstable macro cycle.

Barriers to Capital Movements

Without international assistance, it is virtually impossible to prevent capital from fleeing the country in a crisis; it is much more feasible to construct obstacles to slow it down (at least) as it comes in. In the recent period, Chile and Colombia have had some success with prior deposits and taxes on inflows, especially when they are short-term. In a not much more distant past, Asian economies had fairly effective restrictions on how much and how easily households and firms could borrow abroad. In non-crisis times, acquisition of foreign assets can also be monitored.

The key task is to prevent a "locational" mismatch in the macro balance sheet, with a preponderance of foreign liabilities (especially short-term) and national assets. Local regulatory systems can certainly be configured toward this end, and even to cope with off-balance sheet razzle-dazzle. If imbalances are detected, the relevant authorities can direct or encourage players to unwind their positions.

Spreads

Under a fixed exchange rate regime, it is easy to spot a 10 percent differential between local and foreign short-term interest rates or a similarly sized gap between the growth rate of the local stock market index or real estate prices and a foreign borrowing rate. Such yields are an open invitation to capital inflows that can be extremely destabilizing. Whether policy-makers feel they are able to reduce interest rates or deflate an asset market boom is another question, one that merits real concern.

Another source of potential spreads is through off-balance sheet and derivative operations. Here, local regulators can be at a major disadvantage. They don't necessarily know the latest devices and most (but one hopes not all) of the "really smart guys" will be on the other side inventing still newer devices to make more money. Staying up-to-date as far as possible and inculcating a culture of probity in the local financial system are the best defenses here.

The Regulatory Regime

There is of course a serious question as to whether many developing country regulatory systems can meet such goals, especially in the wake of liberalization episodes. Another difficulty arises with timing. It is very difficult to put a stop to capital flows after the financial system has a locationally unbalanced position; at such a point interest rate increases or a discrete devaluation can easily provoke a crash. The authorities have to stifle an FN cycle early in its upswing; otherwise, they may be powerless to act.

Unstable Dynamics

Each balance of payments crisis is *sui generis*; to produce a set of formal descriptions one would have to write a separate model for each episode in each country. Many components, however, would be the same. The simplest classification is in terms of disequilibria between stocks and flows, along with more microeconomic indicators. Here are some examples:

Flow-flow. One key issue here is identifying the internal "twin(s)" of an external deficit. In the country examples discussed in Taylor (1998), the financial deficits were in the hands of the private sector—business or households. The follow-up question is how they are being paid for. Are rising interest obligations likely to cut into savings and investment flows? Are flows cumulating to produce locational or maturity mismatches in balance sheets? Another precursor of crisis is the relationship between the volume of capital inflows and the current account deficit. If the former exceeds the latter reserves will be rising, perhaps lulling the authorities into a false sense of security. It will rudely vanish when interest payments on accumulating foreign debt begin to exceed the amount of capital flowing in.

Stock-flow. Have some asset or liability stocks become "large" in relation to local flows? East Asia's short-term debt exceeding 10 percent of GDP was a typical example; it was a stock with a level that could change rapidly, with sharply destabilizing repercussions. Rapid expansion of bank credit to the private sector as a share of GDP while booms got under way in the Southern Cone, Mexico, and Thailand might have served as an early warning indicator, had the authorities been looking. The causes included monetization of reserve increases and growth of loans against collateral assets such as securities and real estate with rapidly inflating values.

Stock-stock. Besides lopsided balance sheets in the financial sector, indicators such as debt/equity ratios and the currency composition of portfolios (including their "dollarization" in Latin America recently) become relevant here. They can signal future problems with financing investment–saving differentials of the sort presented in Table 10.1. For example, producers of non-traded goods may borrow in dollar terms from the local banking system. In the event of a devaluation, their real incomes would fall and some might not be able to service their debts. A crisis could follow, even if banks held their "dollar" liabilities and assets generally in balance. It could be avoided if the central bank had ample reserves to back an LLR operation in dollars, but many countries are not so lucky.

Microeconomics. Micro-level developments go along with the evolution of these macro changes. Investment coordination across firms may be breaking down, leading to "excess competition"; real estate speculation and luxury consumption may be on the rise.

The problem with all such indicators is that they often lag an unstable dynamic process. By the time they are visibly out of line it may be too late to attempt to prevent a crisis; its management becomes the urgent task of the day.

Moral Hazard Abroad?

Within countries, moral hazard did not play a central role in generating crises. On the side of the lenders, it also did not seem to be important. In the East Asian crisis, international banks were the big offenders. In 1996 there had been a net flow of capital into the five most affected economies of $93 billion. There was a net outflow of $12 billion in 1997, with the most volatile item being commercial bank credit, which shifted from an inflow of over $50 billion in 1996 to an outflow of $21 billion the following year. The overall turnaround of $105 billion was close to the five countries' total reserves of $127 billion and exceeded 10 percent of their combined GDP (about two percentage points higher than the impact of the 1982 debt crisis on the GDP of Latin America). It was a supply shock with sharp contractionary effects on the macroeconomy. Taking advantage of the short-term nature of their credits, the banks ran from their borrowers before they had a chance to default, making default itself, or a massive international bail-out, a self-fulfilling prophecy.

Did the banks enter heavily into Asian lending because of moral hazards from home, or did they just like the spreads? One will never know for certain. Perhaps the Americans were emboldened by the Mexican "rescue" of 1995, which pumped tens of billions of dollars through that economy back to its creditors on Wall Street (the Mexicans themselves are now trying to cope with bad internal debt to the tune of 15 percent of GDP that the rescue left behind). But the same cannot be said about the Europeans and Japanese. The fact that all international players left so fast suggests that they did not place much faith in the "implicit guarantees" that the Asian governments allegedly had offered.

Rescue Attempts

Once a country enters into a payments crisis, it cannot cope with it on its own. International assistance has to be called in. Again, each situation follows its own rules, but there are a few obvious "dos" and "don'ts" for the actions of the rescue team. We begin with the former.

The contrast between the Mexican and Asian "rescues" is striking: the first happened (at least as far as foreign creditors were concerned) and the second did not. Very slow disbursement of funds by the IMF may well have crippled the Asian effort permanently, pushing fundamentally healthy economies from illiquidity into insolvency. Against the $105 billion external shock that the region received in 1997, international financial institutions may disburse around $45 billion in 1998.

The first and most obvious "do" that emerges from crisis experience is to disburse rescue money fast. In Helleiner's (1998) words, "Finance that is supplied only on the basis of negotiated conditions and which is released only on the basis of compliance with them . . . is *not* liquidity." East Asian economies became highly illiquid in 1997. By mid-1998, their position had not significantly improved, despite more than six months of IMF psychotherapy accompanied by liquidity transfusions on a homeopathic scale.

In fact, the transfusions might not even have been required if the rescuers had "bailed-in" the countries' creditors in the sense of forcing them not to call outstanding loans instead of bailing them out. By appealing to G7 regulatory authorities if need be, the IMF presumably has enough clout to prevent international creditors—especially large international banks—from closing out Asian borrowers overnight. This is a sort of "do" that should be built into rescue protocols before the next crisis strikes.

After a crisis, countries often also have an ample load of "bad debt," typically non-performing assets of the banking sector. Domestic re-financing via a bond issue to the non-bank private sector, an administratively enforced credit roll-over, and price inflation are three ways of dealing with the problem. The latter two would almost certainly require re-imposition of tight controls on outward capital movements, which the international community would have to abet.

Distributional questions also come to the fore. As nations, the Asians are big and visible. But what about small, poor, raw material or assembled goods exporters in sub-Saharan Africa, Central America, the Pacific, and the Caribbean? Several have been hit by rapid reversals of private capital inflows. Presumably they merit international help as much as Korea or Thailand. They are not now receiving it.

Within all afflicted countries, income generation and employment problems are critical. The authorities can repress their peoples, up to a point, but ultimately will have to offer them a degree of social and economic support. Such an effort goes diametrically against the emphasis in Fund-type packages. As Singh puts it:

> To provide such assistance effectively and on an adequate scale will require not only considerable imagination but also a large expansion in government activity and often direct intervention in the market processes. Such emergency safety net programs may include wider subsidies, food for work schemes, and public works projects. How to pay for these measures within the limits of fiscal prudence, let alone within IMF fiscal austerity programs, will be a major issue of political economy for these countries. (1998, p. 19)

The most obvious "don't" is not to liberalize the capital accounts of the affected countries further. If the single most apparent cause of crisis was a door three-quarters open, the last thing one wants to do is move it the rest of the way. A similar observation applies to attempts to restructure economic institutions in depth in crisis-afflicted economies. This strategy is now being pursued by the IMF in Asia, Russia, and elsewhere, using conditionality-laden credit disbursements as bait. This effort runs directly against well-entrenched social structures. It will undoubtedly fail, leaving a big store of political resentment to be paid in the future.

Changing the Global Regulatory System

The foregoing observations lead naturally to five suggestions for re-structuring international financial arrangements.

First, recent experiences demonstrate that the global macroeconomic/financial system is not well understood. "Miracle economies" one month turn into incompetent bastions of "crony capitalism" the next, and the commentators don't skip a beat. Under such circumstances, an immediate recommendation is for humility on the part of the major institutional players (Eatwell and Taylor 1998). There is no reason to force all countries into the same regulatory mold; international institutions should whole heartedly support whatever capital market, trade, and investment regimes that any nation, after due consultation, chooses to put into place.

Second, international agencies should support national regulatory initiatives. There was a lot of information available from the BIS and other sources about the gathering storm in Asia; it was not factored into either the private or public sectors' calculations. If national regulators are made more aware of what is happening in their countries, perhaps they can take prudent steps to avoid a pro-cyclical bias in their decisions.

Third, the IMF seems unlikely to receive large additional sums of money to allow it to serve as a (conditional) lender of last resort. It will therefore have to become more of a signaller to other sources of finance, especially central banks and the Bank for International Settlements. That opens room for new forms of regional cooperation such as Japan's summer 1997 proposal for an Asian bail-out fund, which died after being opposed vigorously by the U.S. government and the IMF. Such institutional innovations should be thought through seriously, and very possibly put into place.

Fourth, specific changes in international regulatory practices may make sense. One obvious modification to the Basle capital adequacy provisions is to permit 20 percent as opposed to 100 percent backing on loans to non-OECD countries for maturities of (say) only three months or less, as opposed to one year at present. Such an adjustment should substantially reduce incentives for banks to concentrate their lending to developing countries in the short term.

Finally, there is no independent external body with power to assess the IMF's actions. More transparency (especially regarding relationships between the American government and the Fund) and independent evaluations of the IMF are sorely needed in light of its largely unsuccessful economy-building enterprises in post-socialist nations and now in East Asia.

Notes

This chapter was first published as an article in vol. 22, no. 6, pp. 663–676, 1998, of the *Cambridge Journal of Economics*. Permission to print this article is granted by Oxford University Press.

This paper draws heavily on the results of a project on International Capital Markets and the Future of Economic Policy, Center for Economic Policy Analysis, New School University, with support from the Ford Foundation. Comments by Alice Amsden, Jane D'Arista, Thorsten Block, Ha-Joon Chang, Sandy Darity, Roberto Frenkel, and Gerry Helleiner are gratefully acknowledged.

1. The "Δ" term signifies a change over time, e.g., $\Delta H_h = H_h(t)-H_h(t-1)$ where $H_h(t)$ and $H_h(t-1)$ are money stocks at the ends of periods t and t–1, respectively.

2. The following discussion concentrates on "first generation" speculative attack models. "Second generation" models make the fundamentals sensitive to shifts in private expectations, thereby allowing extrinsic, random "sunspot" shocks to generate multiple equilibria. The mathematical complications are intriguing to the professorial mind but add little to attempts to understand historical crises.

3. Pieper and Taylor (1998) present a fairly up-to-date review. In various numbers of its World Economic Outlook, the IMF is up-front about attributing crises in both Latin America and Asia to "incompatibilities" between macro policies and the exchange rate regime as well as "excessive regulation" and "too little competition" in the financial sector.

4. For analysis in the Asian context, see Islam (1998). There may also be problems with maturity structures of claims, especially if local players borrow from abroad short term. Nervous foreign lenders may then compare a country's total external payment obligations over the next year (say) with its international reserves. Such ratios proved disastrous for Mexico in 1995 and several Asian countries in 1997. A maturity mismatch in which local players borrow short term abroad and lend long term at home may be less significant—a property developer will default on his or her loan if the property market crashes, regardless of whether it is formally of short or long duration.

References

Chang, Ha-Joon, Hong-Jae Park, and Chul Gyue Yoo. 1998. "Interpreting the Korean Crisis: Financial Liberalization, Industrial Policy, and Corporate Governance." *Cambridge Journal of Economics* 22, no. 6 (November): 735–746.

D'Arista, Jane. 1998. "Financial Regulation in a Liberalized Global Environment." New York: Center for Economic Policy Analysis, New School for Social Research. Mimeo.

Dooley, Michael P. 1997. "A Model of Crises in Emerging Markets." Santa Cruz: Department of Economics, University of California at Santa Cruz. Mimeo.

Eatwell, John, and Lance Taylor. 1998. "International Capital Markets and the Future of Economic Policy." New York: Center for Economic Policy Analysis, New School for Social Research. Mimeo.

Frenkel, Roberto. 1983. "Mercado Financiero, Expectativas Cambiales, y Movimientos de Capital." *El Trimestre Económico* 50, no. 4 (October–December): 2041–2076.

Helleiner, Gerald K. 1998. *The East Asian and Other Financial Crises: Causes, Responses, and Prevention.* Geneva: United Nations Conference on Trade and Development.

Islam, A. 1998. *Dynamcis of Asian Economic Crisis and Selected Policy Implications.* Bangkok: Economic and Social Commission For Asia and the Pacific.

Krugman, Paul. 1979. "A Model of Balance-of-Payments Crises." *Journal of Money, Credit, and Banking* 11, no. 3 (August): 311–325.

———. 1998. "What Happened to Asia?" Cambridge: Department of Economics, Massachusetts Institute of Technology. Mimeo.

Minsky, Hyman P. 1986. *Stabilizing an Unstable Economy.* New Haven: Yale University Press.

Neftci, Salih N. 1998. "AFX Short Positions, Balance Sheets, and Financial Turbulence: An Interpretation of the Asian Financial Crisis." New York: Center for Economic Policy Analysis, New School for Social Research. Mimeo.

Pieper, Ute, and Lance Taylor. 1998. "The Revival of the Liberal Creed: The IMF, the World Bank, and Inequality in a Globalized Economy." In *Globalization and Progressive Economic Policy: What Are the Real Constraints and Options?* ed. Dean Baker, Gerald Epstein, and Robert Pollin. New York: Cambridge University Press.

Rude, C. 1998. "The 1997–98 East Asian Financial Crisis: A New York Market-Informed View." New York: Department of Economic and Social Affairs, United Nations. Mimeo.

Sharma, K. 1998. "Understanding the Dynamics Behind Excess Capital Inflows and Excess Capital Outflows in East Asia." New York: Department of Economic and Social Affairs, United Nations. Mimeo.

Singh, Ajit. 1998. " 'Asian Capitalism' and the Financial Crisis." New York: Center for Economic Policy Analysis, New School for Social Research. Mimeo.

Taylor, Lance. 1998. "Lax Public Sector, Destabilizing Private Sector: Origins of Capital Market Crises." New York: Center for Economic Policy Analysis, New School for Social Research. Mimeo.

ABOUT THE EDITORS AND CONTRIBUTORS

Isabella Bakker is associate professor of political science at York University in Toronto, Canada.

Heather Boushey was a student of David Gordon's and is now an economist at the Economic Policy Institute in Washington, DC.

Samuel Bowles is professor of economics at the University of Massachusetts at Amherst.

Herbert Gintis is professor of economics at the University of Massachusetts at Amherst.

Ellen Houston is a labor economist at the Economic Policy Institute in Washington, DC, and a former graduate student of the late David Gordon.

David R. Howell is professor at the Robert J. Milano Graduate School of Management and Urban Policy of the New School University in New York.

William Milberg is associate professor of economics at the New School University in New York.

Thomas I. Palley is assistant director of public policy at the AFL-CIO in Washington, DC.

Juliet B. Schor is senior lecturer on women's studies at Harvard University and professor of the economics of leisure, Tilburg University, Netherlands.

Jim Stanford is an economist with the Canadian Auto Workers in Toronto, Canada.

Lance Taylor is Arnhold professor of international cooperation and development at the New School University in New York, and director of the Center for Economic Policy Analysis.

INDEX

A

Altruism
  reciprocal, 83, 88
  unconditional, 81, 82, 83, 91, 99
Argentina, 196
Axelrod, Robert, 87–88

B

Bank for International Settlements, 255
Bank loans, 127, 129–30
Basic needs generosity, 81, 82, 98, 99, 101
Bond market, 130
Bureaucratic burden, 24–26, 62n.4

C

Capital accumulation
  classical Marxist theory, 119–21
  discrimination and, 143–44, 145, 146
  Marxist-Kaleckian synthesis, 124
  neoclassical theory, 115
  See also Social structure of accumulation (SSA)
Capital movement, 239, 250

Classical Marxist theory
  aggregate demand, 121
    Kaleckian synthesis, 124, 127–30
  capital accumulation, 119–21
    Kaleckian synthesis, 124
  contested exchange theory, 120
  income distribution, 120
  interest rate, 119, 120–21
    Kaleckian synthesis, 125–26, 127–28, 129, 130
  investment spending, 119, 121
    Kaleckian synthesis, 124, 127–28, 129
  Kaleckian synthesis, 124–30
    aggregate demand, 124, 127–30
    bank loans, 127, 129–30
    bond market, 130
    capital accumulation, 124
    credit market, 127, 129–30
    debt, 129–30
    employment, 124
    financial sector, 125–32
    goods market, 124, 126–29
    inflation, 127–28
    interest rate, 125–26, 127–28, 129, 130
    investment spending, 124, 127–28, 129
    labor market, 124, 126–27

261

264   INDEX